Empty Promise

Empty Promise
The Growing Case against Star Wars

THE UNION OF
CONCERNED SCIENTISTS

Edited by John Tirman

BEACON PRESS BOSTON

Beacon Press
25 Beacon Street
Boston, Massachusetts 02108

Beacon Press books are published under the auspices
of the Unitarian Universalist Association
of Congregations in North America.

92 91 90 89 88 87 86 8 7 6 5 4 3 2 1

Library of Congress Cataloging-in-Publication Data

Empty promise.

Bibliography: p.
Includes index.
1. Strategic Defense Initiative. I. Tirman, John.
II. Union of Concerned Scientists.
UG743.E46 1986 358'.1754 86-47555
ISBN 0-8070-0412-X
ISBN 0-8070-0413-8 (pbk.)

Text design by Sara Arrand

Dedicated to the memory of

HERBERT ("PETE") SCOVILLE, JR.
(1915–1986)

Author, scientist, public servant,
and warrior for peace

Contents

Foreword

Since early 1983, the Union of Concerned Scientists has been deeply involved in the international debate over space weapons, an involvement that has produced technical and policy studies, congressional testimony, articles and books, legislative and legal advocacy, grass roots organizing, and other activities. In a report written and released by a panel of experts in May 1983, UCS was one of the first organizations to address the emerging issue of antisatellite weapons. The following year, another distinguished UCS panel assessed the Reagan administration's vision for space-based missile defense—again, one of the earliest and most authoritative of such analyses. These two studies were later combined with new material and published in October 1984 as *The Fallacy of Star Wars*, which remains one of the most prominent technical critiques of the Strategic Defense Initiative (SDI). "The conclusions of this group of experts have already played an important role in the defense debate," the journal *Foreign Affairs* commented in 1985. "*Fallacy* presents an argument which the proponents of the Administration's SDI have yet to successfully refute."

The SDI has proven to be something of a moving target, however, and the debate itself has evolved since the president made his Star Wars speech in March 1983. In early 1985 we began to address in greater detail specific aspects of the SDI that were not handled at length in *Fallacy*. These short analyses, called the Papers on Strategic Defense, convinced us that another book on the topic was necessary, one that would sharpen our focus on several key areas of the SDI. Whereas *Fallacy* was a broadbrush, technical critique, the new book would regard the particularly troublesome spots in the administration's program—the intrinsic problems, any one of which could spell the end of the president's vision. The result of this effort is this volume, *Empty Promise: The Growing Case against Star Wars*. We have examined the "weak links" in the strategic defense project, both the weak policy areas and those technical topics that recently have received new attention. And to present "state-of-the-art" analysis, we have again called on expert colleagues outside of UCS to contribute.

One of the ironies of the SDI debate of the last three years is that the critics are gradually being proven correct, while the program itself continues to receive ample appropriations from Congress. Major problems—cost, strategic stability, system vulnerability, and physical limitations on certain weapons—are slowly but surely being acknowledged by the program's managers, either explicitly or through revisions in the SDI's priorities, goals, and design. With this more finely tuned assessment, we hope to further contribute to the public's and policymakers' understanding of strategic defenses and, as a result, to contribute to the nation's security.

The fundamental moral tenet in the president's speech of March 23 is that it is better to *save* lives than to *avenge* them, and, to that end, he called upon the nation's scientists to develop a space-based defense that "would render nuclear weapons impotent and obsolete." He was referring to a dramatic shift in long-standing nuclear policy, away from deterrence and toward strategic defenses. Nuclear deterrence rests upon a simple, if terrifying, premise: one's nuclear-armed adversary (the Soviet Union, in particular) will not attack with nuclear weapons because the result of such an attack will be a devastating nuclear retaliation.

President Reagan hoped, as many policymakers in the post-Hiroshima era have hoped, that this balance of terror could be replaced with defenses, technologies that would intercept nuclear missiles before they wrought their destruction. Star

Wars is a vision of a space-based defense (weapons, sensors, computers, etc., based on satellites in outer space) that would intercept Soviet ballistic missiles in their boost phase and warheads in their postboost, midcourse, and reentry phases (see fig. F.1). The SDI is thus a *strategic* defense program, indicating that the system would defend against intercontinental weapons—in this case, missiles and warheads. (Strategic defenses could also include technology used to intercept bombers—air defense—or cruise missiles, although these possibilities are not as yet explicitly included in the SDI.)

In the actual conduct of the SDI, the president's idealistic hope is apparently not being sought. As we demonstrated in *The Fallacy of Star Wars*, the possibility of constructing a perfect, or near-perfect, defense that could save populations from nuclear attack is not a realizable goal. Limited defense, probably meant to protect military targets, is the actual goal of the

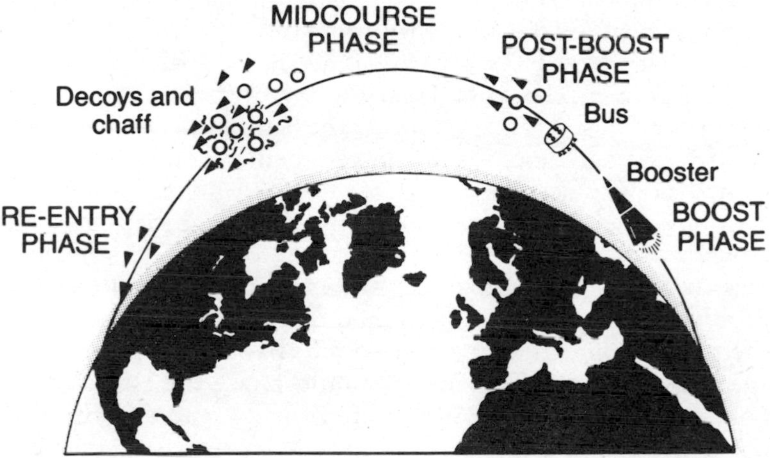

FIG. F.1. The ballistic flight of missiles includes a boost phase, which now would last about 3 to 5 minutes, a postboost period in which warheads are released from a "bus," a 20-minute midcourse phase through outer space (at about 200 miles apogee), and the reentry phase through the atmosphere toward the targets. With fast-burn boosters, boost phase might be reduced to 50 seconds and the release of the warheads could occur inside the atmosphere, which would foil many weapons envisioned for boost-phase interception (see chap. 6). In midcourse, hundreds of thousands of decoys and chaff would confuse Star Wars sensors and complicate targeting.

program. However nobly intentioned the president's plea might have been, the purported morality of defense versus deterrence is really a red herring: long before the United States could deploy any kind of defense, a new arms race and new provocations would almost inevitably ensue, driving the superpowers closer toward nuclear war. That, obviously, is not an ethical course.

The nation has faced similar issues before. During the 1960s, strategic missile defenses were proposed and, in fact, programs to build them in the United States and the Soviet Union were begun. These, however, were ground-based antiballistic missile (ABM) systems, which purported to shoot down warheads in their reentry, or terminal, phase. In the opinion of most experts at the time, defenses were considered "destabilizing" because they created an incentive for a nation to "preempt" with its nuclear weapons in a severe crisis. Unrestricted strategic defenses would also block any hope of negotiating limits or reductions in offensive missiles, since the best way to defeat a defense is with more offense. As a result, the Antiballistic Missile Treaty was signed in 1972, along with the SALT I accord. The ABM Treaty today limits each nation to one ground-based ABM system. As the bedrock of nuclear arms control, the agreement is at the very center of the Star Wars controversy.

In any case, the debate about Star Wars and the SDI itself now focuses on limited defense. Many of the technological tasks are essentially the same, so we continue to explore such problems. (The reader is cautioned that chapters 3 through 6, the more technical analyses, may be challenging to the nonspecialist, but careful reading should repay the effort.) As a policy concern, however, it is important to note that we take the aims of the SDI, insofar as they can be lucidly delineated, to be something less than perfect defense—something, in the words of an SDI manager, that would not replace deterrence, but "enhance" deterrence. SDI has, as a result, become a policy issue every bit as much as a technical matter; indeed, its coherence and fate must be assessed on such grounds. This book is roughly divided into three sections: politics and program, technology, and strategic relations. These indeed are the weak links that we believe will ultimately undo the Star Wars vision.

This book was a group effort. In addition to the eight contributors, many of whom reviewed each others' chapters, I especially thank Nancy Maxwell of UCS for her excellent editing and Nancy Stockford for a variety of perfectly executed tasks. Thanks are also owed to Rebecca Driscoll for the graphics, the UCS board of directors for its encouragement, the board of the Winston Foundation for allowing me the time to fulfill this obligation before taking up new ones, and Caroline Birdsall and her colleagues at Beacon Press for their prompt and expert transformation of this from manuscript to published book.

Most of all, we thank you, the citizen, for taking the time and effort to engage this complex and vital issue.

John Tirman
Cambridge, Massachusetts
June 1, 1986

1
The Politics of Star Wars

JOHN TIRMAN

EVOLUTION OF THE DEBATE

Never has there been a more galvanizing presidential address on military affairs than that delivered by Pres. Ronald Reagan on March 23, 1983, when he called on American scientists to find the means to "render nuclear weapons impotent and obsolete." It set in motion an entirely new and massive technocracy, potentially unprecedented allocations of the nation's treasury, the beginnings of a transformation in relations with America's most powerful adversary, and fresh debates on the dimensions of strategic doctrine, the possibilities for nuclear war, the role of advanced technology in defense, and the obligations of science. Perhaps no single program of post–World War II government has so absorbed the nation's technical elite, while promising to absorb—to soak up—a vast share of its economic resources. And no single project is likely to dominate our discourse and deliberations about defense policy in the rest of this century as the exotic, limitless idea of "Star Wars"—a space-based shield to destroy nuclear missiles.

The sense of excitement and challenge the president stirred in much of the defense community was more than matched by outrage and defiance in other circles. In the days following the speech, independent scientific and policy experts—many with decades of experience in strategic defense research—expressed deep skepticism about the idea. Wolfgang Panofsky, a leading academic physicist and high-level defense consultant, put it plainly: "I know of no developments, no technical advances, that would change the present balance of terror to an umbrella of security." Outside of the weapons labs, the federal bureaucracy, and a few fringe "think tanks," the informed opinion was uniformly derisive. A representative example of Fourth Estate opinion could be found in a *Los Angeles Times* editorial: "it is far from clear that the crash program proposed by Reagan makes sense." The habitually cautious *Time* magazine warned of a space weapons race in which "the danger is that both will lose, each aggravating the insecurity of the other as it strives to keep up. That is a danger that will loom long before the scientists and generals know whether the system they are so feverishly developing will actually work."

Even with the first rush of analysis, it was assumed in many quarters that President Reagan was not seriously contemplating this "Buck Rogers" concept. One report quoted an administration official as saying that the March 23 speech was "an attempt by the president to 'regain the political offensive' on the defense issue." The White House was worried about the nuclear freeze movement and polls showing "a steady decline of public support for the president's defense stand," the report explained. A prominent southern newspaper went so far as to say that the missile defense plea "can be dismissed as the speech's gimmick." A lead article in *The New Republic* probably summed up many observers' sentiments two weeks later: "The New Federalism faded fast, and in six months Mr. Reagan's Star Wars nuclear defense scenario will be dimly remembered."[1] For a time, it seemed that view was prophetic.

Several key figures within the administration saw the unexpected Star Wars speech as an opportunity to accomplish many diverse objectives, however, and so the president's quixotic vision soon had the force not only of an Oval Office imprimatur, but of ideological conviction and Pentagon power. The purely political goal of blunting the freeze's gains was perhaps one contributor, but a number of other considerations were every bit as important in giving the idea the institutional backing it required to survive and thrive. The origins of the space-based defense idea have been attributed mainly to Edward Teller, the old cold warrior, "father" of the H-bomb, and founder and intellectual couturier of the Lawrence Livermore National Laboratory, one of the major centers of nuclear weapons design. Teller had long been fascinated by "third-generation" nuclear weapons, and his enthusiasm for an X-ray laser pumped by the explosive power of a hydrogen bomb had apparently caught President Reagan's attention. (The weapons labs' enthusiasm for SDI is sometimes described as the outgrowth of a persistent ennui suffered in their work on by-now tedious nuclear weapons design; Star Wars was something new.) Another alleged influence on the March 23 call to arms was retired air force general Danny Graham, who had fashioned a "high frontier" concept in which kinetic energy weapons would provide a space-based defense. Whatever the influences on the president, the idea took on a life of its own after that spring of 1983. By all accounts, the armed services were not enthralled by the president's speech. But soon it was realized in the defense policy apparatus that a variety of objectives could be pursued under Star Wars: creating a new impetus for military technology, badgering the Soviet Union, dominating outer space, and, for some, destroying arms control.

Immediately after the president's speech, the experts had quickly divided along familiar lines, lines long ago drawn and persisting to this day. After all, the notion of a technological defense against strategic (intercontinental) ballistic missiles was not new; almost from the moment the United States dropped two atomic bombs on Japan to end World War II, the weaponeers of that era considered how a nation might defend against such mortal attacks. A few days after Japan surrendered, J. Robert Oppenheimer, the physicist who headed the Manhattan Project research, and three colleagues wrote to the secretary of war. "We have been unable to devise or propose effective military countermeasures for atomic weapons," they wrote. "It is our firm opinion that no military countermeasures will be found which will be adequately effective in preventing the delivery of atomic weapons."

The view that nuclear offense would always defeat strategic defense largely held sway through almost forty years of research and development of strategic defenses. The U.S. military doggedly pursued air defenses against bombers and ground-based defenses against missiles, a pursuit that culminated in the deployment of an antiballistic missile (ABM) system to protect Minuteman ICBM silos in Grand Forks, North Dakota, in the 1970s. The Grand Forks complex was the one strategic defense system allowed under the ABM Treaty, an accord that put to rest an acrimonious debate begun with a decision to deploy the Safeguard ABM system in the late 1960s. That debate raged from the time Secretary of Defense Robert McNamara announced the program in 1967, through the Nixon administration, and until the ABM Treaty, along with SALT I, was signed in 1972. And that debate took a form much like today's: ABM advocates claimed the technology was "feasible" and would enhance deterrence; its critics charged that Safeguard would not work adequately, would upset the stability of deterrence, and was a waste of money. For the most part, the critics won out because the ballistic missile defense (BMD) concepts could never convince policymakers that protection for military facilities was possible, given all the things an attacker could do—the "countermeasures"—to defeat the system. Even after the ABM Treaty was signed, however, a substantial research effort continued, if for no other reason than to guard against Soviet "surprises." By the time the Reagan administration revived strategic defense as an option, U.S. scientists had more than thirty years of experience exploring in detail the technology—its feasibility, utility, and desirability.

After a few weeks the nascent debate on Star Wars quieted down, but it revived when it became clear, toward the end of 1983, that the administration was fully intent on pursuing the president's plea. Two White House panels reported favorably on the idea—a Defense Technologies Study Team headed by the once and future NASA chief, James Fletcher, and a Future Security Strategy Study headed by Fred S. Hoffman. The Fletcher panel report first sparked renewed attention when parts of it were leaked to the trade journal *Aviation Week*; among other intriguing revelations, the price of Star Wars

R&D was pegged at $26 billion for five years, a figure that dwarfed all previous military research programs. The panel investigated the technical prospects for a ballistic missile defense based in space by beginning with highly optimistic assumptions about future technology advances. As a result, there was little surprise when the Fletcher study concluded that defense was feasible technically and desirable strategically. Despite its less-than-rigorous origins, the Fletcher report was to serve as a benchmark for the program's future progress. In any event, the release of these official assessments rekindled a barely smoldering national debate.

At the same time the Fletcher and Hoffman panels were exploring strategic defenses, the armed services were revamping their $900 million pre–Star Wars BMD program to conform with the new impetus from the White House. A move toward short-wavelength lasers—such as the X-ray laser—and away from chemical lasers, for example, was reportedly underway by August 1983, although chemical lasers continued to receive ample funds for two more years. The Joint Chiefs of Staff were considering, and later established, a unified Space Command, which ultimately could have Star Wars under its wing. Antisatellite (ASAT) weapons gained new attention (including a sudden plea from the Soviets to ban them), not only as a key technology in the military's quest for outer space hegemony, but as a way to test similar weapons techniques for Star Wars.

With specifics beginning to emerge from the military and science apparatus in the administration, a series of contradictions appeared, which soon became characteristic of the program. A government report leaked shortly after the president's speech touted the chemical laser, saying that research problems did not exist and that only lack of funds prevented the weapon's fruition; but a year later the major component of the program was canceled due to lack of promise, and the chemical laser itself was later "downselected"—no longer a serious candidate for boost-phase interception. The BMD project managers in the Pentagon, agreeing to the direction set by Congress in the summer of 1983, were emphasizing ultraviolet and X-ray lasers over chemical (infrared) lasers; but the president's science adviser, George Keyworth, insisted that the nuclear-pumped X-ray device had no "critical role" in the program. In mid-1983 some Pentagon officials and Keyworth spoke enthusiastically of a five- or six-year research phase to prove the feasibility of laser weapons and all the other systems (sensors, computing, battle management) required for Star Wars; but the Defense Department's chief scientist, Richard DeLauer, told a House committee in November 1983 that it was at least two decades away.[2]

The niggling question of whether Star Wars would defend people and cities—as President Reagan promised—or defend missile silos, which was what researchers and defense officials were saying, was the most fundamental and persistent contradiction of any. The conflicting findings of the Hoffman and Fletcher reports, which occupied center stage by the beginning of 1984, merely lent an air of authority to the confusion. Whereas the widely publicized Fletcher panel spoke of a 99.9 percent effective defense, the Hoffman panel spoke of beginning with current technology to build defenses to protect military targets in the United States and Europe. "It is difficult," concluded one scholar, "to interpret the Hoffman report as anything but a skeptical dismissal of President Reagan's proposed comprehensive defense of the American people."[3]

Nevertheless, the two reports propelled the concept forward in the political arena and had the effect of giving expert blessing to Star Wars. Combined with the new budget request of $1.8 billion, submitted in January 1984 for Fiscal Year 1985, the Star Wars idea, seemingly dead in the water only the summer before, was up and running. The program was given a name, the Strategic Defense Initiative (SDI), and a champion, new director James A. Abrahamson, a three-star air force general who certainly seemed to have the right stuff: test pilot, war veteran, chief of the F-15 fighter-jet program, and head of the space shuttle. Abrahamson was the perfect man for the job. Bright, articulate, soft-spoken, almost boyish in appearance, he was the antithesis of the Curtis Lemay–style stereotype of a multistarred general out to teach the Russians a lesson. General Abrahamson's task was daunting: fashion an advanced R&D program to fit an unknown design to fulfill contradictory goals, combine BMD projects dispersed through the military-industrial world, cope with the usual interservice rivalries and inefficiency, try to recruit a highly skeptical scientific community, and sell this morass, an extraordinarily expensive morass, to an always difficult Congress.

The fresh attention given Star Wars by the administration and the press coincided with the release of independent studies mostly critical of the idea: an analysis by Congress's Office of Technology Assessment (OTA), a study by a panel of experts convened by the Union of Concerned Scientists, and a book of essays on strategic defense issued by the Brookings Institution, among others. Each was particularly devastating to the hope for a comprehensive population defense. Together they had considerable impact on opinion makers, given the eminence and thoroughness of the contributors to each. Some of the critics, such as Hans Bethe, Richard Garwin, and Raymond Garthoff, had researched BMD concepts for decades at the highest levels. It was difficult to discard such advice.

The studies—which stirred considerable controversy and a concerted attack from right-wing columnists and the Pentagon—in some ways reflected the fixation, especially apparent right after the March 23 speech, with feasibility and the notion of perfect defense, the latter being, of course, the president's often-stated goal.[4] Indeed, the technical argument at times resembled a theological dispute, with hypothetical exchanges on how many BMD satellites would be needed to destroy the Soviet ICBM fleet or the weight penalties the boosters would suffer if decoys were bundled along with warheads into its payload. Even though such arcana dominated the first year of the debate, however, the critics' logic nonetheless hit home. And perhaps in response to the growing consensus that effective population defense was impossible, top officials gradually changed their tune on the SDI's objectives. Within a week of each other in May 1984, for example, Defense Secretary Caspar Weinberger and General Abrahamson acknowledged that the "short-term goal" of SDI was to protect U.S. offensive nuclear forces, though this retreat to partial defense to "enhance deterrence," rather than replace it, was in all likelihood the only realizable objective of the program.

To be sure, the abandoning of the hope to render "nuclear weapons impotent and obsolete" was more often unceremonious and subcabinet. One of the political advantages any administration possesses is that it can speak with many voices, and the Reagan team exploited this advantage willfully. While the president maintained that a comprehensive defense of populations was still his aim, and Secretary of Defense Weinberger could echo that sentiment in more hedged language, the managers of the SDI could reassure the knowledgeable audiences in the defense community and Capitol Hill that space-based defense concepts were being pursued to buttress the U.S. deterrent. This equivocation served an immensely important political need, allowing the president to harvest the popularity of defending people, while the Pentagon could entice the defense industry and members of Congress who knew the SDI would protect only missile silos and other military targets. With this retreat, however, came a shift in the terms of the debate, for once perfect defense was no longer sought, feasibility became less important. A defense of 60 or 70 percent effectiveness was considered more doable than one of 99 percent or more.

Another ironic twist on the feasibility question, which became evident during the summer of 1984, benefited the SDI's public image. The very notion of "feasibility" in an emerging technology project like the SDI is open-ended. The ostensible purpose of the program was to research BMD concepts, so SDI managers could say, as they did, that "we don't know if we can build these systems, but we're trying and we're hopeful." Critics who doubted that the technology could achieve any meaningful success were accused of being closed minded. How could anyone say the project was impossible if it had not yet been tried? Stories of inventors who endured the ridicule of contemporaries were invoked, as was the often-quoted claim of Lord Rutherford that nuclear fission was impossible. (Of course, the critics only said that *perfect* defense was impossible.) At the end of the summer, CBS and NBC each aired Star Wars documentaries, programs replete with dazzling images of lasers, earnest scientists in high-tech labs, and animations showing the system working. The message was subliminal, but powerful: when Americans put their mind to something, they will make it work. The other crucial considerations—costs, strategic relations, Soviet responses—were nearly subsumed in the confusion over feasibility, which only played into the Strategic Defense Initiative Organization's (SDIO) hand.

The expert criticisms of strategic defense nonetheless found receptive ears on Capitol Hill, and Abrahamson was faced with a formidable measure of congressional skepticism. The Fletcher report's $26 billion over five years would extend to a ten-year R&D price tag of perhaps $70 billion. Such sums were bound to elicit close scrutiny. Groups of senators and representatives were also agitating for space arms control; they were going so far as to enact legislation to limit ASAT testing. Although Congress tended to vacillate on such issues—first resolving to curtail the incipient space-weapons competition, then acquiescing to the White House—it was obvious that Star Wars would require careful political planning on the part of the military bureaucracy. The time-tested method of guaranteeing budget support was soon applied to the SDI, with attempts to spread out contracts through congressional districts, tout the economic benefits of the program, and "ramp up" the SDI budgets with annual twofold increases. The intended result: a forceful momentum built into the program, attracting the commitment and formidable lobbying power of the aerospace and electronics industries, while establishing SDI as a permanent fixture in the Pentagon.

Indeed, it seemed that there could be no other reason for the huge budget increases of 1985 and 1986. After receiving a first-year appropriation of $1.4 billion in FY 1985, the SDIO (and the related programs in the Department of Energy) requested nearly $4 billion for 1986; Congress appropriated $3 billion for that year, and in the following budget cycle the request totaled $5.4 billion. Such rapid escalations sparked brushfires of dissent in Congress, particularly since such sums could not be efficiently spent. James Schlesinger, secretary of defense under Nixon and Ford, made the point plainly in Senate testimony, saying that such R&D programs "cannot profitably expand" more than about 35 percent each year. And there were persistent reports that SDIO was having trouble spending the money. The inescapable conclusion was that the budget ramping was a political tactic, meant to build momentum that would convince the industry the SDI was here to stay, while also coalescing internal Pentagon support.

In an October 1984 speech, Abrahamson, in responding to some Capitol Hill skeptics who were balking at the SDIO's large requests, said, "we could stretch out pieces of it, but stretching will end SDI. There is only one answer to cutbacks: do it faster and faster and faster." A top Wall Street analyst, who specializes in the defense industry, depicted the momentum issue this way: "The defense contractors follow the Pentagon's lead, but the more they see the dollars growing and the idea becoming respectable, the more they take it seriously. If you're a contractor, you get into this the way you get into a cold swimming pool—very gradually. But the rate of growth in this program has gotten the industry's attention." Indeed it did: by late 1984 and early 1985, business journals were proclaiming the coming SDI cornucopia with headlines such as "Money From Heaven"; seminars were being conducted nationwide to teach contractors where and how to get in on the bonanza; and private firms were soon queuing up to participate. Most important, the aerospace industry, the most influential lobbyist in Washington, was on board, ready and willing to exert pressure on behalf of the growing Star Wars budget.[5] As James Schlesinger said repeatedly, production of a Star Wars system could cost as much as $1 trillion, an unbelievable windfall for aerospace and related industries. It was no wonder they found the SDI worth fighting for.

At the same time the SDIO was pursuing specific technologies, testing "subcomponents" of systems and otherwise pursuing a largely mission-oriented program, it suddenly announced in the fall of 1984 an elaborate, three-phase "racehorse" competition for private contractors to define the basic structure of the Star Wars system. The forty-three-page request for proposals, titled "System Architecture Studies," stated how embryonic the thinking about a *system* really was: "The purpose of this effort," the document read, "is to provide *an initial definition* and assessment of several alternative constructs of systems (architectures)." Ten contractors won the lucrative contracts to figure out for the Star Wars bureaucracy what it was supposed to be aiming for. The lack of a conceptual design did not deter SDIO from its now-habitual public face of technical optimism, nor did it restrain the spending of hundreds of millions of dollars on specific techniques that could be devalued by the architecture studies still a year from completion. This was, to put it charitably, a peculiar method of management—avidly pursuing particulars while not settled on the general.

Just as the feasibility question was transformed over time, the cost question was as well. In February 1985 Paul Nitze, the administration's chief arms-control adviser and a Washington policy-making veteran, established what appeared to be the cost standard for proceeding with Star Wars. In a Philadelphia speech, Nitze declared that Star Wars must be "cost effective at the margin," that is, it should cost less for the United States to shoot down a Soviet missile than it would for the USSR to build that additional missile. In the parlance of strategic analysts, this is the "cost-exchange ratio," and by all accounts, it strongly favors the offense. Building an ICBM—even with countermeasures such as decoys and boosters hardened against lasers—is probably less expensive than the increment in space-based weapons, in part because satellites themselves are so costly and because the technology of missiles is more mature than that of directed-energy weapons and the other techniques Star Wars demands. Nitze also said that a space-based defense must be "survivable," able to withstand the attacks from orbiting ASATs and ground-based weapons the Soviets were sure to deploy if the United States pressed ahead with the SDI.

Nitze's speech had the salient effect of refocusing the debate on considerations that had little to do with technical feasibility per se. It was apparent that even should the lasers, computers, sensors, and so forth, be "possible"—in the narrow sense that they could be invented, constructed, and tested successfully—that would not be enough to convince decision makers to proceed with deployment. The system would have to meet other criteria—in Nitze's view, cost and survivability. Additional considerations were coming to the public's attention as well. Most prominent was the likelihood that Star Wars would merely stimulate a new offensive arms race, since more and better offense (a doubling or tripling of the Soviets' ICBMs, plus new cruise missiles, bombers, and so on) was the most assured way of defeating even a highly effective defense. This became apparent when the U.S.-USSR arms control talks opened in Geneva in January 1985. The Soviets were adamant: Star Wars must go before strategic weapons could be reduced. Right or wrong, they saw SDI not as a replacement or enhancement of deterrence, but as part of a U.S. first-strike capability. Even a leaky defense, the Soviets reasoned, might be suitably effective against a ragged, poorly coordinated Soviet retaliation after the United States attacked them first. As a result, they saw SDI as extremely threatening.

The U.S. critics of Star Wars had been saying these things all along, that a strategic defense could be defeated, that the system would be too costly, that strategic stability and the offensive arms race would only worsen if SDI progressed. Such perspectives were initially muffled by the predominant attention paid to feasibility. But with feasibility questions in limbo, cost and other crucial factors began to receive the scrutiny they deserved.

The cost question was multifaceted, of course, involving far more than the cost-exchange formula articulated by Nitze. There was the fractious question of how expensive the entire ballistic missile defense would be. Schlesinger and such independent analysts as the Council on Economic Priorities had estimated it to be in the hundreds of billions of dollars—perhaps a trillion—while the more outspoken, if not more thoughtful, advocates of the SDI insisted it might be as little as $60 billion, a figure never taken seriously in informed circles. Secretary Weinberger trumped his partners' cards, however, by calling for an additional defense against bombers and cruise missiles, which would cost additional hundreds of billions. At least Weinberger's candor raised the irrepressible fact that a shield protecting the United States from ballistic missiles would not prevent other avenues of assault, including aircraft, the low-flying cruise, depressed-trajectory ballistic missiles launched from submarines near the American coast, or even "suitcase" bombs. The Council on Economic Priorities also raised the indelicate matter of conflicts of interest among defense contractors, to which the administration never adequately responded. Finally, Schlesinger—just one of a phalanx of former defense officials and diplomats skeptical of SDI—raised a troubling question that actually seemed to grow more important after the Gramm-Rudman deficit reduction law was enacted. In a late 1984 speech, Schlesinger recalled his experience with the Safeguard ABM program, noting that it "was well on the way to eating the Army out of house and home at the cost of their conventional capabilities."[6] Clearly, as the cost of the SDI grew, the trade-offs with other military R&D programs would become a greater source of conflict within the Pentagon.

When the first phase of the SDI's "architecture" studies were released in October 1985, the public had, for the first time, a clear view of the trouble the president's vision was in. Here were the comprehensive designs for the space- and ground-based systems, designs including the weapons, sensors, computers, and all the other hardware necessary to thin out a Soviet attack. The studies, the work of ten private firms (five have proceeded with a second phase of architecture studies), were released without fanfare, and understandably so. The favored SDI architecture showed *seven* separate layers, *thousands* of defense satellites, and a fresh emphasis on midcourse and terminal defense. The size and scope of this architecture was stunning. (It had the unintended but salutary effect of putting the dispute over the requisite number of SDI satellites to rest.) It implied not only tremendous economic costs, but a level of complexity that could only mesmerize both battle management planners and software writers. It depicted a task that was, in a word, daunting. The other favorite among the five remaining architectures showed *no* space-based weapons at all, apparently returning to the days of purely terminal defenses.

That one favorite architecture envisions seven layers and thousands of defense satellites, and the other favors a small number of sensors and no BMD weapons in space, indicates the level of confusion about what the Strategic Defense Initiative is supposed to do. The two designs reflect clearly different goals: one—the terminal BMD—probably to provide a defense of military targets only; the other to present the potential for a broader defense of the United States. The two designs also entail greatly differing technical tasks. The battle management, software, sensing, weaponry, and other techniques associated with the purely terminal system are far less demanding than those of the mostly space-based plan. The more the mission is narrowed (and defending a few missile silos is narrow indeed), the more "feasible" Star Wars becomes.

The differing architectures seemed to be symbolic of the disarray within the program itself. Newspaper articles reported worsening spats between the army and the air force over who would take the leading role. Managers of non-SDI military research programs grumbled about the budget priority awarded to the strategic defense programs. Rumors persisted about how once highly regarded technologies were being discarded—"downselected" in the SDIO's bureaucratese. Computer scientists with years of experience in developing programs for military systems publicly disparaged the possibility of writing software for the complex Star Wars battle management. In early 1986 they surprisingly found that the SDI-sponsored "Eastport" study agreed with one of the most important criticisms—that the favorite architectures grossly underestimated battle management tasks. Contracts expected to be awarded early in 1985 had, by summer's end, not been written. A *Wall Street Journal* report that summer summed up the disorder with its headline: "High-Tech Star Wars Program Is Challenged By Low-Tech Woes—Bureaucracy and Politics."

The mounting case against SDI on grounds of cost, strategic stability, survivability, and technology badgered the program chiefs throughout 1985 and 1986. Public opinion polls showed ambivalence among the American people about even the utopian version of Star Wars. An in-depth national poll conducted for ABC News and the *Washington Post* revealed deep reservations: 50 percent of the Americans sampled said they opposed SDI outright; another 25 percent said they opposed it if it would violate the ABM Treaty. A *Newsweek* survey found a more even split, but the skepticism was nonetheless apparent. A 1986 poll of the nation's physicists uncovered pervasive doubts about the SDI; some 80 percent concluded that Soviet countermeasures could defeat any space-based defense.[7] One had to wonder who was supporting the program, and why Congress was appropriating most of what SDIO requested in a time of severe budget austerity, when the SDI had the backing of neither the public nor the experts.

What marked the evolution of the Star Wars debate in its first three years was a steady retreat from the president's idealism, indeed, an almost schizoid quality in the administration's protestations that the government really *is* pursuing population defenses, while it was actually developing limited defenses, very likely intended for military targets. This persistent distortion of Star Wars' goal was only one dimension of the controversy, however. The SDIO was able, with the same straight face, to maintain that feasibility questions were being conquered at a whirlwind pace and simultaneously to downgrade the very techniques critics had previously shown o be unworkable. But this was not merely a matter of saving face. It became the centerpiece in the politics of Star Wars.

THE USES OF TECHNOLOGICAL OPTIMISM

Throughout the Star Wars debate, the most characteristic attitude of the SDIO was its optimism. The can-do, pioneering spirit and the futuristic quality of the program appeal to a deeply ingrained value in American political culture, that of Yankee ingenuity. Even the project's name—Strategic Defense *Initiative*—imparts an indelible sense of boldness, adventure, and risk taking. Appointing General Abrahamson, the chief of the shuttle, which until January 1986 also stirred the awe and reverence long associated with space exploration, was in keeping with that image. And the SDI's progress has been touted by administration officials as steadily fulfilling their exalted expectations of rapid, ground-breaking progress.

Optimism does not merely drive the program, but is shaped to justify it. Without "breakthroughs" and "sooner than expected" results, Congress would be leery of granting the enormous budget requests and the exclusively high priority the SDI demands. The infectious, often endearing optimism of the president can take any program just so far; in a time of budget austerity, big ticket items—and SDI is now the biggest in the Pentagon—must be rationalized. And one piece of evidence Congress readily accepts is progress. Thus, optimism has become not only the motivating spirit for many within the program, but a key element of the SDI's official ideology.

The most accessible way to show progress to Congress and the press—who, after all, would be unlikely to understand scientific lab results—is to present a demonstration of technology. Although treaty obligations constrain many weapons tests, there is great latitude in this area, and the SDIO has moved quickly to produce displays of laser techniques in particular. These shows, frequently staged in late spring or early autumn when Congress is about to vote on the program, have not always achieved the intended effect, however. Indeed, the rush to test has itself become a source of controversy, for many within the program and the skeptics outside it view these demonstrations as politically motivated, rather than scientific. In the words of one SDI scientist, they appear to be "sleazy stunts." In fact, the strategy of testing may be even more scandalous.

A number of SDI tests have demonstrated old technologies in development for many years. In June 1984, for example, the army tested a direct-ascent homing vehicle at the Kwajalein test range in the Pacific. This third stage of a rocket rose to hit a descending, dummy warhead of a known trajectory just above the atmosphere. The test, hailed by its commander as "an absolutely tremendous success," was immediately publicized as proof that Star Wars technology could work. The project, called the Homing Overlay Experiment, was the culmination of a six-year, $300 million effort that had previously suffered three failures. The test certainly showed that one interceptor can stop an attack consisting of one warhead; a controlled test, however, bears little resemblance to the saturation attacks, with high-altitude nuclear bursts, that would characterize an actual attack. Most important, perhaps, it was a terminal, ground-based system; the distinguishing feature and technological challenge of Star Wars is that it is intended to be space based in order to intercept missiles in their initial, boost phase.

A year later the SDIO tried to bounce a laser beam off a mirror on the space shuttle to demonstrate that "we can track a fast-moving target with a laser on the ground," even though the same laser, atop a ten-thousand-foot mountain in Maui, had "painted" Soviet satellites with the beam previously. Such low-power lasers had also been used against drone helicopters and the like since 1973. Despite that experience, the first SDIO attempt failed: an error had the shuttle mirror pointing outward, toward space, rather than toward the laser. A second try fulfilled the test mission, but proved little, since the physical principles were not in doubt. Television pictures of the blue-green laser reflected off the shuttle were widely distributed nonetheless, and newspaper headlines, such as that of the *Washington Post*, hailed the demonstration as a "success" and a "first for 'Star Wars.'"[8]

A far more spectacular video image was availed in a September 1985 test of a chemical laser at the White Sands Missile Range in New Mexico. This navy program, dubbed MIRACL, had been mothballed by Congress two years before but was dusted off by the SDIO at the same time the defense community was reaching a consensus on the uselessness of chemical lasers as BMD weapons. In the test, one stage of an old Titan booster, rigged up with cables, was the target. The laser, which according to one report "looks more like a giant diesel engine than a futuristic weapon" and required dozens of delicate mirrors, 370 people, and 9,000 gallons of water to operate, was then focused "for several seconds" on the Titan until the cables holding it up snapped and gave the impression that the "missile" was exploding. SDIO distributed videotapes of the explosion to television networks, which showed the tape without explaining its significance. In congressional testimony a month later, General Abrahamson maintained that the White Sands test "demonstrated graphically the lethality of this technology," and exclaimed to a Philadelphia audience that it was a "world-class breakthrough."

Abrahamson's hyperbole apparently reached its apogee that autumn, a rhetorical initiative matched with the technology demonstrations, which in turn coincided neatly with appropriations votes in Congress and the Reagan-Gorbachev summit in Geneva, where rumors persisted that SDI might be traded for deep cuts in strategic nuclear weapons. SDI was making "very steady progress," Abrahamson told a November press conference. "Inventions and innovations are coming along at just an incredible pace." The strategy began to backfire, however, as scientists *inside* the program criticized such meaningless "showmanship"—particularly the MIRACL demonstration. "These tests have the potential to be what we call strap-down chicken tests, where you strap the chicken down, blow it apart with a shotgun, and say shotguns kill chickens," mused one Sandia Lab scientist. "But that's quite different from trying to kill a chicken in a dense forest while it's running away from you."[9] Several scientists openly worried about the effect of the SDIO's false claims of "breakthroughs" on science's credibility.

No episode was more revealing of the public relations thrust of the SDI—and the potential damage to science—than that of the X-ray laser scandal. The technique is one of the most exotic of the entire Star Wars enterprise, one that would focus the energy of a hydrogen bomb explosion to create a powerful laser whose "light" is in the X-ray wavelength. Although far from proven—and facing many of the practical limitations of other candidate BMD weapons—the X-ray laser, due to its light weight and potential power, has been thought especially promising and has earned the favor of Edward Teller and his Livermore protégés. Under the direction of Lowell Wood and a few young colleagues, the X-ray laser project—code-named Excalibur—suddenly gained prominence in April 1985 when Teller, in a speech at a California campus, revealed that a highly classified test of the new device had been successful—that is, the X-rays had been focused into sufficient "brightness" to greatly encourage Excalibur enthusiasts. Even Hans Bethe, the dean of American physicists and an SDI critic (and an old adversary of Teller), seemed favorably impressed when briefed about the device's progress that spring.

One of Livermore's directors, using the test as evidence, in July pushed SDIO into higher allocations for the project after Teller had gone directly to the president to request more funds—some $60 million more, nearly doubling the project's budget. Lowell Wood was openly boastful about the X-ray laser, at times sharply chiding critics for their earlier skepticism. Ironically, the SDIO has tended to soft-pedal this technology, given its nuclear weapon source in a program the president says is non-nuclear, and the Department of Energy (DOE) oversees Excalibur, as it does all the lab's nuclear research.

Then, in November 1985, the roof fell in. Jeffrey Smith, the defense reporter for *Science* magazine, and Robert Scheer, who has written widely on nuclear policy for the *Los Angeles Times*, published articles in which scientists at Los Alamos and Livermore violated "top secret" strictures—and risked prison sentences—to reveal that the March X-ray laser test was flawed and indeed did not confirm the brazen claims of breakthroughs that its adherents had advertised. More important, independent studies of the test results at Los Alamos and Livermore led scientists to warn the experimenters repeatedly—and immediately—that the test was miscalibrated and that the results were therefore distorted. Indeed, lab physicists had warned Wood and his cohorts *before* the test about such calibration errors. Yet Teller's petition for funds and that of other Livermore chiefs proceeded with the full knowledge that the X-ray laser "breakthrough" was phoney.

The scandal caused a tremendous stir in the defense-science community. Astonishingly, the government's response was to crack down on the lab scientists who had leaked the classified information to reporters. According to one lab scientist not involved in the controversy, "the DOE security forces were using Gestapo-like tactics" to ferret out the leakers, even though those who were guilty of security breaches to put the X-ray laser in a favorable light the spring before were not punished. Roy Woodruff, nominally the head of the X-ray laser project at Livermore, resigned in November, reportedly because he was "fed up" with Teller's and Wood's interference and embarrassed by the revelations that month. In December, Livermore officially acknowledged that there were "unresolved scientific issues associated with the difficulties of measuring some properties of X-ray lasers."

The intentional misrepresentation of Excalibur's progress—and the exposure of that fraud in the press—did not daunt its advocates, however. Livermore proceeded with further tests of the device, and the 1987 budget request was boosted to $300 million; the project will consume 30 percent of all SDI directed-energy research dollars by 1988. Program managers also responded to the scandal by clamping down on public comment. A January 1986 letter from DOE's assistant secretary for nuclear weapons research to the director of Livermore is revealing: "we do not believe the discussion of nuclear directed energy weapon concepts during media interviews is in the best interests of the Department of Energy, [Livermore], or the national SDI program," the letter stated. "Involvement by the DOE and the nuclear weapons laboratories in the SDI program has received more media attention than we believe is prudent." The directive was dutifully followed.

Though of a far more serious nature, the X-ray laser scandal was in keeping with the administration's effort to exaggerate the progress of the program. As Robert Scheer reported, "most scientists in the [X-ray laser] program agree on the need for research, but they argue that the program has fallen victim to politics and that the search for 'spectacular results . . . has overridden careful physics.' "[10] That sentiment echoes the criticisms from *inside* SDI leveled at Abrahamson and others in their promotion of the MIRACL, the Homing Overlay Experiment, and others. However, such a promotional mindset is not alien to the military; in fact, the Senate Armed Services Committee, in its Fiscal Year 1986 authorization, specifically requested "near-term" demonstrations of technology. One could argue, therefore, that SDIO was doing nothing unusual in the suspect experiments and the following hyperbole.

Star Wars is not just another military R&D project, however. Flashy demos and high-toned claims have several inimical effects. First, they give the impression that SDI is progressing so well that all it needs is a full pocketbook to get the job done. Congress is reluctant to forego "a good thing," and once underway such momentum tends to become self-perpetuating. The colorful displays of "successful" experiments tend to overshadow the sober, often painfully detailed examination necessary to make responsible decisions about the program. Second, the rush to make a decision in the 1990s—the "schedule-driven" nature of the program for which optimism is a primary engine—may preclude exploration of techniques requiring a longer time to mature; thus, even those who support an aggressive BMD research program worry that the expedited schedule produces "bad science." It also, apparently, is forcing good people in the program to leave.[11] Finally, the public optimism sends a message to the Soviets, one that is essentially threatening and likely to produce a more assertive, perhaps preemptively hostile, response.

The incessant use of technological optimism also serves another purpose: to divert attention from the most troubling aspects of the program, aspects that could be a death knell to any form of space-based missile defense. One such problem is the "back end" of Star Wars, the very unglamorous realm of transportation and logistics. It is frequently overlooked that the Star Wars armada must first be boosted into space and, while there, repaired, changed, supplemented, and so on, as the months and years roll by. A Senate staff report puts the requirements most sharply, stating that they include "massive launch and recovery operations, an industrial complex to build the weapons and sensors, refurbish operations for maintenance and conversions . . . inter-orbit operations and intra-orbit operations, communications operations . . . plus an extensive ground transportation system."[12] The difficulty with this panoply of tasks is not feasibility so much as cost. Boosting any material into orbit is very expensive, upwards of $3,000 per pound. If, as some SDI architecture studies suggest, several thousands of satellites are needed for space defense, then as much as 200 million pounds of hardware must be lofted into low and high earth orbits, at a present cost of as much as $600 billion for as many as 5,000 shuttle flights.

These numbers, which are now high-end estimates, could nonetheless be conservative if the military does not reverse the series of failures of its boosters. In August 1985 and April 1986, Titan boosters carrying military cargoes into space exploded shortly after lift-off. A Delta booster lifting a weather satellite blew up in May 1986. And, of course, the shuttle program was set back by the catastrophic failure of the *Challenger* in January 1986. These were the vehicles SDI enthusiasts were depending on for Star Wars deployment, yet the reliability—let alone future costs to ensure better performance—of these systems is very much in doubt. By the time Star Wars could be deployed early in the next century, the performance problems of boosters would presumably be solved. But the cost problems are nagging. A senior SDI official, in speaking of a new space cargo ship for SDI, admitted the "costs are going to be staggering." They may also be hard to predict. The shuttle was projected by James Fletcher, the head of NASA when the shuttle was first being considered, to achieve boosting costs of

$100 per pound, with 60 flights per year. By 1986, even before the *Challenger* disaster, the space orbiter had been consistently over budget and had experienced several technical setbacks—many of them computer software glitches—which delayed its flight schedule repeatedly. Even the most favorable projections of flights and costs were nowhere near the promises made when the shuttle was in development. It was precisely such technological optimism on the part of Fletcher and his colleagues, however, that sold the shuttle program to Congress.

General Abrahamson has promised to present "cost goals," in contrast to realistic estimates, with the 1988 budget and has tried an end run around Nitze's cost standard by insisting that SDI need only be "affordable," regardless of how it compares with Soviet offensive forces—perhaps a tacit admission that the cost study was not producing acceptable figures. This attempt to circumvent the proper criterion signals that when the cost goals appear, it is likely that optimism will once more be invoked—this time to project new technological capabilities that will achieve massive cost reductions. Again consider the case of transportation and logistics. In order to deploy—much less maintain, alter, or supplement—the Star Wars armada now envisioned, the nation's "lift capacity," *at a minimum,* will have to be tripled and its cost will have to be reduced by a factor of ten. As indicated earlier, the demands could be far more severe. To achieve such goals, however, would require revolutionary technical innovations in the production of both boosters and the defense satellites, a new way to "get humans out of the loop" in the support operations (there were, for example, 26,000 people in the shuttle program alone), and a transformation of the typical military procurement effort, which routinely accepts 300 to 500 percent cost overruns and poor levels of performance. As the Senate staff study addressing these concerns concluded, "It appears that the transportation-support-logistics system for a comprehensive strategic defense may well be as complex and unprecedented as the defense itself."

The political uses of technological optimism, so incessantly employed by the SDI's bureaucrats, may in fact be a legacy of the Fletcher panel. It was that report that set the ambitious timetables and budgetary targets, and it is by Fletcher that SDI measures its "progress." It is instructive, then, to regard the basis of that report's investigations. For it was not a coldly dispassionate assessment, but rather one that was a "best-case" analysis. In the unclassified version, the panel states that "*by taking an optimistic view* . . . we concluded that a robust BMD system can be made to work eventually." Indeed, it was, in one analyst's view, "a rather candid document from experts who made every effort not to embarrass the president."[13] Whatever its source, the Fletcher report established a context for operating the Star Wars project, a dreamy state of can-do boosterism, where criticism is disparaged as disloyalty and modest technology demonstrations are hailed as world-class breakthroughs.

Optimism alone could not convince Congress and the American people, however. Soon after the Fletcher report was issued, an old device in a new form suddenly made an appearance, one that grew in importance as the president's utopianism diminished in significance as the SDI's raison d' être. That device was, ironically, the flip side of optimism: fear. In this case, it was a manufactured fear of a Soviet "Star Wars" that would disarm America.

THE SOVIETS AND STRATEGIC DEFENSE

The infusion of a strong dose of Russophobia was perhaps inevitable. SDI advocates could not coast for long on the president's resilient idealism, and the other ostensible rationales for Star Wars remained as untenable as ever. By the time General Abrahamson was selected to head the effort, the Soviet menace was being relentlessly offered as a primary reason for Star Wars. But it was not the threat of a Soviet attack per se; as Abrahamson told a House subcommittee in May 1984, "my specific charge is to examine the possibility of early deployments in case there is a breakout of the Anti-Ballistic Missile Treaty on the part of the Russians." The administration line was simple: the Soviets have for years had a major BMD research program much larger than SDI; they already have a missile defense system ringing Moscow (as allowed under the ABM Treaty), which provides a basis for a nationwide strategic defense system (not allowed under the treaty); as evidence of their intentions, one need only regard the Krasnoyarsk radar in Siberia, which is clearly illegal and a step toward the tracking systems needed for a nationwide defense. At times, administration spokesmen have gone so far as to claim that the USSR is "ten years ahead" of the United States in the BMD field. Conclusion: "We have no choice" but to pursue the SDI vigorously.

Like the United States, however, the Soviet doctrine favors a posture of deterrence: nuclear war is to be avoided, and the most logical way to prevent it is to deter attack by maintaining large and capable offensive nuclear forces. These forces—predominantly land-based ICBMs—may be used preemptively or in retaliation, the former preferred if the United States appears ready to strike.

Additionally, the Soviets have avidly pursued the research and development of BMD techniques and deployed allowable systems. These actions, however, should be regarded in the context of Soviet military policy and experience to assess the level of threat they pose to U.S. security. It is useful to recall, for example, the nation's historical experience and what they consequently consider as necessities of defense. "The terrible air raids that the Russian people suffered during World War II, particularly in Moscow and Leningrad, made it clear that the technical means for coping with attack from above was going to become an essential part of war in the future," writes Sayre Stevens, who was the CIA's deputy director for intelligence. "This judgment was coupled with the commitment by the Soviet leadership to protect the homeland from the terrible ravages that it had suffered in World War II, a commitment probably made stronger by perceptions of Soviet unpreparedness at the outset of the war."[14] This deeply ingrained outlook has inevitably informed Soviet strategic policy.

The Galosh system of missile defense ringing Moscow—sixty-four direct-ascent, nuclear-tipped missiles intended to intercept and destroy incoming warheads above the atmosphere—is evidence of this emphasis. The system, which is being upgraded and expanded to use one hundred interceptors, also employs radars near Moscow and on the USSR's periphery to track warheads and guide the missiles. This

Galosh modernization is one of the sources of concern for many in the West who fear that it signals the beginning of a countrywide "breakout" from the constraints of the ABM Treaty.

Another concern is the construction of a new "phased array" radar near the town of Krasnoyarsk, a radar that is neither close to the ABM complex in Moscow nor on the periphery of the country, as allowed by the ABM Treaty. Along with five other such radars, which are legally positioned, the Krasnoyarsk facility appears intended to fill a gap in the Soviets' early warning network; as a result, it is potentially a key element in a comprehensive BMD network. The Soviets claim the facility is for space tracking, which seems unlikely. The Reagan administration has made Krasnoyarsk the core of its list of alleged Soviet violations of arms control treaties, making the installation somewhat more important than even its limited ABM potential alone could confer. There are many possible explanations for why this radar is built as it is, but the proper diplomatic channels to resolve this dispute have not been exhausted by either side.

Soviet research and development on directed energy devices raise questions too. "The USSR's laser program is much larger than U.S. efforts and involves over 10,000 scientists and engineers," at a cost equal in U.S. terms to $1 billion, a high-level administration report asserted in 1985.[15] The descriptions provided by the U.S. government imply that the USSR has very aggressive ambitions for ground-based lasers and other advanced techniques, either as antisatellite weapons or as part of a ballistic missile defense.

A final area of concern is the Soviets' surface-to-air missiles (SAMs), which are part of its extensive air defense system intended to shoot down U.S. bombers during wartime. SAMs may have some inherent BMD capability and, like the Galosh upgrade, may represent a potential for breakout. Seen in concert with the other Soviet activities, however legal, the SAMs appear to indicate a strong and possibly growing emphasis on strategic defense.

These "worst-case" assumptions—perhaps necessary for any military planner, East or West—can easily be converted into the specter of a grand Soviet design to trash the ABM

Treaty and deploy a nationwide defense that would deprive the United States of its offensive nuclear potency, particularly its retaliatory capability after a Soviet first strike had destroyed U.S. land-based ICBMs. But does the USSR's defense program signal an imminent breakout, which in turn justifies America's crash program of the SDI?

To answer that pivotal question, consider air defense and the SAM-as-BMD scenario. The Soviets' air defense system is certainly a reflection of their greater emphasis on strategic defense generally. The improvements in Soviet SAMs, however, respond to U.S. actions. "An aggressive U.S. program to improve strategic aerodynamic attack capabilities has been responsible for the vigor with which the Soviet Union has sought increasingly capable air defenses," Sayre Stevens concludes. "A series of U.S. weapons systems . . . has put increasing pressure on Soviet air defense technology." Herbert York, who has held several high-level defense posts, makes a similar point: "For nearly four decades, the Soviets have been investing vast sums of money in the deployment and improvement of air defenses. Never during all that time have they been capable of seriously blunting a U.S. air attack."[16]

The Galosh upgrade is similarly unthreatening. The United States abandoned its one allowable ABM system (which was completed near Grand Forks, North Dakota, to protect Minuteman silos) in 1975 precisely because it was widely concluded that such a terminal defense system was useless against a saturation attack of Soviet warheads. The Galosh complex surrounding Moscow suffers from the same disadvantage, and efforts to extend these technologies more widely (probably to protect military facilities) hold only marginal promise. Even with its improved Galosh system, the Soviets cannot defend against anything more than "small-scale attacks on key targets around Moscow," according to a 1985 CIA analysis.[17]

The research on directed-energy weapons must also be considered warily. The estimate of ten thousand scientists working on lasers is derived from estimating the floor space used in research centers and assigning values—scientist-hours, in effect—to the type of research conducted in those centers. It has little to do with the actual product of those facilities, which in fact appear to be no more menacing than the similar lines and levels of research the United States has pursued in the same period. Indeed, *the official U.S. comparisons of key BMD-related technologies consistently has shown the United States more advanced than the Soviet Union* even before the SDI was off the ground.[18]

Two principal tendencies in Soviet doctrine are also worth examining to assess the significance of their BMD activities. First, most experts agree that the Soviet Union values the ABM Treaty highly, in part because it precludes a costly defense weapons competition with the United States. Constraints on strategic defenses also lend high confidence to offensive nuclear capability and strategic stability, a key argument used to convince the Soviets to sign the ABM Treaty to begin with.[19] With the singular exception of Krasnoyarsk, Soviet BMD activities to date show compliance with the treaty constraints as well as eagerness to maintain as effective strategic defenses as the treaty allows. This latter emphasis derives from their view that defenses and offenses are closely linked. "Strategic defence is inexorably linked to the offence in Soviet thinking," explains sovietologist Stephen Meyer. "[Strategic defence's] value is to protect forces and warmaking potential while buying time to switch to the offensive."[20]

The second tendency is even more speculative: the Soviet response to the SDI. Virtually every expert sees the Soviets eventually emulating the SDI if an agreement to constrain such aggressive R&D programs cannot be reached at Geneva. The Soviets view military might as the primary arena for a "successful" competition with the United States, and, as a consequence, they will not allow the United States to gain a decisive advantage in any major weapons technology. Since they view SDI as potentially capable of limited success (able, for example, to intercept 60 percent of their warheads), the Soviets will pursue an offsetting response—namely, the countermeasures used to defeat a U.S. strategic defense. "Despite wishful thinking to the contrary," Stephen Meyer writes, "it is very unlikely that SDI will weaken the offensive emphasis in Soviet military thinking," which means, among other possibilities, "that SDI will lead to further emphasis on innovation in Soviet offensive missions, as well as defensive missions."[21]

The consensus of informed opinion points to a Soviet wait-and-see attitude: If SDI is sustained in the U.S. Congress, the Soviets will undertake a more aggressive program both to transform their offensive nuclear forces to attack and penetrate Star Wars and to deploy their own (perhaps ground-based) BMD system nationwide. Most certainly, they will not permit Star Wars to proceed unchallenged.

One must always regard the Soviets warily, of course, but the Reagan administration's depiction of the Soviet BMD program as a *justification* for the SDI seems contrived. The Soviet Union has strong incentives to adhere to the ABM Treaty, not least to avoid another dimension of an arms-technology rivalry. Their activities will always test the boundaries of treaty obligations, but their work on SAMs, Galosh, and radars—including Krasnoyarsk—present no militarily significant challenge to U.S. deterrence, certainly nothing to warrant the SDI extravaganza.

THE IDEOLOGY OF STAR WARS

If the Soviet strategic program—both offense and defense—does not constitute a worrisome threat to U.S. security, then what are the rationales driving Star Wars? Four clear tendencies seem apparent in the administration's subrosa ideology that account for the great risks and costs the government is willing to undertake to pursue space-based missile defense.

The first of these is the hope to dominate outer space militarily. Space has been viewed as the "new high ground," an advantageous position from which one or the other of the superpowers could gain a stronghold. The military uses of space have a long history, indeed, space activities were always viewed by policymakers as military first, civilian second. Beginning with the ballistic missile itself—which merely travels through space—satellites' growing capability enabled uses including communications, command and control of conventional and nuclear forces, reconnaissance, early warning of attack, and so on. Antisatellite weapons were developed in the early 1960s as well, so the "militarization" of space is not novel. The growing technical capability wrought by microelectronics in particular has made space more accessible, however, and as a result the realm above the atmosphere has become far more attractive.

With the inauguration of Ronald Reagan in 1981, a more aggressive military space policy was soon underway. Although the Carter administration had initiated a new ASAT weapon program—a homing vehicle, meant to destroy Soviet satellites, that is launched from the belly of an F-15 aircraft—it viewed ASAT arms control as desirable and was purportedly funding the ASAT R&D to encourage the Soviets to negotiate an ASAT ban. This attitude changed markedly under President Reagan. Within two years a new policy was established: arms control was no longer desirable (a Soviet draft treaty was summarily dismissed), and antisatellite weapons were given fresh impetus. As a 1982 White House statement put it: "The United States will proceed with development of an antisatellite (ASAT capability), with operational deployment as a goal. The primary purposes . . . are to deter threats to space systems of the United States and . . . to deny any adversary the use of space-based systems that provide support to hostile military forces." The policy had even more sinister overtones, however. The new emphasis on space was consonant with the administration's fixation on *war-fighting* capability, the doctrine that envisions the United States fighting a protracted, global nuclear war. Such a doctrine necessitates many varieties of weapons, including space weapons. In a leaked "Defense Guidance" report, for example, the Defense Department stated: "We must achieve capabilities to ensure free access to and use of space in peace and war; deny the wartime use of space to adversaries . . . and apply military force *from* space if that becomes necessary."[22]

Star Wars offered the military-space enthusiasts a grand opportunity for the kind of massive R&D and the revision of doctrine necessary to realize the "weaponization" of space. Once the president's unfocused desire was set in motion, it was obvious that a panoply of space weapons could be developed under the rubric of space-based ballistic missile defense. That the ultimate SDI objective could—and probably would—fail was not a deterrent to those who envision the United States dominating outer space, since the varieties of technologies—lasers, kinetic energy weapons, sensors, and so forth—the SDI might nurture would neatly conform to the demands of antisatellite weapons and other possibilities for "military force *from* space." The March 23 speech, in short, handed a carte blanche to the military to delve into the space weapons business without restraint.

A second motive behind SDI involves an attitude toward the Soviet Union, a posture of noncooperation and competitiveness that extends into every sphere of U.S.-USSR relations. Those who knew that Star Wars could cost hundreds of billions of dollars and that the Soviets would have to react, possibly with commensurate expense, foresaw an *economic* rivalry that the United States was bound to win. The Soviets simply cannot keep up with America, this argument reasons, and the already stressed Russian economy will be disabled by the space arms race. The United States will have the pleasure of harassing the Soviets with superior technology and, perhaps, a public relations edge as well. At the same time, the U.S. defense industry will benefit handsomely, with an accelerated shift of national resources from social needs to military use. It is doubtful that economic considerations originated the Star Wars effort, but it is likely that they have energized many in the administration and, of course, in the industry. More certain, however, is the view that harassing the Soviets is a legitimate tactic, and SDI looms as a quite intimidating form of harassment that does in fact force the Soviet leadership to choose among limited options of response.

In both of these thrusts—the drive to dominate space and to badger the Soviets—another rationale is apparent. That is the unwavering preference for the use of technology as the main tool of policy. The United States' seemingly innate talent for invention and innovation presents military opportunities simply not available to the relatively backward Soviets; with the high-tech revolution, moreover, the technology gap has widened. So SDI is embraced as the culmination of a resilient American tendency to rely on science and engineering to solve problems of all varieties. It is welcomed, too, as an initiative that—regardless of its fate—will spin off all sorts of techniques usable in defense. The more significant utility, however, bears on the Soviet rivalry: by leveraging this technical virtuosity, the United States can establish a permanent state of military superiority. This attitude not only employs technology as the elixir of policy-making, but as the antidote to its poisonous alternative: diplomacy.

It is no secret that the Reagan presidency is marked by an undiluted disdain for arms control. Throughout the 1980s, the United States' stance toward the critical arms issues—strategic weapons, intermediate nuclear forces (INF) in Europe, the comprehensive test ban, and ASAT—has been obstreperous. Even existing treaties—SALT II and the ABM Treaty, in particular—have been under relentless assault. The administration's hostility to arms reduction and restraint as the modus vivendi of superpower relations is now so well documented and virtually accepted in Washington that it would be naïve not to draw very direct connections between Reagan's febrile drive for military superiority and the Strategic Defense Initiative. The president and his top advisers must, of course, pay lip service to the notion of nuclear disarmament: the desire for arms control is simply too strong in American political culture to ignore.

As a result, the obfuscation in official arms policy tends to phrases such as "such an agreement is not verifiable," as in the case of antisatellite weapons, or "such an agreement is not in the interests of national security," as was the response to the Soviets' unilateral moratorium on tests of nuclear explosives. In most such cases, no further elaboration is offered; for the purposes of public relations, none is probably needed. The issues as a whole are complex, and the public cannot be blamed for not being experts. The administration has as its allies, moreover, a large cadre of right-wing polemicists who give the administration's position a public face. Former diplomat George W. Ball's description of what he calls the "secular fundamentalists" concisely reveals the predominant view pervading the White House and Pentagon. "Since they share a vigorous repugnance to dealing with the Kremlin, the leading secular fundamentalists are now joining in a loud and well-orchestrated chorus, proclaiming that all past efforts at nuclear arms control have been futile and that most such efforts have benefitted the Soviet Union against the interests of the United States," Ball wrote in 1985. "The leitmotif running through all [their] statements is the obsessive urge to build up our nuclear arsenal and to reject efforts to halt the arms spiral through diplomacy. Just how these militant intellectuals conceive that the process will finally end is the great unanswered question."[23] Edward Teller, in November 1983 testimony to the House Armed Services Committee, put the idea concisely: "There are," he told the panel, "numerous advocates of arms reduction to be accomplished by negotiations and treaties with the Soviet Union. We pursued this path for more than a quarter of a century. The results have been a shift of military power to the Soviet Union and a steadily increasing danger to world peace."

The relationship of this attitude on arms control to the SDI is direct and unambiguous. Proceeding with a space-based missile defense will, without a doubt, wreck the ABM Treaty, and it will do so years before the knotty matters of feasibility and the effects on strategic stability are understood. SDI could also wreck any chance for future weapons limitations, or reductions, because the multiplication and innovation of offensive forces are among the ways the Soviets can defeat a missile defense. Progress toward a test ban on antisatellite weapons has been summarily halted by the Reagan administration, in part because it would hamper testing of technologically similar Star Wars techniques. And the Soviet moratorium on nuclear explosives testing, which Secretary Gorbachev invited the United States to join, was turned down, again due partially to the SDI—many nuclear tests will be needed to advance the X-ray laser. The scorecard shows a nearly complete sweep for Star Wars versus negotiated and verifiable arms control.

These several rationales have cohabited with the administration's policy-making apparatus. And because the top policy spokesmen are willing to equivocate about the goals of the SDI, the administration's adherence to the ABM Treaty, its negotiating position with the Soviet Union, and other such matters, any number of "reasons" for pursuing Star Wars can be maintained simultaneously.

What is becoming increasingly apparent, however, is that as the program matures the government's ability to have its cake and eat it too will diminish. For the "weak links" in the SDI are showing signs of stress. The program management itself has repeatedly shifted priorities and is apparently unable to spend its ample resources efficiently, which is merely characteristic of any decrepit bureaucracy. The scientific community is balking at the program, and the most prestigious scientists and academic departments are resolutely refusing to participate, denying SDI their sorely needed talent. The technical difficulties of space-based defense—recognized as troublesome right from the start—are no nearer resolution. Some of these technical matters, moreover, look more daunting than they did at first glance, particularly the computer software requirements, the difficulty of managing the system, the vulnerability of any space-based armada to counterattack, and the many other cost-effective measures the Soviets can take to enable their offensive weapons to penetrate even a high-tech defense. Finally, there is the utter vacuity of strategic reasoning behind Star Wars: a less-than-perfect defense is not needed to enhance U.S. security; it is anathema to our allies; it is extremely provocative to the Soviet Union, which views it as a component of a U.S. first-strike capability; and it will drive the offensive and defensive arms race to new heights of frenzy and peril.

The politics of SDI do not comprise an admirable chapter in American history. It has, so far, been marred by government equivocation, even duplicity, in explaining its intentions to the American people. The informed skeptics of the program have been officially depicted as embittered Cassandras and charlatans, and even accused of disloyalty, although their skepticism repeatedly proves correct. And the very economic health and strategic security of the nation is increasingly placed in jeopardy with every day that Star Wars is allowed to proceed. Whether this bleak chapter is a brief folly or a lengthy disaster depends in large part on exactly when one of the SDI's weak links finally breaks.

2
Scientists and Star Wars

JONATHAN B. TUCKER

In his farewell radio and television address to the American people on January 17, 1961, Pres. Dwight D. Eisenhower offered a distillation of the wisdom gained during his years of public service and his hopes and fears for the future. One of the trends that most troubled him was the growing political influence of the military. "The conjunction of an immense military establishment and a large arms industry is new in the American experience," he said. "We recognize the imperative need for this development. Yet we must not fail to comprehend its grave implications. . . . In the councils of government, we must guard against the acquisition of unwarranted influence, whether sought or unsought, by the military-industrial complex. The potential for the disastrous rise of misplaced power exists and will persist."

Eisenhower also warned about the dangers of the expanding partnership between science and government. During World War II, scientific research had been responsible for a technological revolution in America's military and industry, symbolized by the awesome power of the atomic bomb. But in the process, science itself had been transformed. Eisenhower noted that research was becoming "more formalized, complex, and costly" and that a steadily increasing share was conducted "for, by, or at the direction of, the Federal government." He concluded: "The prospect of domination of the nation's scholars by Federal employment, project allocations, and the power of money is present—and is gravely to be regarded."

A quarter century later, Eisenhower's warnings seem remarkably prescient. University research is increasingly shaped by government priorities, and the nation is channeling almost half its research expenditures into military systems. Nowhere have Eisenhower's premonitions been more starkly fulfilled than in the Strategic Defense Initiative. In a short time, SDI has evolved from a gleam in the president's eye into a massive government-managed and -sponsored research effort that already dwarfs the Manhattan Project and the Apollo Program.

The decision to launch SDI was not preceded by an objective assessment of the technical feasibility of a population defense against ballistic missiles. While the Reagan administration sought advice from well-known enthusiasts of strategic defense, such as Edward Teller, knowledgeable skeptics were excluded from the policy-making process. Administration officials did not inform or consult top scientists in the Department of Defense, nor did they discuss the proposal with the White House Science Council, an advisory board of eminent scientists that met only a few days before the president's March 23 speech. When the speech aroused a critical response from the technical community, the administration belatedly sought scientific legitimacy for the proposal by appointing two expert study panels to evaluate the feasibility and strategic implications of ballistic missile defense (BMD). George Keyworth II, the White House science adviser, also became an outspoken advocate of SDI. Because he considered himself a member of the White House "team" rather than a representative of the scientific community, Keyworth failed to communicate to the president the widespread skepticism among scientists about the feasibility of an effective population defense.

Although SDI has enjoyed political and budgetary success, its technological future appears less promising. Even the president admits that an effective defense against ballistic missiles will require a vast array of advanced technologies that today lie far beyond the state of the art. Bringing these technologies to fruition, if possible, will require the dedicated participation of the nation's best scientific minds. Yet SDI has failed to win the political support of a sizable fraction of the scientific-technical community—the very people the president is counting on to make his dream a reality. Indeed, not since the height of the Vietnam War have scientists and engineers been so deeply divided over an issue of national policy.

Dramatizing the intensity of the scientific opposition to SDI has been the willingness of thousands of physicists, computer scientists, and engineers across the country to sign a pledge refusing to solicit or accept SDI-related research grants. At a time when alternative sources of research support are dwindling, these individuals have expressed their personal opposition to SDI at a potentially significant cost to their careers. Although the research boycott has failed to cripple the program, it has called attention to the growing schism within the scientific community—a "weak link" that may ultimately threaten the initiative's future.

DECIPHERING THE SDI BUREAUCRACY

In the spring of 1984 the Pentagon created a new agency called the Strategic Defense Initiative Organization to centralize management of BMD research, including twenty-seven existing programs that had previously been scattered throughout the defense bureaucracy. SDIO was structured into five technical Program Elements—System Analysis and Battle Management; Sensors and Surveillance; Directed Energy Weapons; Kinetic Energy Weapons; and Survivability, Lethality, and Key Technologies. In late 1984 SDIO created a sixth division called the Innovative Science and Technology Office (IST) to manage research on "highly innovative, high-risk" concepts and technologies that would have to be nurtured for SDI to work. Appointed as IST director was James Ionson, an astrophysicist on leave from the NASA Goddard Space Flight Center.

While the five SDIO Program Elements fund research and development conducted by the national laboratories and the major defense contractors, IST money is targeted primarily at universities. IST's research goals are simultaneously basic and applied: it supports work on the cutting edge of the fundamental sciences, yet in support of a specific military mission. Academic scientists are encouraged to explore novel concepts and technologies broadly relevant to strategic defense, in the hope that their ideas can eventually be transferred to industrial contractors for hardware development. Even before the creation of IST, the Pentagon was seeking greater participation by the universities in military R&D, having concluded that defense contractors often have an insular view of military technology and could benefit from a regular infusion of new ideas.

University involvement in SDI research has grown rapidly. By mid-1986, scientists and engineers at seventy-three academic institutions throughout the United States were engaged in IST-sponsored projects. The IST budget has also tripled in two years, from $28 million in fiscal year 1985 to $91.8 million in FY 1986. A leading recipient of IST funding is the Massachusetts Institute of Technology (MIT), where on-campus IST contracts totaled approximately $850,000 in 1985 and are expected to exceed $3 million in 1986.[1] In addition, since 1983, university-affiliated research centers (including MIT's Lincoln Laboratory) have received more than $540 million in contracts from the other SDIO Program Elements. When these various sources are combined, SDIO funding for university research already exceeds $200 million a year.

The organizational structure of IST suggests that its goals and priorities may differ substantially from the image the agency has tried to convey to the academic community. In numerous speeches and interviews, Ionson has implied that IST's primary mission is to provide grants for scientists engaged in unclassified research in areas of broad relevance to strategic defense. But a brief glance at the agency's organizational structure, which went into effect October 1, 1986, suggests an emphasis on more focused research and development.

In addition to a Program Support Division, which is responsible for program analysis and international programs, IST's research program is managed by three closely coordinated divisions. The Science and Technology Division funds basic university research of potential importance to SDI—including 135 three-year research grants in FY 1986—and administers the SDIO Small Business Innovation Research Program. Although these programs are centrally managed by

IST personnel, they are implemented by "science and technology agents" on the staffs of other government agencies, including the Office of Naval Research, the Army Research Office, the Air Force Office of Scientific Research, the Defense Nuclear Agency, NASA, and the Department of Energy.

The Science and Technology Division also organizes Research Consortia: joint R & D projects involving the collaboration of several university, industrial, and government labs. Over the past two years, IST has established consortia to investigate a variety of topics, including nuclear and nonnuclear space power, optical computing, highly reliable electronic circuits, high-strength composite materials, particle beams, rocket propellants, and ultra-shortwave lasers.[2]

Once the fundamental research sponsored by the Science and Technology Division has spawned new concepts and devices, IST's Integrated Technology Division applies and combines these technologies into a form suitable for experimentation and demonstration. For example, the planned Space Technology Experiment will demonstrate the production of high levels of electric power in space. Finally, the Applications Division selects the most promising technologies and directs advanced engineering and further demonstration to facilitate technology transfer to one of the five SDIO Program Elements. In sum, this organizational structure suggests that IST views unclassified basic research not as an end in itself, but merely as the first step on the road to developing actual military hardware.

IST's method for soliciting research proposals during the first year and a half of the program (FY 1985–86) was also revealing. In order to attract a large number of proposals, IST initially spared university researchers the laborious task of preparing a formal proposal document, which normally includes an extensive description of the planned research and a detailed budget. Instead, applicants were asked to submit preproposals or "white papers"—informal summaries limited to ten pages of technical content (including "a clear description of how the research relates to the overall SDIO program") plus a one-page summary of funding requirements. Because the white papers were short, IST officials could screen them in large numbers, identifying the salient features of the proposed research and its relevance to the SDI mission. Investigators who passed the initial screening process were then invited to submit a formal proposal.

This streamlined process enabled IST to winnow down the number of applicants to a manageable level (about twice the available amount of funding) so that formal proposals could be reviewed more efficiently. Although the use of white papers was not new, having been employed by agencies such as the National Science Foundation, IST departed from established procedure by soliciting the proposals directly from researchers rather than through university channels. In so doing, IST bypassed the normal institutional review process in which university administrators check grant proposals for consistency with school policies, such as those regarding classification and the use of university facilities. (In FY 1987, IST will abandon the white-paper process and require submission of full proposals.)

IST also differs from civilian research agencies such as the National Science Foundation in that it does not subject formal proposals to "peer review" by outside scientific experts, who are supposed to recommend funding strictly on the basis of scientific merit. Instead, IST funding decisions are made by in-house technocrats and are based in large part on the relevance of the proposed research to the goals of SDI. This strong mission orientation has been criticized because it tends to reward salesmanship at the expense of good science. Notes one critic, "When the decisions are made by people who have a mission, they tend to give the money to the people who make the biggest promises."[3]

In addition to sponsoring university research of value to SDI, IST has a second mission: to build political support for the SDI program within the academic community. Indeed, some observers believe that this is IST's primary role. Jack Ruina, a professor of electrical engineering at MIT and once a high-ranking Defense Department official, contends that "although long-term unclassified research is hardly viewed as central to the success of SDI, it is seen as lending the program legitimacy and prestige."[4]

In the spring of 1985, the IST office launched an aggressive campaign to recruit the participation of university scientists and engineers in SDI research. Between February and June, IST dispensed some $62 million in long-term contracts to Research Consortia involving twenty-seven universities in sixteen states. And on March 29, IST held a "Technical Review for Universities" to familiarize the academic research community with its "wish list" of research topics. The day-long seminar was held at a hotel in New Carrollton, Maryland, an industrial suburb midway between Baltimore and Washington, D.C. In attendance were more than 240 administrators and faculty members from 124 academic institutions in forty-seven states.[5]

IST director Ionson chaired the meeting, which included a speech by science adviser George Keyworth and presentations by the IST agents for the various research areas. The attendees were told that IST would distribute a total of about $100 million in university research grants during fiscal years 1985 and 1986. In addition, Robert Hughey of the Department of Energy announced that DOE was launching a parallel New and Innovative Concepts Program to fund university research on energy technologies of relevance to SDI. Funded at $3 million to $5 million annually, this DOE program provides contracts running one to three years and ranging in size from $50,000 to $500,000.[6] Although a few researchers attending the New Carrollton seminar expressed concerns about restrictions on publication of research data, the initial response was positive. IST received more than 3,000 white papers, from which about 400 formal proposals were requested, and about 200 ultimately funded.

Despite this success, however, IST also aroused considerable controversy by its clumsy efforts to manipulate the academic community for political ends. On April 23, 1985, for example, IST announced to the press that the California Institute of Technology had agreed to participate in a Research Consortium on optical computing. In fact, although one Caltech professor had accepted a subcontract from the consortium, the university administration had not signed an agreement with IST. Caltech president Marvin L. Goldberger fired off an angry letter to SDIO chief Lt. Gen. James Abrahamson and Defense Secretary Caspar Weinberger, accusing IST of making "manifestly false" statements about the university's participation in SDI in order to win political support for the program on Capitol Hill.

IST director Ionson also made a serious gaffe when he told a reporter attending the New Carrollton seminar that university participation in SDI research would have an important political impact. "We're trying to sell something to Congress," he said. "If we can say that this fellow at MIT will get money to do such and such research, it's something real to sell."[7] Angered by Ionson's remarks, MIT president Paul E. Gray issued a strong rebuttal. In a speech at MIT's graduation exercises on June 3, 1985, he accused IST of trying to "short-circuit debate and use MIT and other institutions as political instruments in an attempt to obtain implicit institutional endorsement." Gray insisted that "this university will not be so used. Any participation by MIT in SDI-funded research should in no way be understood or used as an institutional endorsement of the SDI program."[8]

An MIT official speculated that Ionson's remarks "were more driven by naïveté than by machiavellian instinct." Whatever Ionson's motives, it has become increasingly clear that IST funding has political strings attached.

THE CLASSIFICATION CONUNDRUM

Until recently, most Pentagon funding at universities has been for basic research with potential military applications but no direct links to specific weapons systems. For example, the Office of Naval Research supports fundamental research in biology and oceanography, while the Defense Advanced Research Projects Agency (DARPA) has long funded basic research in the field of artificial intelligence.

Although IST claims to be in this relatively benign tradition, there is an important difference. Because IST-funded research is closely linked to the SDI mission, the results will be inherently more sensitive. Indeed, IST officials have refused to rule out the possibility of classification at a future date. The same applies to DOE's parallel New and Innovative Concepts Program. At the March 1985 seminar in New Carrollton, pro gram manager Robert Hughey warned that security classification "is going to be a problem for SDI research projects sponsored by DOE" and hinted that some research begun openly might have to be classified later.[9]

The ambiguous status of IST-funded research stems in part from the fact that all SDI research is funded out of the DOD budget category for advanced development (designated 6.3), which is normally classified, rather than out of the budget categories for basic research (6.1) or exploratory research (6.2), which are normally not classified. SDIO officials claim that these budget categories are somewhat artificial and that for administrative convenience every large military research program is given a single budget designation. Since SDI comprises a wide variety of activities ranging from basic research to large demonstration projects, the "average" budget category of 6.3 has been applied to the whole program. But one reason for the 6.3 designation might be to make it easier for IST to impose security restrictions on research projects at a later date.

IST director Ionson tried to dampen the smoldering concerns about classification but inadvertently ended up fanning the flames. In a policy memorandum issued on August 8, 1985, he stated that IST-funded projects at universities, "although funded out of budget category 6.3, will be treated as fundamental research." Yet in the next paragraph Ionson qualified this statement by adding that a prepublication review clause could be specified in the research contract before the work begins. In such cases, IST retains the right to classify research results "when there is a likelihood of disclosing operational capabilities and performance characteristics of planned or developing military systems, or technologies unique and critical to defense programs." If the prepublication review option is not agreed to in advance, it will not be imposed retroactively, Ionson said.[10] Still, this policy statement clearly leaves the door open for IST to require a prepublication review clause in future contracts.

In another ambiguous policy statement Ionson said that although there was no requirement for principal investigators working on IST-funded research projects to obtain security clearances, "it might be advisable for them to have secret clearances so that we can let them know what is going on and they can access classified documents."[11] Access to secret information, he explained, would enable faculty members to guide graduate students away from potentially sensitive research topics. But the implicit pressure for principal investigators to obtain security clearances would clearly erode the ban on classified research in effect at the great majority of universities. It would also discourage non-U.S. citizens from participating in IST-funded projects, damaging both the quality of research and the open university environment. At MIT, for example, about one-third of all graduate students are not U.S. citizens.

Because of IST's ambiguous policy on classification, uncertainty hangs over the program like a darkening thundercloud. Once large numbers of IST-funded projects are under way at universities, will IST suddenly change the rules of the game and decide to stamp the results secret on a blanket, or project-by-project, basis? The consequences would be serious. According to Kenneth A. Smith, MIT's vice president for research, if research projects are classified retroactively, MIT has "a bail-out clause in the contract that says we're going to get out of the project, and they have to give us close-out costs. The individual researchers may be damned unhappy, but that's what we're going to do."[12]

Such abrupt terminations of funding would leave university scientists stranded in midexperiment, faced with a Hobson's choice of abandoning their research after a major investment of time and effort or pursuing it at a classified facility where they would be unable to publish their findings, the key to advancement in academia. Graduate students would be even worse off. Since Ph.D. dissertations must be publishable in the open literature, students working on belatedly classified projects could not earn credentials for an academic job. They would therefore have to "sanitize" their research, switch topics entirely, or reconcile themselves to a career in a classified government laboratory.

The risk that security restrictions may eventually be imposed on unclassified IST research has been heightened by the agency's strong emphasis on Research Consortia. Since most universities forbid classified work on campus, IST has organized the consortia so that the most sensitive projects are "quarantined" within secure government or industrial labs. Asserts MIT's Smith, "We wouldn't get into a consortium in the first place unless we felt that the statement of work for the portion to be done here was sufficiently clear that classification was not anticipated."

But what happens when university-based scientists participating in a Research Consortium generate results that IST considers "militarily critical"? Presumably the research will be classified and transferred to a secure industrial or government lab within the consortium. For example, an IST-funded project at MIT might be moved to Lincoln Laboratory, an off-campus facility run by the university but devoted almost entirely to classified military research. The net effect of many such transfers would be a significant flow of research funds and skilled scientists from the open university environment into secret defense labs. This civilian-to-military "brain drain" would, in effect, punish the universities for their success in SDI research.

Of course all such scenarios remain somewhat speculative. At the large majority of universities that ban secret research on campus, IST officials may be deterred from formally classifying research projects by the threat of protests and bad publicity. But they could also resort to less draconian alternatives. "IST obviously can't eliminate the classification barrier overnight," says Sheldon Krimsky, associate professor of urban and environmental affairs at Tufts University. "But they have a number of instruments other than formal classification to restrict the flow of scientific information outside of this country."[13]

The Export Administration Act, for example, empowers the federal government to control the export of unclassified technical information that could endanger U.S. national security. In addition, the Pentagon may restrict the presentation of unclassified papers at U.S. scientific meetings attended by foreign nationals. A particularly controversial application of this law occurred during an April 1985 meeting of the Society of Photo-Optical Instrumentation Engineers. In the middle of the conference, Pentagon officials suddenly intervened and prevented scientists from delivering forty-three unclassified papers in open session. A dozen papers were withdrawn entirely, while presentations of the others were restricted to U.S. citizens. After heated protests from the scientific community, the White House issued a policy statement in September 1985 limiting the security restrictions that can be imposed on unclassified research. Under the new policy, if a research project requires tight controls to protect national security, it must be formally classified; the government cannot restrict publication retroactively by simply ordering researchers not to release their results. This policy change reassured many scientists, but it did not end the Reagan administration's insistence that some types of unclassified technical information, such as that involving microelectronics, be presented only at sessions from which foreigners have been excluded.[14]

A few American universities permit and even encourage classified research on campus and have been amply rewarded by the Pentagon for their cooperation. One such institution is the Georgia Institute of Technology, which has received eight SDI contracts worth a total of $35 million.[15] As other universities become increasingly dependent on DOD funding, they may also be tempted to loosen their strictures on classified research. Indeed, Carnegie-Mellon University's Software Engineering Institute, which is heavily supported by the Pentagon, set an ominous precedent when it agreed to submit potentially sensitive research papers to the DOD for prepublication review—and if necessary, censorship.

Given the dwindling number of nondefense funding sources, critics fear that if the military support of academic science continues to grow at the present rate, the Pentagon will soon find itself in a very strong bargaining position. By threatening to transfer valuable research contracts to academic institutions that already permit secret research, the DOD may be able to pressure other universities into accepting tightened security restrictions on publication. Because the free exchange of information has long been a key strength of U.S. research, such Pentagon-imposed restrictions could undermine the position of the United States as a world leader in science and technology. The ironic result could be a net decline in our national security.

THE DISTORTION OF RESEARCH

One frequently voiced concern about mission-oriented military research is that it will distort the structure of academic science. Although universities try to be evenhanded in their allocation of resources, the types of funding available largely determine the areas of inquiry that can be actively pursued.

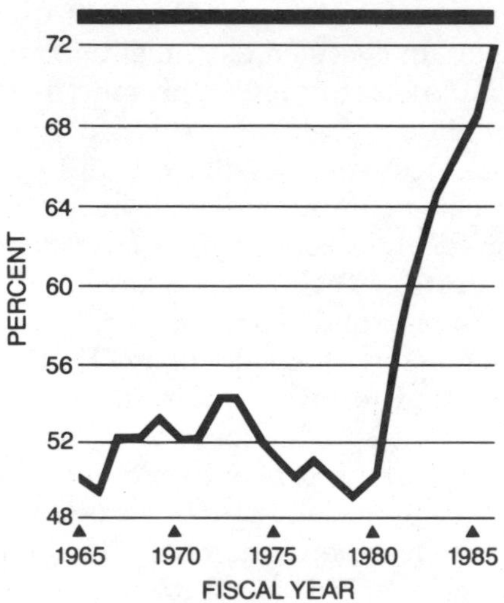

FIG. 2.1. Defense research and development as a proportion of all federal R&D. SOURCE: *Science* (May 2, 1986).

In recent years, military R&D has accounted for an ever-larger slice of the total federal research pie, growing from 50 percent in FY 1980, to 67 percent in FY 1985, to 72 percent in FY 1986. At the same time, federal support for civilian R&D as a percentage of GNP has steadily declined, so that the United States now trails Japan and West Germany.[16] Although the vast bulk of the Pentagon's research budget is channeled to the private sector, DOD allocated $970 million in FY 1986 to support university research, a sum equivalent to 16 percent of all federal funding on campus. Over the past twenty years, DOD funding at universities as a fraction of total federal support has followed a U-shaped curve, reaching a peak of 16 percent in 1969, at the height of the Vietnam War, falling to a low of 10 percent in 1980, and then climbing back up to 16 percent by 1983.

This share of DOD support for campus research—one out of every six dollars of government money—may seem too small to warrant alarm, but several factors increase its significance. First, dependence on the Pentagon is particularly great in

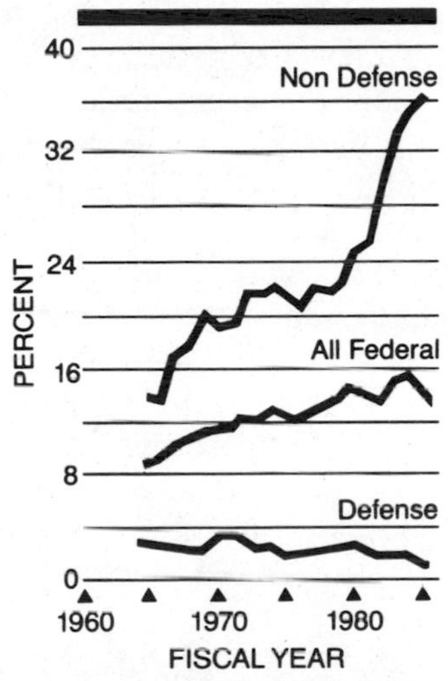

FIG. 2.2. Basic research as a proportion of defense, federal, and nondefense R&D. SOURCE: *Science* (May 2, 1986).

certain research areas: engineering research generally is 38 percent funded by DOD, while the proportion of military support is very high in the specialized fields of astronautical engineering (82 percent), electrical engineering (56 percent), materials engineering (48 percent), and computer science (46 percent).[17]

Second, between 1980 and 1985, Pentagon support for university research grew by a total of 89 percent, or 2.5 times faster than that from any other source. While the DOD research budget has continued to grow, research budgets of U.S. agencies in health, science, and space have leveled off or declined. At the same time, these nondefense agencies have slanted some of their programs to meet military requirements. The Department of Energy now devotes two-thirds of its $10.5 billion budget to nuclear weapons programs, and nominally civilian programs such as NASA's space shuttle and the planned space station are largely driven by military requirements.

A third worrisome trend is that the Pentagon has placed increasing emphasis on applied research and development at the expense of pure science. While basic research received 6 percent of the military R&D budget two decades ago, it accounts for less than 3 percent today. This shift in DOD's emphasis toward applied research began with the 1970 Mansfield Amendment, which required Pentagon-funded university research to have some clear relevance to military missions, but the trend has accelerated sharply under the Reagan administration. For example, DARPA, long the leading sponsor of basic research on artificial intelligence (AI) recently launched an applied research program to demonstrate the utility of AI systems for performing specific military missions. Initial demonstration projects include an autonomous land vehicle for the army, a carrier battle-management system for the navy, and a computerized pilot's associate for the air force.[18]

Finally, the Pentagon's growing involvement in the support of university research means that large amounts of federal money are being channeled into a limited number of fields. SDI research, for example, is narrowly focused on seventeen technologies of potential importance to strategic defense. "The funding has been doubling every year, which is more than these areas can absorb," argues Vera Kistiakowsky, a professor of physics at MIT.[19] Rather than spawning a large amount of high-quality work, she says, the excess funding has resulted in waste and duplication.

Although the IST budget is not yet large enough to distort the balance of research at universities, such highly selective funding will cause harm in the long run, particularly if support from alternative funding sources continues to decline. Whenever the federal government makes large-scale shifts in the nation's research priorities, it attracts into the targeted areas scientists who otherwise would have pursued other interests. Over a period of years, these shifts could significantly alter the relative sizes and composition of university departments, impoverishing the overall diversity and vitality of academic life. Says Kistiakowsky: "The purchase of the participation of scientists through the availability of money from SDI and its nonavailability from other sources is completely contrary to the basic freedom of scientific opportunity that has made our research effort so strong."

Unfortunately, because science is so dependent on federal support, it has become inextricably embedded in national politics. Postwar presidents have established a tradition of launching major mission-oriented research programs as part of their domestic or foreign policy. Kennedy spent billions racing the Russians to the moon, Nixon declared a War on Cancer, Carter poured money into research on solar energy and synthetic fuels, and Reagan created SDI. In each case, the concentration of funding and effort in one area was politically inspired and not necessarily consistent with the best use of the nation's financial and scientific resources.

Indeed, mission-oriented research is rarely a cost-effective way to improve scientific understanding. The failure of the War on Cancer attests to that fact; basic research in cell biology, immunology, and molecular genetics has yielded far more knowledge about the underlying causes of cancer than applied research on specific tumors. Mission-oriented research can also be harmful to scientific inquiry because it often forces scientists to alter their research in procrustean ways to meet the specific needs of the funding agency. Although such slanting of research is hardly new, Frank Perkins, dean of the graduate school at MIT, contends that there are many more strings attached to research grants today than in the past. "It used to be that scientists were funded in a general area and could select the specific topics that were likely to be the most productive, with very few constraints," he says. "But faculty are no longer free to simply pick a research topic and work on it."[20]

IST's mission orientation, for example, sharply delimits the types of research that are supported. Laser scientists seeking IST money must work on systems "capable of handling power levels and operating at wavelengths that are of interest for strategic defense," an IST prospectus states. "Consequently, approaches that are inherently limited to low powers and/or to specific (inappropriate) wavelengths are not acceptable."[21] Because of these constraints, the scientific gains from IST-funded research are likely to be far smaller than could be achieved with unrestricted research grants.

A BRAIN DRAIN?

In addition to consuming a vast share of the United States' financial resources, the military-industrial sector diverts large numbers of technically skilled individuals from the civilian economy. As of 1984, some 14 percent of the nation's 4 million scientists and engineers were engaged in military R & D, and a third of all new engineers entering the job market between 1984 and 1987 are expected to find employment in the defense sector. Despite a growing need for technically skilled personnel in civilian industry, most private firms find it hard to compete with the premium salaries, "perks," and challenging problems offered by military contractors. SDI will exacerbate the shortage of technically skilled workers in the non-defense sector. According to a projection by the Council on Economic Priorities, a New York–based public-interest group, more than 18,000 scientists, engineers, and technicians will be engaged in SDI-related research by 1987.[22] This diversion of talent could carry high opportunity costs, impairing the nation's ability to deal with an array of pressing technological problems including a deteriorating infrastructure, environmental challenges such as toxic waste and acid rain, and an obsolescent industrial base that is increasingly incapable of competing effectively in world markets. Indeed, while billions are being invested in military electronics research, the U.S. consumer electronics industry has been overwhelmed by competition from Japan, South Korea, Taiwan, and other rising economic powers.

In the past, national research efforts on the scale of SDI were supplemented by federally funded education programs designed to increase the supply of scientists and engineers. During the 1960s, for example, the Apollo, Minuteman, and Polaris programs were backed up by the National Defense Education Act, which generated enough new talent to keep the civilian economy strong. But the Reagan administration has failed to create a comparable education program to mitigate the adverse impacts of its massive defense buildup. As a result, the huge increases in military spending associated with SDI may siphon off irreplaceable science and engineering talent from the civilian economy.

The projected benefits of SDI for the economy appear to have been oversold. SDIO officials have suggested that the research will yield important technological spinoffs, enabling the United States to carve out major new markets in microelectronics, computers, and telecommunications. This argument has been effective in convincing Great Britain, West Germany, Israel, and Italy to jump on the SDI bandwagon. But most military technology is now so complex and designed to such demanding specifications that it is rarely suited to mass-produced commercial products or consumer needs. A widely noted example is the $7,622 coffeemaker that one defense contractor manufactured for the air force, but less notorious cases abound. As for revolutionary new SDI technologies, most will certainly be classified. If commercial spin-offs do emerge, developing them through SDI will be enormously more inefficient and costly than direct investment in civilian R&D. In an editorial on the economic impact of SDI, the British science journal *Nature* concluded that "the most likely (and sombre) course of events is that great skill will be locked up in a programme of little economic value. The chances that people will pick up skills they never had, and will afterward deploy them in civil applications, are small. Technically, SDI is more likely to be a diversion than an opportunity."[23]

Meanwhile the growth of defense-related research at universities such as MIT is already having a significant impact on young scientists and engineers. Increasing numbers of undergraduates and graduate students are relying on DOD fellowships and research grants to finance their educations and advance their careers, thus expanding the Pentagon's influence. "Most MIT students are supported as research assistants," explains Dean Perkins. "So if there's a lot of defense-related research on campus, it will be the source of a large number of assistantships."

Working on defense-related projects socializes students to accept the appropriateness of military work on campus and also makes them more likely to consider a career in the defense industry. According to statistics compiled by the MIT Placement Office, between 3 and 5 percent of MIT graduates in science and engineering go to work at federally funded weapons labs (such as Draper, Lincoln, Lawrence Livermore, and Los Alamos), while about 25 percent are employed by private aerospace and defense contractors. Although students may realize that military R&D involves significant drawbacks, such as restrictions on publication and lack of contact with colleagues in the civilian sector, it also offers attractive benefits, including high salaries, excellent working conditions (including access to the best computers), challenging problems, and the ability to do one's own research without having to search continually for funding.

Although these benefits make military R&D appealing to many of today's brightest engineering students, the defense boom is unlikely to last forever. Real military expenditures have risen 50 percent since 1970, but the budget cuts mandated by the Gramm-Rudman-Hollings deficit reduction act have already begun to slow the momentum of the Reagan buildup. The current rapid expansion of SDI research could therefore be followed by an equally precipitous decline.

Indeed, postwar history has shown that politically inspired, mission-oriented programs are vulnerable to sudden shifts in the political winds. Many middle-aged American engineers have bitter memories of at least one such "boom and bust" cycle. During the early 1960s, when the cold war was being fought on two technological fronts—the moon race and the arms race—the aerospace industry underwent a massive expansion to meet the government's seemingly insatiable demand for boosters, spacecraft, and ICBMs. Flush with cash, the industry lured top-quality scientists and engineers from throughout the United States and Western Europe. But the aerospace boom could not be sustained, particularly once the United States became mired in the long and costly war in Vietnam, and with the end of the Apollo Program, government contracts dropped off. By the early 1970s, thousands of aerospace engineers found themselves in unemployment lines, most of them ill equipped for jobs in consumer-oriented industries. Nobel laureate physicist John Bardeen has warned that the rapid expansion of the SDI program may have a comparable impact on America's R&D community and that the human consequences of the eventual "bust" could be just as devastating.

TWO ETHICAL DILEMMAS

The fact that IST-funded research at universities is linked to the development of a particular weapons system distinguishes it from other DOD-sponsored research activities. IST-funded research raises more acute moral concerns because its ties to military application are close and explicit rather than remote and implicit.

The ethical dilemmas surrounding SDI and the universities are both institutional and individual, and involve conflicts between the values of academic freedom and social responsibility. At the institutional level, most university administrators have taken a "neutral" stance toward IST-funded research, arguing that it should be the prerogative of individual investigators to decide for themselves whether to participate. In October 1985, for example, the board of regents of the University of Michigan passed a resolution supporting any faculty member who wished to engage in unclassified SDI research, on the grounds that the principle of "academic freedom" must be protected. "I have no idea whether Star Wars is good or bad, whether it will work or won't work, whether it's in the best or worst interests of our strategic balance," said regent Thomas Roach. "But the right to do research should not be infringed." Similarly, MIT president Paul Gray, although highly critical of IST's attempts to use the university for political ends, defended the right of faculty members to engage in unclassified IST-funded research. "It would be wrong for a university—as an institution—to proscribe certain research sponsors on grounds which are essentially political in nature," he wrote in a statement issued in December 1985. "There should be no political tests for research."[24]

Critics respond that universities cannot remain politically

neutral while allowing faculty members to solicit IST contracts. Despite disclaimers that accepting grant money from IST is not tantamount to endorsing SDI, participation in research unavoidably identifies the institution with the goals and missions of the program. "By providing space and services for SDI research and taking overhead money, MIT becomes part of the process," argues Vera Kistiakowsky. "That's why President Gray's statement that MIT 'will not be used' is simply not accurate." Critics also contend that university participation lends credibility and prestige to the SDI program, making it easier for the Reagan administration to sell its budget requests to a skeptical Congress. Indeed, IST's early attempts to use academic research contracts for public-relations purposes made it clear that university participation does have a political impact.

MIT vice president Smith concedes that because of the political ramifications of SDI, the universities are in a bind: they will be seen as making a political statement whether they permit IST-funded research on campus or not. For his part, Smith argues that participating in IST-funded research should be an individual ethical judgment, not a decision imposed from above by the university administration. Although some critics have countered that academic freedom is not absolute and must be weighed against the social responsibility of the university, most SDI opponents have backed away from seeking a total ban on IST-funded research for three reasons. First, such an uncompromising position would be divisive and futile at a large university like MIT, where the faculty is deeply split over the merits of SDI. Second, making research funding decisions contingent on broad political considerations (extending far beyond existing ethical, safety, and environmental criteria) would raise complex administrative problems. Third, it would set a dangerous precedent, making it easier for political extremists to block controversial research programs in the future.

A broad consensus has therefore emerged that participation in IST-funded research should be a matter of individual choice. In confronting this choice, however, scientists have responded in very different ways. Some ignore the political issues on the grounds that IST is just another funding source that will support research they would pursue in any case. Others have qualms about the feasibility or strategic wisdom of SDI but argue rather cynically that since the program's goals are remote and probably unattainable, there is no harm in using IST money to support worthwhile research. "Many scientists [with IST contracts] argue that their research is objective and apolitical," notes Fran Bagenal, a visiting scientist at the MIT Center for Space Research. "But I think they should consider the political consequences of what they're doing—the fact that their research lends credibility to a misguided policy, and contributes to the deception that the public is getting more security for its money."[25]

Scientists and engineers who actively oppose SDI on political or ethical grounds may find themselves in a painful ethical dilemma. Because there are few alternative funding sources in fields such as free-electron lasers and plasma physics, some researchers have been forced to choose between their work and their consciences. One university physicist who opposes SDI was faced with a difficult choice when he was told that his funding from the Office of Naval Research had been cut off and that he should apply for an IST grant. Because he did not want to fire all of his graduate students and postdoctoral and technical staff, he decided to apply for the IST funds despite strong misgivings. Young scientists who have not yet established a track record of publication are vulnerable to cutbacks in research funding and may see no alternative to IST support. "To some extent, they feel compromised—that what they are doing is prostitution of science," Bagenal says. Despite such pressures, however, increasing numbers of scientists have expressed their opposition to SDI by refusing to participate in IST-funded research.

SCIENTISTS SPEAK OUT

In the spring of 1985, physicists at Cornell University and the University of Illinois (Champaign-Urbana) independently began to circulate petitions calling the SDI program "deeply misguided and dangerous" and asking physicists, mathematicians, computer scientists, and engineers to pledge not to solicit or accept IST contracts. An academic research boycott, it was believed, would have an impact on the national debate by demonstrating that a significant fraction of the scientific community was opposed to the SDI program.

Because the first petitions began to circulate in May, shortly before the universities let out for the summer, the launching of a major effort was delayed until fall. On September 12, 1985, campus organizers held a press conference in Cambridge, Massachusetts, and announced a national campaign to win support for a research boycott. The pledge petition was circulated at more than a hundred research universities across the country.

By the spring of 1986, the pledge had been signed by more than 3,700 tenured professors in the hard sciences and engineering, as well as 2,800 junior faculty, postdoctoral fellows, and graduate students. Signers are in the majority at 109 physical science and engineering research departments at 72 campuses. Overall, scientists at 110 institutions are participating in the research boycott; these institutions collectively receive 75 percent of the academic physical science and engineering funding dispersed by DOD and the National Science Foundation.[26] Particularly striking are the large numbers of physicists at the so-called prestige universities who have signed the pledge. (See table 2.1).

Given the historical reluctance of most scientists to speak out on matters of public policy, the success of the research boycott has exceeded expectations. Zellman Warhaft, a Cornell engineer, called it a "watershed" in the history of modern weapons research. There are two historical precedents for scientific activism on this scale: the atomic scientists' campaign in the late 1940s to urge international control of nuclear weapons and the protests against ABM and the "electronic battlefield" in Vietnam in the late 1960s. Even so, the SDI pledge campaign is the first research boycott against a specific weapons system to be truly national in scope.

On some campuses, the petition drive has aroused tensions among the faculty, particularly when organizers have pressured reluctant colleagues to sign the pledge. Some scientists argue that such tactics violate the academic freedom of scientists who wish, for whatever reason, to seek IST funds. For example, MIT professor Jack Ruina, an outspoken critic of SDI

TABLE 2.1 Pledge Results in the Nation's 20 Top Physics Departments[a]

Rank	Institution	Faculty Signatures Number/Total	%
1	Harvard University	19/37	51
2	Cornell University	35/49	71
3	California Institute of Technology (Caltech)	28/47	60
4	Princeton University	41/56	73
5	Massachusetts Institute of Technology (MIT)	37/92	40
6	University of California-Berkeley	33/66	50
7	Stanford University	8/21	38
8	University of Chicago	32/44	73
9	University of Illinois-Urbana	54/73	74
10	Columbia University	17/32	53
11	Yale University	14/37	38
12	SUNY-Stony Brook	44/55	80
13	University of California-San Diego	12/32	38
14	University of Pennsylvania	32/48	67
15	University of Washington	27/43	63
16	UCLA	6/42	14
17	University of Wisconsin-Madison	30/46	65
18	University of Maryland	31/54	57
19	University of Michigan-Ann Arbor	27/53	51
20	University of California-Santa Barbara	19/35	54
Total		546/962	57%

[a]Ranking by the *Chronicle of Higher Education*

SOURCE: Lisbeth Gronlund, John Kogut, Michael Weissman, and David Wright "A Status Report on the Boycott of Star Wars Research by Academic Scientists and Engineers," *Chronicle of Higher Education*, (May 13, 1986), p. 22.

on technical and strategic grounds, wrote an editorial in the MIT alumni magazine, *Technology Review*, in which he said that it is harmful to the academic enterprise "when peer review extends to judgments of what cause is just, and collegial pressure is exercised to influence research for reasons other than academic merit." In a more rhetorically heated commentary, Sidney Hook, a senior fellow at the Hoover Institution, wrote in the *New York Times* that the research boycott was designed "to intimidate those willing to serve their Government, [and] to mobilize pressure by building up a climate of hostile opinion on campuses," thereby violating the academic freedom of scientists who support SDI.[27]

Boycott organizers have defended their right to make the case against SDI as forcefully as possible, noting that SDI is not a detached research effort but a controversial political program. "I think it's a little unfair to invoke academic freedom for something that you want to see continue, if you're not going to invoke it for everything," says Vera Kistiakowsky. "The pledge campaign hasn't prevented anybody from doing anything, but it has made a lot of people sit up and take notice."

A few scientists have expressed concern that if they openly oppose SDI, the federal government may retaliate by cutting off their research support from other sources or otherwise obstructing their careers. Although these fears may seem exaggerated, an incident at the University of Illinois in the summer of 1985 is telling. The U.S. Army Corps of Engineers runs a Construction Engineering Research Laboratory (CERL) on campus that has long engaged in collaborative research with University of Illinois scientists. On July 14, however, the laboratory's director, Col. Paul J. Theuer, issued a confidential memorandum prohibiting further collaboration between CERL personnel and any university faculty members who had publicly opposed the SDI program. "As part of the Executive Branch, we have to support the President," the memo explained. After the document was leaked and widely publicized on campus, Colonel Theuer retracted the offending policy, and the controversy faded. A more explicit threat was proffered by Under Secretary of Defense Donald E. Hicks, head of the Pentagon's research and development program. He told a Senate committee during his confirmation hearings in the summer of 1985 that "I am not particularly interested in seeing department money going to someplace where an individual is outspoken in his rejection of department aims, even for basic research." Although Hicks later clarified that it is not official

DOD policy to deny funding to scientists critical of SDI, he reiterated his personal views in an interview, saying, "I have a tough time with disloyalty."[28]

What has been the effect of the research boycott? SDIO officials insist that it has had no real impact. But MIT vice president Smith believes that the scientific protest has had a sobering effect on the Pentagon. "The whole set of responses—the petition, Paul Gray's graduation address, and so forth—made it clear that they were in trouble with the academic community," he says. "So I think they've become more sensitive about how they're going to have to deal with that community in order to have a reasonable working relationship."

There are also telltale signs that SDIO may be more worried about the research boycott than it is willing to admit publicly. Reportedly, IST has had trouble attracting top-quality grant proposals and is trying to bolster its research effort by funding contracts initiated by other agencies (such as the Office of Naval Research), sometimes without even informing the grantees of the switch. As a result, some university researchers have discovered they are receiving SDI money, with all its implications, even though they did not solicit it. According to John Kogut, a physics professor at the University of Illinois, two groups at Princeton learned that their research contracts were being funded by SDIO only after the university business office noticed that the codes on the contracts had changed. "Some of the principal investigators were upset about this, but none of them took a public stand on the issue," Kogut says.[29]

Since IST-funded university research accounts for less than 3 percent of the SDI budget, an academic research boycott cannot hope to cripple the program. Still, it may slow SDI's headlong momentum and inspire greater public and congressional scrutiny. Kogut contends that the pledge campaign has already heightened awareness within the academic community. "Whenever Abrahamson or Ionson tries to sell the program to new institutions, the pledge always comes up," he says. "So they're being faced with a series of more difficult questions than they have been in the past." Combined with opinion surveys showing that a large majority of scientists oppose SDI, the research boycott indicates a growing attitude of noncooperation that will inevitably hurt the program.

THE PENTAGON'S AGENDA

Research programs as large as SDI rapidly acquire a political momentum that makes them extremely difficult to stop. Nevertheless, some scientists believe that SDI in its present form will not outlive the Reagan administration because only the president believes strongly enough in the feasibility of a population defense to make it a top national priority. There have also been persistent rumors from the outset that the armed services perceive SDIO as a competitor for scarce resources. Combined with growing pressures on Congress to reduce the federal deficit and the defense budget, the lukewarm attitude among many high-ranking officers may lead to a major reconsideration of SDI by the time the next administration takes office in 1989.

Still, the threat to university science posed by SDI transcends the specifics of the program itself. Critics see SDI as only the most visible component of a pervasive effort by the Pentagon to gain greater university participation in military R & D. The decision by most universities in the late 1960s to refuse classified research contracts created a barrier between the defense establishment and academia, but the growing involvement of university scientists in mission-oriented military research is rapidly eroding that divide.

"SDI has much more significance as a political program than as a weapons program," says Tufts University's Krimsky. "DOD is probably getting a good deal of what it wants, which is to make the universities feel more comfortable about doing defense-related research. I think that's ultimately the real goal, whether or not they ever build SDI." In the long run, critics worry, the Pentagon would like to return to the pre-Vietnam era, when the great research universities were seen as "scientific arsenals of democracy" that could be harnessed to develop the next generation of weaponry.

There are also fears that the growing military influence on campus will convert the universities into a pork-barrel constituency of the Pentagon, undermining the key role of academic institutions in a free society as open forums for discussion and debate of national issues, including defense policy. The personal involvement of many faculty members and students in defense-related research could have a chilling effect on dissent. "I would like to think that people wouldn't hesitate to speak out, but I'm also a realist," says Dean Perkins. "I think it will vary tremendously from individual to individual. But let's face it—if you're receiving support from a particular place, you're going to think twice before criticizing it."

Finally, the growth of mission-oriented military research has broad philosophical implications for the future of American science. In his book *The Technological Society*, French sociologist Jacques Ellul contends that pure science is becoming increasingly subordinate to the search for technical applications. "Research is blind; it advances gropingly and by means of a thousand experiments which miscarry," he writes. "But . . . technical exigence is dead set against science in this respect, because technique cannot tolerate the gropings and slow tempo of science." Ellul argues that pure science is gradually being displaced by what he calls *Zweckwissenschaft* (practical science), a regimented form of research in which "the state mobilizes all technicians and scientists, and imposes on them a precise and limited technical objective. . . . It forbids all research which it deems not to be in its own interests and institutes only that research which has utility. . . . Ends are known in advance; science only furnishes the means." Ellul concludes that "we too are advancing progressively towards this conception, which may in the long run prove to be ruinous despite the dazzling fireworks it produces today."[30]

As Eisenhower asserted in his farewell address, excessive government control over science makes for both bad science and bad government. Given the Reagan administration's refusal to heed that warning, it may be up to the university research community to prevent Ike's dark prophecy from becoming tomorrow's reality.

3
A Tangled Network: Command and Control for SDI

ROBERT ZIRKLE

One of the often-overlooked dimensions of Star Wars is that it must work as a *system*. It is not enough to have space-based lasers, sensors, computers, and the many other components working individually. Rather they must work together smoothly and in ways mutually reinforcing, or the enterprise as a whole will surely fail. Yet this requirement for integration, this network for command, control and communications, is itself an immensely complex undertaking, fraught with uncertainties and vulnerabilities.

A strategic defense must successfully perform its mission the moment it is activated. No time will be allowed for "learning under fire." It must perform successfully on short notice, at a time and place chosen by the opponent, and against a wide variety of possible attack patterns and countermeasures. It must perform its mission while under attack itself, in the unknown environment of nuclear war. In peacetime it will be necessary to verify that the system works as intended and maintains this peak condition for years. In addition, it will be necessary to ensure that the system does not fire accidently or without proper authorization. A survivable, reliable, and effective command and control system for managing the defense is, in short, fundamental to Star Wars.

Command and control cannot be examined in a vacuum, separate from the military strategy, structure, and weapons that it must serve. A major difficulty in assessing command

and control for the Strategic Defense Initiative is that, because the program remains in the research and development stage, the strategy, structure, and weapons are continually evolving. Due to the nascent state of space-based defenses, detailed analysis of its command and control is not possible, but a general sketch of the problem is feasible, along with possible solutions and their attendant costs and risks.

The command and control system for strategic defense has evolved, on paper, from a highly centralized, tightly coupled system requiring tight coordination between all its elements to a more decentralized arrangement in which clusters of weapons and sensors are invested with a large degree of local autonomy. Either arrangement will lead to a vastly complex system. The existing command and control system for *offensive* nuclear forces serves as an indication of this complexity, and, indeed, many of the issues confronted by a command and control system for strategic defense are similar to those faced by the offensive command and control system. Nevertheless, because the defense must react much more quickly than the offensive system, many of the solutions to these issues will differ. And importantly, the offensive and defensive command and control networks will coexist and commingle, an interaction that will affect the performance of both.

MILITARY COMMAND AND CONTROL

Command and control of military forces can be defined as the rules, procedures, hardware, personnel, and communication networks used in the operational management of military forces. They can be thought of as the brain and central nervous system of a military force, while the sensors act as the eyes and ears and the weapons as the muscle.

The effective command and control of military forces is a problem as old as social conflict itself. From the time humans first began banding together to oppose other groups by force, a central concern has been how to manage and direct these forces. Advances in technology that could aid this management—communications, information collection, handling, and so forth—have been largely offset by vast increases in the size and complexity of modern military forces and conflict.

Certain characteristics inherent in war also make the problem of successfully managing military force difficult.

War is unpredictable and chaotic. The rapid pace of events leads to uncertain and even contradictory information reaching the higher echelons of command. Frequently, there is a complete absence of information concerning critical areas of the battle, as the disruption or destruction of communication networks cuts off commanders from crucial engagements. Historically, commanders have seldom been able to follow, let alone manage, conflicts as they have unfolded. These features of battle were aptly described by the nineteenth-century military theorist Karl von Clausewitz as the "fog of war." The attempt to operate in this "fog," to manage the uncertainties of war, is a major function of any military command and control system.

A defining feature of a command and control system is its structure or organization. All military organizations have a hierarchical, or pyramidlike, structure. Within this broad structure, lower levels of the hierarchy can have more or less autonomy. The military historian Martin Van Creveld, after examining military structures ranging from the Roman centurions to the U.S. command structure in the Vietnam War, concluded that two types of military command and control structures have evolved to handle the uncertainty of war: a highly centralized system in which authority and control are tightly held at a single point, and a decentralized system in which various components of the military structure can and often do act autonomously within the broad objectives specified by higher authorities.[1]

In a centralized command structure, all decision making is performed at the highest level of the organization. This requires that all assessments regarding the state of the battle (threat or intelligence assessments) be made at the top. In order to make the threat assessment, the commander and his staff must receive all intelligence data; this places extraordinary demands on the communications links between the intelligence collectors and the command center. Demands on the links between the command center and the forces are also great, especially if the commander attempts to manage the smallest details of the battle as it unfolds. Owing to the vulnerabilities of communications and intelligence systems, and to the limits of a command center to integrate the vast amount of necessary data, forces under a centralized command structure usually adhere to rigid, detailed plans drawn up prior to the battle.

In contrast, a decentralized command structure allows lower levels to perform threat assessments and exercise authority during the conflict. A measure of local autonomy allows decisions to be made at the level of the command structure best able to assess the local conditions. This structure reduces the stress that communication systems must bear. The drawback to this type of system is the potential loss of higher-level coordination that some military operations might require. Van Crevald concluded that, in general, the decentralized command structure led to successful military operations more often than did centralized systems.

The command and control system in place for strategic nuclear offensive forces represents the first of the command and control structures Van Creveld describes: a tightly coupled, highly centralized system. The nature of nuclear weapons and nuclear war dictates this type of structure.

During peacetime, two factors argue for a highly centralized system. First, the incredibly destructive power of nuclear weapons, as well as the political repercussions of their use, requires that they remain under tight political and military control at all times to prevent accidental or unauthorized use. Second, the destructive power of nuclear weapons also means that a seemingly small threat can have widespread effects on the entire nuclear force. A single Soviet submarine off the U.S. coast has, for example, enough destructive power (though not the range) to decimate the U.S. strategic bomber force. Such situations led the nuclear command structure to attempt, in the words of one analyst, "to 'manage' every small threat in detail by centralized direction, reliance on near real-time warning, and dependence on prearranged reactions."[2]

Tight control is also necessary during wartime. The advent of nuclear ballistic missiles, with their short flight times, presents the potential for rapid escalation of nuclear conflict to the level of total conflagration. Under these circumstances, tight control of the military forces is required to ensure that the use of military force remains commensurate with political ends. This task of restraint is especially problematic in scenarios of nuclear war fighting, scenarios that envision multiple, sustained nuclear conflicts around the world at various levels of destructiveness. Nevertheless, the theories underlying various nuclear war-fighting strategies assume that a centralized command system will survive and operate effectively even during wartime.

The command and control structure for offensive nuclear forces consists of four elements: decision-making centers, warning sensors and intelligence collecting systems, communication systems, and plans and procedures.

Decision Making

The decision-making or command centers for strategic command and control are elements of the overall U.S. military command structure. Commands relevant to strategic nuclear forces include the Strategic Air Command (SAC), the Aerospace Defense Command, and the new U.S. Space Command. The commander in chief of SAC has under his command all land-based ICBMs as well as all strategic bombers. Aerospace Defense Command was the United States' component of the joint U.S.-Canadian North American Aerospace Defense Command (NORAD). Headed by a U.S. general, NORAD has primary responsibility in three areas: missile warning and attack assessment, air defense of the United States and Canada, and monitoring of all human-made objects in space. The U.S. Space Command, activated in September 1985, oversees all operational U.S. military space systems. More important, in the future this command may be assigned operational control of antisatellite weapons and may serve as the command for any space-based defensive system.[3] The Aerospace Defense Command was deactivated in 1986 and most of its missions reassigned to the Space Command. Each command has a primary command post, and most also have less vulnerable backup facilities to ensure that the functions of each command would continue if the primary centers were destroyed. Many of these backup centers are airborne—for example, the SAC "Looking Glass" aircraft, which is kept on a twenty-four-hour airborne alert.

Final authority for nuclear weapons rests with the National Command Authority (NCA), consisting of the president and the secretary of defense, or their designated successors. To ensure survival of the NCA, a modified Boeing 747 serves as an airborne command post. The president and secretary of defense, or their successors, would board this aircraft once an attack was underway. From here, the NCA would direct the response to a Soviet nuclear attack, in conjunction with the SAC Looking Glass aircraft.

Warning and Intelligence Collection

In order to carry out their assigned tasks under a centralized system, the decision-making authorities require up-to-date information on the international military and political situation. These data are provided by the warning and intelligence-collecting component. A vast array of intelligence-collecting systems exist, providing both strategic intelligence (indications of Soviet force dispositions and preparations that could provide initial intelligence of an impending attack hours, days, or weeks in advance) and tactical intelligence (indications that an attack is underway, providing up to thirty minutes warning of an ICBM attack). Strategic intelligence systems include ground-, sea-, air-, and space-based assets that collect radar and communications signals, as well as space-based photographic reconnaissance. Because strategic warning signals are often ambiguous, such indications are not sufficient to launch U.S. nuclear forces in a so-called preemptive attack. The likely U.S. response to strategic warning would be to initiate procedures to increase the preparedness (alert levels) of U.S. forces.

The U.S. command structure requires immediate tactical warning of an attack before responding with nuclear weapons. To decrease the chance of false alarms, tactical warning is governed by the principle of "dual phenomenology": before an attack can be confirmed, it must be detected by two separate warning systems relying on two distinct physical phenomena. Initial tactical warning of ballistic missile launches would be provided by infrared sensors aboard one of three Defense Support Satellites stationed in geosynchronous orbit (at an altitude of 36,000 km). Such satellites can detect a missile's hot plume shortly after liftoff, or about thirty minutes before a land-based ballistic missile could reach its target in the continental United States.

Ten to fifteen minutes later, as ICBMs appeared over the horizon, additional confirmation of an attack would be acquired by the Ballistic Missile Early Warning radars located in Alaska, Greenland, and Great Britain. The launch of submarine-based ballistic missiles would be confirmed by a set of radars located along the U.S. coasts. Early warning of bomber attack relies primarily upon a series of radar installations stretching across northern Alaska and Canada.

Communications

To ensure that commanders maintain continuous contact with the nuclear forces, an elaborate set of communication networks exist. Different types of nuclear strategies pose different communication requirements. A simple policy of massive retaliation would at least require that the "emergency action message," a simple encrypted "go" code to launch, be received by the major portion of the surviving forces. More complex strategies, such as those involving retargeting of surviving forces or extended nuclear war fighting, could require high-data-rate communication, communication facilities capable of extended survival, or the ability for two-way communication between the responsible authorities and the forces.

A variety of methods exist for communicating with the land-based ICBM force. Leased commercial land-lines are the primary transmission links during peacetime, but this network is expected to be largely destroyed following a nuclear attack. Communication satellites could provide a backup capability, but the frequencies used are vulnerable to various nuclear effects, which could disrupt these links for minutes or hours. The most likely method for communicating to the missile forces during or immediately following a nuclear attack would be through an airborne network consisting of the Looking Glass and the president's command aircraft, relay aircraft stationed between missile fields, and airborne launch-control aircraft circling above these fields.

Bombers present a greater challenge for communication systems. To avoid being destroyed on the ground, these aircraft would be launched as soon as initial tactical warning is received. Once aloft, they would fly to preassigned areas high above northern Canada. After takeoff, messages can be sent only through satellite links or by passing messages north via aircraft or ground stations using line-of-sight communications.

Submarines pose still a different set of requirements, due to the opacity of seawater to many types of communication frequencies, the submarine's great distance from U.S. shores, and their need to remain undetected while on patrol. As the frequency of electromagnetic waves decreases, the depth to which they penetrate seawater increases, but the rate at which they can transmit messages, in turn, decreases. During peacetime, ground-based systems are relied upon for transmitting low-data rate, one-way messages from shore to submarine. But these ground-based antennas are extremely vulnerable. During crises and attacks, one-way submarine communications rely upon TACAMO (for Take Charge and Move Out) relay aircraft deployed over the Atlantic and Pacific oceans. Two-way communications are available through satellite links, but these are rarely used because a large antenna must be placed above the surface of the water, potentially giving away the submarine's position. Additional, highly classified means exist for submarine communications, and some of these may allow the vessel to communicate back to shore.

Procedures

A major element of any command and control system is the set of procedures used by the system. One set of procedures central to the command and control system for offensive nuclear forces relates to the use of nuclear weapons. Underlying many of these procedures are the opposing notions of positive and negative control. Positive control can be thought of as the safety catch preventing the unauthorized or accidental use of nuclear weapons. In contrast, negative control ensures that the finger is on the nuclear trigger and that the weapons are released when deemed necessary.

Examples abound of procedures ensuring positive control over nuclear weapons. For instance, within an ICBM launch-control center the launching of a missile requires that two widely spaced keys be turned simultaneously, an action that can only be performed by two people. Furthermore, all land-based missiles are equipped with electronic locks, known as Permissive Action Links (PALs). To unlock the weapons, the launch operators must punch in the correct sequence of codes, a sequence unknown to them until they receive the emergency action message. Although bombers could be sent aloft following an early indication of attack, they are required to return to their bases unless they get a specific order to proceed from their loitering positions to the USSR. Submarine-based ballistic missiles do not have PALs, but the launching of SLBMs requires the cooperation of many crew members. Perhaps the most important positive control is the presence of human beings in the decision-making loop.

Illustrations of negative control are harder to find because of the sensitive nature of the subject, but one example may be inferred from the absence of PALs on submarine-based ballistic missiles. Some officials and analysts have indicated that PALs are not present on these weapons in order to keep open the possibility (if not in fact, then at least in the minds of Soviet political and military leaders) of a submarine under very tightly circumscribed conditions, firing its weapons without higher authorization. For example, sub commanders might fire their weapons both if they knew the United States was under attack and if they had lost communications with authorities, which they were unable to regain after exhausting all possible means. In this way, even in the most extreme case of a Soviet first strike eliminating all bombers, land-based ICBMs, and command centers, the Soviets could never be sure the United States would not retaliate.

Another crucial set of procedures involves the threat assessment process and the alerting of nuclear forces. The system's centralized threat assessment requires that a vast amount of data flow into a small number of "data fusion" centers, which are tightly linked to each other. In peacetime, the central element in this matrix of data fusion centers is the NORAD headquarters. It reportedly takes about ninety seconds for tactical warning data to be collected, processed, and transmitted to NORAD.[4] The data also are displayed simultaneously on screens at SAC, the National Military Command Center at the Pentagon, and the Alternate Military Command Center at Fort Ritchie, Maryland. If monitors and displays at NORAD suddenly indicate an attack against the United States, a process is set in motion that simultaneously evaluates this threat and gradually places military forces on higher states of alert.

The first stage in this process is the convening of a telephone conference between the commander in chief of NORAD and the commanders of the other three sites receiving sensor data. The commander of NORAD, in consultation with the other commanders, attempts to discern whether the data are real or the result of system error. To aid in decision making, incoming data from the tactical warning sensors are integrated with data from strategic warning systems and from human sources. The data are assessed within the context of the general political and military environment. For instance, are U.S.-Soviet relations nonconfrontational and the international scene relatively crisis-free? Are NATO–Warsaw Pact forces engaged in conventional conflict in Western Europe?

If the NORAD commander feels that the situation warrants it, he will then call a *threat assessment conference* consisting of the four military commanders as well as the chairman of the Joint Chiefs of Staff. It is here that a final decision is made by the NORAD commander as to whether an attack is underway. Between October 1979 and mid-1983, six threat assessment conferences were convened.[5] For example, on November 9, 1979, programs used to test the data processing and threat assessment system were mistakenly fed into the NORAD computer, leading NORAD display screens to show an incoming Soviet attack. On June 3, 1980, a faulty computer chip caused display screens at two of the four command centers (SAC and the National Military Command Center) to display a massive attack.[6]

Should the threat assessment conference conclude that the United States is under attack, the president is notified and convenes a *missile attack conference*. The president, in consultation with all five military commanders, would in that circumstance choose the appropriate response to the Soviet attack—the final stage in the process leading to nuclear war.

VULNERABILITIES IN COMMAND AND CONTROL

Several authors have recently pointed out a number of threats and potential dangers within the command and control matrix. Their concerns arise from two features of the system: its vulnerability to nuclear attack and its complex, tightly coupled nature.

The vulnerability of the command and control system is particularly acute given the nuclear war-fighting strategy it is increasingly designed to serve. Over the last decade, succeeding administrations have evolved a nuclear strategy consisting of measured controlled responses to Soviet nuclear attack. As one analyst has written, "*Controlled escalation* has become the central operational concept in current U.S. strategic doctrine."[7] Such a strategy requires a highly flexible command and control system capable of enduring nuclear attacks for prolonged periods while maintaining centralized control and threat assessment. This last requirement—maintaining centralized information assessment—is especially crucial, for U.S. nuclear war-fighting strategies are based "so fundamentally on having centralized knowledge of damage inflicted and received and on knowing the relative numbers of surviving warheads available to each nation."[8]

As noted earlier, however, it is rarely possible to maintain centralized information assessment during battle. The destructiveness of nuclear weapons leaves little hope for attaining this objective in nuclear war. As a result, the extreme vulnerability of the intelligence systems, command centers, and, more important, the communication systems to nuclear attack makes a controlled nuclear war highly improbable. Following an exhaustive study of the vulnerabilities inherent in the U.S. command and control system, Desmond Ball concluded that the "control of a nuclear exchange would become very difficult to maintain after several tens of strategic nuclear weapons have been used, even where deliberate attacks on command-and-control capabilities were avoided."[9]

The vulnerability of the command and control system, coupled with the deployment of highly accurate "counterforce" weapons with very short flight times, has raised an even more troubling possibility: an attack could render the United States unable to respond at all. Though this outcome is doubtful, a decapitating attack—one deliberately aimed at the command and control system—might result in a ragged, uncoordinated, and much less effective U.S. response. If the Soviets ever came to believe that nuclear war was imminent, they might decide that an uncoordinated U.S. response would be preferable to a highly coordinated one, and thus launch a first strike against the U.S. command and control structure.[10]

The complex, tightly coupled nature of the command and control and nuclear force structure gives rise to a different set of concerns, which can be illustrated by two examples of the results of false alarms. The 1979 false alert, caused by an operator error at NORAD, resulted in ten fighters being sent aloft from three separate air bases and a higher level of alert for all U.S. missile and submarine bases. The faulty computer chip that caused one of the 1980 false alerts resulted in, among other things, the preparation for takeoff of almost one hundred B-52 bombers as well as the president's command aircraft.[11]

Highly complex, tightly coupled systems are especially prone to "normal" accidents (as opposed to simple human error, or equipment or design failures). Such accidents are caused by the introduction of random shocks to the system, the result of design, equipment, or operator error, which become amplified in "incomprehensible, unpredictable, unanticipated, and unpreventable ways" owing to the tightly coupled, highly interactive nature of the system. The nuclear accident at Three Mile Island in 1979 represents the quintessential case of a "normal" accident.[12]

As these examples suggest, the nuclear command and control system may not be immune to "normal" accidents. During calm periods the chance of a false alert leading to inadvertent nuclear war is extremely remote, owing to the positive controls embedded within the system. If a crisis were to heat up and the threat of war between U.S. and Soviet forces intensified, however, many of these checks would be loosened or removed altogether. As U.S.-Soviet tensions increase, the perceptions of threat and possible attack also increase, making both sides more responsive to worst-case assessments and indications of attack. When controls are loosened during a serious crisis, there is a much greater likelihood that a few random, unexpected stimuli could cascade through the system with unforeseen and catastrophic results.[13] Simultaneous, random events could be construed to form a pattern of increased hostility where none actually exists.

The dangers of tightly coupled forces are compounded by the fact that both the United States and the Soviet Union possess such command systems and that these systems interact through their warning and intelligence networks. Each side monitors the force readiness of the other to discern changes in alert levels. These observations are then fed back into the observer's command system and are used to establish the appropriate alert level of its own forces. During a crisis, should one side suddenly increase its force readiness, the change would be instantly picked up by the opponent, resulting in changes in its alert levels. Such a move could, in turn, lead the first country to increase its alert further, and so on.

This ratcheting action is dangerous enough by itself, but, as shown, errors can occur within the warning systems and inaccurate intelligence assessments can be made. During a period of superpower tension, similar mistakes could lead to very dangerous outcomes, especially when the results of such errors could be detected and magnified by the intelligence systems of the opponent. As a result, the rapid escalation of U.S.-Soviet alert levels could be spurred either by an actual increase in one side's readiness or by errors in the adversary's intelligence and warning system.[14]

COMMAND AND CONTROL FOR STRATEGIC DEFENSE

Any command and control system for strategic defense must be able to perform a number of functions. First, it is necessary to maintain and test the system during peacetime. The ability to improve and revise the system is also essential because technologies and threats evolve. The existence of space-based components in this system makes maintenance, station keeping, and upgrading considerably more difficult. More important, the command and control system must guarantee that weapons are not accidently fired during peacetime operations, as well as ensuring that only authorized release of weapons can occur. At the same time, the reliability of the system must remain very high; authorities must feel confident that the system will activate when needed. In short, the command and control system must maintain both positive and negative control.

The command and control system must detect missile launches, track the missiles or warheads, distinguish between real missiles or warheads and decoys, assign weapons to targets, conduct kill assessment, decide between conflicting or contradictory data, and hand off data to other elements of the system when necessary. In addition, the command and control system must be able to detect threats to the defense itself and undertake measures to counter them. Finally, the system must be at least as survivable as the weapons it is managing. It will do no good to have many survivable weapons if the command and control system managing them can be quickly destroyed.

There are five general concerns about SDI's command and control tasks: the most appropriate structure of the command and control system, the sheer complexity of strategic defenses, the mechanisms of weapons release, reactions to false alerts, and the system's relationship to command and control of offensive forces.

Structure

A major issue in the development of command and control for strategic defense is the degree of coordination required between components of the system. There is a wide range of possibilities between the two extremes of a tightly coupled defense system and one that is completely decoupled with each weapon system engaging targets totally independent of other elements of the defense. The issue involves complicated trade-offs between costs, vulnerabilities, efficiencies, and overall effectiveness.

The more tightly coupled a system is, the more it is susceptible to complete disruption from a small, but well-placed, defense suppression attack. (This is precisely the case with the offensive system, giving rise to fears of a "decapitating" first strike.) Also, the more complex and tightly coupled a system, the more susceptible it is to "normal" accidents, producing unexpected and, potentially, disastrous results. On the other hand, as the system becomes more decentralized it also becomes less efficient, requiring the use of more assets and driving up costs. There is great uncertainty about the efficiency of a decentralized battle management system, with estimates as low as 20 percent.[15]

Decentralization may also result in a system unable to successfully perform its mission. Higher-level coordination may, for instance, be required to prevent saturation of terminal defenses around key ground sites. More important, a decentralized system may not cope well with decoys. As one countermeasure to a defense, the Soviets are likely to dispense a vast array of decoys along with warheads from each missile's "bus" (estimates on the size of the "threat cloud"—the number of warheads plus decoys—range from 100,000 to 1 million).[16] It is even possible that, through antisimulation techniques, Soviet warheads could be disguised to look like decoys to the defense's sensors. In order to ensure that all warheads are targeted while wasting as few shots as possible on decoys, the defense must be able to distinguish warheads from decoys. One method for doing so requires "birth-to-death" tracking: spotting each target as it leaves the postboost bus (when it may prove easiest to distinguish warhead from decoy) and keeping a running file on each warhead until it is destroyed. This task requires that information on decoys and warheads, acquired by passive sensors, be passed along from postboost phase to the midcourse phase to the terminal defense. Thus, a high degree of network coordination is necessary, which in turn necessitates a higher order of centralized control.

Less coordination could be tolerated if a new technology, known as interactive discrimination, is successfully developed. Interactive discrimination involves the use of laser or particle beams that, while not strong enough to destroy a target, would cause it to react differently depending upon whether it was a warhead or a decoy. Because this technique could be used at any point along the target's path through space, it would drastically reduce the amount of information transferral required. In the extreme case, each local defense constellation might be able to perform its own discrimination, though this would also increase the complexity and cost of each local group. However, interactive discrimination has been described as "little more than an interesting and promising concept."[17] If interactive discrimination fails to develop, this could prove a fatal impediment to decentralizing command and control.

A first cut at the problem of the structure of a defensive command and control system was produced by the Fletcher committee's Panel on Battle Management, Command, Control, and Communication (C^3), and Data Processing. This structure was a highly centralized, tightly coordinated system. Though such a system was merely suggested as an "ideal," many contractors adhered to this formulation during the first phase of architecture studies conducted in 1984–85.

This system has now been abandoned as vulnerable, unworkable, and unnecessary. The Eastport panel, commissioned by SDIO in the summer of 1985 to study the command and control and battle management issues, released its report in early 1986, recommending a more decentralized, "open and distributed system that takes advantage of the strategic defense system's special characteristics, such as dynamics, size, and the lack of need for global consistency and synchronization."[18] Though under tight control in peacetime, the management of the defensive system during war would be dispersed to local "battle groups" made up of battle stations, sensors, and command and control assets. Consistent with the notion of decentralized authority in wartime, threat assessment would also be performed locally, once the system is activated. The panel's report also gave a few examples of areas in which tight coordination is still required—for instance, the central authority to activate the system and the processing of multiple sensor data within a battle group. The panel also recognized that a higher order of coordination may be required during the midcourse phase to gather and process decoy-discrimination data, in an abbreviated version of birth-to-death tracking.

This decentralized architecture is based upon the concept of "partitioning"—the breaking down of the defense problem into a series of separate, local engagements based upon distance and function. For example, defenses engaging ballistic missiles launched from missile fields in the southeastern portion of the Soviet Union need not be concerned with engagements taking place over missile fields in the western portion of the Soviet Union, or with engagements involving submarine-launched ballistic missiles at sea. Further partitioning might prove feasible, such as between layers of the defense. Unfortunately, it is difficult to specify boundaries exactly without further elaboration of SDI technologies and architecture, such as solutions to discrimination. Nevertheless, the Eastport panel's discussion of defensive battle groups, similar to naval carrier task forces, implies the use of partitioning down to a low level.

Complexity

A key characteristic of any space-based defense is its sheer complexity, which places tremendous demands upon command and control. The burden that this feature places on computer software will be described in chapter 5. Equally demanding requirements are placed upon the system's communications network.

Any network must provide communications among thousands of space-, air-, and ground-based assets located around the globe. Weapons in orbit above the Soviet Union, for example, must remain in contact with ground-based command authorities located in the United States. The network must be secure against attempts to intercept and tamper with signals or jam transmissions. The network must be able to cope with destruction of assets as well as innocent failures of components. Because satellites will be stationed in many different orbits, they will be moving relative to one another. Consequently, the composition of defense constellations, or battle groups, will change many times during the course of an engagement, as assets move in and out of constellations. Since communications must be maintained between relevant components, the network must be capable of dynamically rearranging itself. The need for high-data-rate communications implies the use of extremely high frequency (EHF) and laser communications, both having very narrow beam widths; this further increases the difficulty of maintaining links between assets in relative motion. The Eastport panel recognized that the ability to meet these and other requirements is far from being realized with current communications technologies.

Because of the difficulty of fully predicting the behavior of large dynamic networks, the panel recommended the development of a man-machine interface to allow human operators to adjust the network to unforeseen events. And, to reduce the vulnerability and complexity of any given platform, the Eastport panel recommended a dedicated network of communication satellites instead of a network based on the battle stations and sensors.

The complexity can be appreciated through a glimpse of the command and control system at work. The workings of each layer of the defense are similar; in each, low-orbit sensors will track potential targets and try to discriminate between targets and decoys. In the boost and postboost phases, sensors may have to track hundreds of objects and discriminate between missiles with warheads and missiles without. During midcourse, the number of warheads and decoys could expand into the hundreds of thousands. The discrimination task can be eased if information is coordinated among battle groups, especially if information can be passed along from battle groups able to detect the objects as they leave the postboost bus.

Sensor data will be transmitted to space- or ground-based battle management computers, which will integrate data from multiple sensors, separate good data from spurious data, and decide which sensors are viewing which objects. They will also assign weapons to targets according to some set of rules, perhaps a very simple one. After weapons have fired, the sensors and battle management computers will undertake kill assessments, reassigning weapons to surviving targets.

While all of these tasks are being performed, the individual battle groups will be continually rearranging themselves as satellites move in and out of them. The defense itself will be under attack, also setting in motion battles with antisatellite weapons. Weapons will be assigned the task of protecting the defense system, and the effort will be coordinated. Attrition will occur, nonetheless; some lost functions will be reassigned, but some degradation in performance will have to be accepted.

This description is just a sample of the complexity involved in the defense system. This complexity will exist regardless of whether the system is tightly or loosely coupled. The difference will lie in whether complexity is characteristic of higher or lower levels of the defense. A tightly coupled system is likely to be prone to the dangerous, unforeseeable "normal" accident, while the loosely coupled system may simply be inadequate.

Arming and Weapons Release

Another set of issues common to any type of strategic defense involves ordnance safety and the arming and release of weapons. The Fletcher commission's panel on C^3 and battle management characterized the authorized release of weapons and ordnance safety as the two functions "absolutely critical to the safety, credibility, and effectiveness of a BMD system."[19] As in the case of strategic offense, the twin notions of positive and negative control arise, but they are complicated by the speed with which a defense must react. Two factors make quick reaction essential: the need to engage missiles in the boost phase, which may last only one to three minutes, and the need to react against defense suppression attacks.

It is apparent that under pressure to attack missiles in the boost phase, the elaborate procedures now undertaken to confirm a missile attack and to ensure a degree of positive control over the release of offensive weapons would be unworkable for defensive systems—time would simply not allow it. This is true only for indications of large-scale ballistic missile launches, however. In cases where a single launch or even a few simultaneous launches are indicated, the time constraints are not as acute. The midcourse portion of a fully deployed system should be able to handle a small number of launches. This fact would allow an additional ten to fifteen minutes to assess the warning data before activating the system, and the current threat-assessment system requires much less time to operate. This procedure would require the development of rules of engagement defining thresholds for either activating boost-phase interception or consulting higher authorities.

A second factor that could shorten reaction times is the need to counter defense suppression attacks. The opening phase of any first strike is likely to include attacks against the defensive system, to increase the offense's chances of survival. A number of methods could be used to reduce the vulnerability of space-based defenses, but the effectiveness of each countermeasure depends upon the type of antisatellite (ASAT) attack used by the offense. When both sides possess a "shoot-back" capability—defense satellites using their lasers to attack ASATs, for example—a large advantage may lie in shooting first. Two U.S. responses are possible: relying upon survivability measures other than shooting back, accepting some early attrition, and shooting back only when fired upon first; or immediately attacking potential space-based ASAT threats, including Soviet BMD assets. The United States would be forced into accepting the latter response if a situation arises in which both the United States and the Soviet Union have deployed in their space-based defense neutral particle beam weapons having an ASAT capability. This case has been described by one SDI official as similar to "the re-enactment of the 'Shootout At The OK Corral.' "[20] BMD stations would have a strong incentive to attack nearby space mines as well. Such situations would greatly increase crisis instability, posing clear advantages to the side that shoots first in a crisis.

The emphasis on quick reaction has raised the possibility of completely automated decision making, seemingly sacrificing positive control to negative control. Supporters of this idea, such as Edward T. Gerry, chairman of the Fletcher panel's boost-phase systems panel, contend that there "is no time for man in the loop."[21] One analyst has suggested that presidential authority over the release of weapons can be maintained by having the president specify precisely the conditions for certain actions; these specifications would then be written into the computer software for weapons release.[22] Nevertheless, both the Fletcher panel on battle management and the Eastport panel rejected the notion of relinquishing all human control. Maintaining some level of human control over weapons release while also ensuring that the system is activated in time is obviously a troublesome dilemma.

Other solutions exist for resolving the trade-off between positive and negative control, although each has its drawbacks. For instance, the president could retain authority over weapons release, choosing a defensive response from a short list of options (perhaps no more than two: fire or do not fire) upon receiving initial tactical warning. But there probably would not be time enough to locate the president and undertake this procedure. A second method would be to maintain presidential authority over weapons release only until evidence of strategic warning of an attack is received. At that time, authority over release would be delegated to lower command levels, in a process somewhat comparable with the alerting procedures for offensive forces. However, this solution would prove ineffective in the case of a surprise attack, in which no strategic warning or, more likely, ambiguous and conflicting warning was received. A third method would be to permanently assign decisions concerning system activation to lower command levels, perhaps with the same type of strict presidential orders suggested for automated control. Taken to the extreme, decisions regarding weapons release could be made by single individuals far down in the command structure. It should be noted that any defense that employs X-ray lasers pumped by nuclear explosives without requiring direct presidential authorization for their release would be setting a very dangerous precedent.

In each of these schemes, additional procedures to enhance positive control could be utilized. For example, when authority is delegated to lower command levels, threat assessment could be made by one command and the necessary response undertaken by another, much as the NORAD commander now makes the necessary threat assessment that allows the SAC commander to "flush" the bombers. Also, the warning concept of dual phenomenology could be maintained, provided that a space-based radar could be deployed and that this radar could detect missiles during the boost phase. In the case of decision making and system activation by a single individual, it has been suggested that data could be fed to this observer through three redundant sets of software. Each software package could be produced by a different software development group in the hope that no two sets of software would fail in exactly the same way.[23]

False Alarms

Unfortunately, no warning system, no matter how redundant, is fail-safe. The lack of time available for double-checking warning data almost assures that the defense will, at some point, be mistakenly activated. What are the dangers of false alarms and mistaken activation? Many SDI supporters, especially those who call for fully automated weapons release, see little risk involved in such an event. If the system is activated when no threat exists, then the defense simply fires at targets that are not there. Many would agree with the claim of Edward Gerry that "we are talking about a nonnuclear defensive system which is incapable of inflicting damage to anyone or anything on earth."[24] In their view, the dangers of false alarms must be balanced against the much greater dangers of the system failing to activate in time when a real threat exists.

Depending upon the type of defense deployed and its rules of engagement, the risks of incorrectly activating the defense, particularly in a crisis, may be greater than these SDI supporters claim. To begin, mistakenly activating any boost-phase defense that includes pop-up systems could lead to serious consequences. In order to ensure that these weapons would be available for the boost phase, pop-up systems would have to be based on submarines. The sudden launching of submarine-based missiles during a crisis could be seen by the Soviets as the beginning of an offensive first strike. Though the claim is debatable, some even suggest that optical lasers could penetrate the atmosphere and do extensive damage on earth.[25]

A more serious problem arises in attempts to counter defense suppression attacks, which are likely to be part of the initial stages of any ballistic missile attack. If, as part of the defense's rules of engagement to protect against ASAT attacks, activation of the U.S. BMD system results in immediate attacks upon Soviet BMD assets, then mistaken activation of the system during a crisis would look to the Soviets very much like the opening moves of a U.S. first strike.

Effects on Offensive Command and Control

A strategic defense will have effects on offensive command and control, particularly control of nuclear war fighting, mutual alerts, and survivability. Deployment of space-based defenses on both sides will have mixed effects on the survivability of offensive command and control systems. On the one hand, as many supporters of SDI claim, an effective defense could increase the survivability of terrestrial elements of the offensive command and control system. It could increase the survivability of key command centers, especially if combined with a terminal defense around these sites. This might result in an increase in the time available to the NCA and military commanders to decide on an appropriate response. In practice though, unless the defenses were extremely effective, increases in decision-making time are likely to be slight. If authorities were not highly confident that they could survive the first salvo, there would remain a strong incentive to complete the decision-making process before the first warheads were expected to strike. The defense could also enhance the protection of some communications assets, although many, such as large ELF and VLF antennas, are too vulnerable for any form of protection. The effects of a space-based defense on the satellite components of an offensive command and control system are nettlesome. If geosynchronous ASAT capabilities are developed and limitations on these weapons are not negotiated, the threat to offensive C^3 satellites is obvious.

Nevertheless, the mutual deployment of defenses places a premium on devising and executing effective decapitation attacks against offensive command and control systems. The easiest type of attack for a defense to handle is one that is ragged and uncoordinated. In turn, the most effective means for ensuring an uncoordinated response is to concentrate a first strike on the opponent's command and control system. Thus, while space-based defenses may increase the survivability of certain portions of the offensive command and control system, they also increase the benefits and the likelihood of attacks against this system.

It has been reported that an attempt is underway within the Pentagon to integrate offensive missiles and the defensive shield into a coherent war-fighting strategy.[26] This attempt will probably compound the problems of controlled war-fighting, not solve it. The existence of defenses on both sides makes target planning enormously difficult. This is due to the tremendous uncertainties associated with the effectiveness of both sides' defenses and their interaction with one another. Additional uncertainty will derive from the fact that U.S. nuclear missiles must pass through a U.S. defense, relying on untried rules of engagement for identifying friend from foe.

In short, the deployment of defenses is unlikely to make nuclear war any more controllable "once a few tens of weapons" land in the United States. A defense may prolong this eventuality, but unless it is both extremely effective and extremely survivable (close to 100 percent), it is unlikely to maintain control. This is all the more likely since the assets needed to control a nuclear war are the targets most attractive to an opponent with a deployed defense.

Finally, it is important to remember that both sides' BMD systems will be coupled, by way of the intelligence systems, into the offensive command and control systems of the opponent. Even an event as seemingly innocuous as the mistaken firing of a defensive weapon into empty space, when coupled with other random events during a crisis, could begin the mutual ratcheting of offensive alert systems discussed earlier. Once begun, the end result could be catastrophic. The potential for loading additional stimuli (either small or very large) into the tightly coupled offensive command and control system is a very serious possible effect of a space-based BMD system on offensive command and control.

From the standpoint of feasibility and military effectiveness, the movement toward a decentralized command and control system for ballistic missile defense appears to be a step in the right direction, though surely a small one. There are many problems left to overcome, problems that may prove insurmountable. If nothing else, the move toward decentralization will certainly boost the cost of a defense by increasing the necessary number of space assets. The extent of integration required to make the defense effective may prove unattainable. The time constraints involved in boost-phase defense and, perhaps, in protection of the defense itself may increase the likelihood of mistakenly activating the system. And while a ballistic missile defense could improve the survivability of offensive command and control assets, it will also increase the benefits of attacking those assets.

The tangled network of command and control for Star Wars demonstrates vividly the complexity and vulnerabilities that proceeding with SDI will inevitably entail. Because the C^3 system may prove not only unreliable, but an inadvertent catalyst for conflict, it shows again that the SDI risks a serious erosion of crisis stability.

4
Could We Trust the SDI Software?

GREG NELSON AND DAVID REDELL

Weapons and sensors alone do not make a ballistic missile defense. Computers would be the central nervous system of Star Wars: interpreting the data from sensors, calculating the numbers and trajectories of warheads, handling communications between the many satellites and ground command posts, assigning targets to weapons, gathering information about how successful the weapons have been, and so on and so on. It is an immense task, given the numbers of warheads, Soviet countermeasures, vast distances of space, and the serious technical barriers that must be surmounted before programmers can begin to write the software. The software itself—the vast array of computer programs devised to process and communicate information—would challenge the best minds of the field for many years to come, and even then it is unlikely that the system could reliably protect the nation from nuclear destruction.To the criticisms of the physicist, the strategist, and the economist must be added that of the computer programmer: Star Wars is too complicated.

The problem of SDI software is widely acknowledged. The government study laying the technical groundwork for the SDI was the Fletcher report, and one of its six volumes was devoted entirely to the computational requirements of space-based defense. The first conclusion of that volume was that "specifying, generating, testing, and maintaining the software for a battle management system will be a task that far exceeds in complexity and difficulty any that has yet been accomplished in the production of civil or military software systems."[1] The report itself expressed guarded optimism, but the difficulties it outlined led many to conclude that the problem was insoluble.

In 1985 the SDIO commissioned a study titled "Computing in Support of Battle Management" by a panel of computer scientists, usually called the Eastport group. The Eastport group concluded in a report released in early 1986 that the computational difficulties were within the technological capability that could be developed within the next several years, but that the complexity of the computer system made battle management and command, control, and communication the "paramount strategic defense problem." David Parnas, a consultant to the Office of Naval Research, had previously resigned from the Eastport group, having concluded that the SDI software would be inherently untrustworthy. The critique that he submitted with his resignation was later published and quickly became a benchmark for those skeptical of the SDIO's optimism.

In addition to the Fletcher report, the Eastport study, and Parnas's paper, numerous articles, public debates, and news stories have fueled an ongoing software controversy that quickly became a pivotal aspect of the larger issue of SDI feasibility.[2] Indeed, the disagreements over SDI software began to dominate the technical concerns about Star Wars in early 1985, and today software remains one of the most troublesome areas of research for the program. And well it should, for the multiple demands of the battle management software are daunting. It is likely to be the most difficult software project ever undertaken and raises fundamental questions about the trustworthiness of large, complex computer systems.

In approaching this controversy, we begin with the points on which the program's critics and supporters agree. While there is some diversity of opinion in both camps, the following three points are accepted by most knowledgeable observers of both persuasions.

First, the defenses being considered for the SDI are so elaborate that their very complexity is a serious liability. The burden of this complexity falls primarily upon the programmers of the computer system: breakthroughs with individual weapons will do no good if we have no confidence in the computer programs controlling the whole system. And SDI's computational requirements are far more demanding than the computational requirements of previous systems, such as the Aegis ship defense, the Divad mobile antiaircraft gun, the Safeguard ABM system, or the Worldwide Military Command and Control System, all of which encountered serious software difficulties.

Second, the development of software is a more fundamental problem than the development of computing hardware; experience shows that it is easier to provide raw computational power than to harness that power to solve complicated problems.

Third, current programming techniques are limited in their ability to deal with extremely large, complex software projects. New developments such as artificial intelligence (the use of computers to mimic human thought or expertise), or methods such as automatic programming and program verification to ensure that software meets its "specification"—the definition of how the software is to satisfy its real-world requirements—do not represent sweeping breakthroughs that will solve this problem.

Three principal existing software engineering methods have been proposed for raising our confidence in an SDI computer system, but these also entail questions that greatly concern independent computer scientists.

System redundancy. Because of the danger that an error in one part of a highly centralized system could cause other parts of the system to fail, an important question is whether an SDI system could be built as a collection of independent, loosely coordinated parts, thus ensuring reliability through redundancy.

Software-fault tolerance. No known or foreseeable technology for software development will allow the construction of large error-free software systems. Thus, an important question is whether reliable performance can be guaranteed in spite of inevitable software errors.

Partial testing and simulation. Testing is essential to ensure software reliability. Full-scale operational testing of an SDI system would be impossible. The major issue is the extent to which partial testing and simulation could substitute for full-scale operational testing.

In this chapter, the computational requirements of the SDI are first analyzed; then, in turn, the techniques of system redundancy, software-fault tolerance, and partial testing and simulation are assessed.

COMPUTATIONAL REQUIREMENTS OF THE SDI

The exact computational requirements depend on the nature and purpose of the ballistic missile defense system, both of which are now uncertain and controversial. Though many of our points also apply to systems at the simpler end of the scale, such as those that provide only terminal defense of missile silos, our analysis is concerned primarily with the computational requirements of a layered defense that includes boost-phase, midcourse, and terminal interception of ICBMs.

We will divide the functions of the system into low-, middle-, and high-level categories somewhat analogous to levels in a management hierarchy. Although the boundaries between the categories are somewhat arbitrary, the classification is still useful.

The low-level functions of the system include:

Aiming and control of sensors and weapons. Simply aiming and activating the sensors and weapons would require computerized control systems of high speed, reliability, and precision.

Processing a high volume of data from sensors. Infrared and radar sensors would generate many millions of data elements per second, requiring processing at very high speed by specialized computers.

Middle-level functions include:

Surveillance and target acquisition. To acquire a target, the system would have to recognize its characteristic pattern in the sensor data (its "signature").

Track formation and decoy discrimination. Information from repeated sampling would be used to calculate the trajectory of each target. This task, called *track formation,* is very demanding, especially when many targets must be tracked simultaneously. The decoy discrimination problem has not been solved, but it is likely that any solution would require that the computer system recognize subtle differences in the patterns of data gathered about the targets.

Kill assessment. After attacking a target, the system would need to monitor changes in its signature to decide whether the attack had been effective, whether to attack again, and so on. Details of this process are highly dependent on the type of weapon employed and the cleverness of the offense's countermeasures.

Scheduling and allocation of weapons and other resources. Given the thousands of targets not discountable as decoys, rapid decisions would be needed to assign weapons to targets in order, based on some set of criteria for establishing priorities, such as estimated impact point or impact time.

Dynamic reconfiguration to compensate for damaged components. During a battle, the system would inevitably suffer damage and disruption. In an attempt to minimize the impact of the damage, the computer system would need to revise communication paths, target assignments, and other decisions.

High-level functions include:

Coordination among system components. Since the defense satellites and targets are both moving, each satellite would periodically shift its attention to a new set of targets. This process would be much more efficient if the components cooperated actively by exchanging data about targets; unfortunately, this would introduce added complexity.

Coordination with command authority. From the vast amount of data arriving at satellites from sensors, the system must produce a comprehensible picture of what is going on and convey it to the command authority. In the reverse direction, high-level commands received from the command authority must be translated into a multitude of specific actions by the various satellites.

Automated weapons release. Since some decisions would

need to be made too quickly for human involvement, some degree of automated weapons release and activation appears unavoidable.

Detection of attacks on the system itself. In addition to defending targets against ballistic missiles and warheads, the system would need to monitor attacks directed against itself—by antisatellite weapons, for example—and activate appropriate countermeasures.

These specific functions interact with several general requirements of the SDI software. Many of the functions have "real-time" performance requirements—that is, the computation must keep up with the pace of external events. Real-time requirements cannot be satisfied by faster hardware alone; the software must be structured intricately to accommodate that demand. In addition, the hardware and software must "tolerate," or compensate for, component failures and defects in the system's design. There must be security against interference, such as jamming or unauthorized commands. Updating the system is another serious difficulty: the contest between measure and countermeasure in the BMD arena would require continual changes in the software. Installing software updates is a difficult problem in any "distributed," or decentralized, system, and the problem would be harder in a system located in orbiting satellites, with access to the computers only through encrypted communication channels.

Moreover, in the SDI software as in most software systems, the interaction between different aspects of the problem adds complexity. Consider the difficulty of meeting real-time performance requirements in the face of the communications delays of the distributed system: distributed systems are designed to tolerate unpredictable communication delays, while real-time systems are based on precise prescheduling of events. The combination of these requirements is much more difficult than either of them individually because they introduce conflicting notions of how the system should be structured.

Another example is the conflict between real-time constraints and fault tolerance. The latter involves self-correcting mechanisms for errors in the computer system, mechanisms that, in general, take time to work. This conflict is illustrated by the Safeguard ABM software, whose designers point out that "system-error responses contribute to system availability, but they may be inhibited during a battle to prevent interruption of tactical operation."[3] In other words, a measure taken to enable fault tolerance is precluded during battle by real-time constraints. Unfortunately, it is during a battle that software errors are most likely to be revealed.

Speed and reliability will conflict in other areas as well. A critical requirement for booster interception is fast response, since the boost phase currently would last less than five minutes, and fast-burn boosters could reduce this interval to one minute or less. It is generally agreed that to meet this requirement, some degree of automation in the weapons release process is inevitable. But the early warning system now in use has produced false alarms because of hardware errors, ambiguous data from sensors, unanticipated natural events, and human error. Similar false alarms can be expected from the SDI computer system. Whatever combination of human control and automation is used, it may take several minutes to determine that an alarm is false. As a result, the system's guarantee that it will engage boosters promptly introduces the danger that it might go off by accident. Even more stringent time constraints would be introduced if the system needed to actively defend itself by attacking hostile missiles or satellites. A false alert triggering preemptive attacks on enemy space or ground assets could easily precipitate a general nuclear war. The reliability requirements to be imposed in this area will, of course, depend on the estimated danger from an accident, but they could well turn out to be impossible to meet.

It is sometimes taken for granted that artificial intelligence (AI) techniques would be used in the automatic weapons-release programs if conventional "pattern recognition" methods are inadequate for the task. But in this event, reliable operation would be even more difficult to guarantee. Current artificial intelligence technology exhibits substantial "brittleness"—that is, it can behave in undesirable ways when confronted with unanticipated situations. While some progress in this area will undoubtedly be made, there is little reason to believe that entrusting the activation of a BMD system entirely to software would be safe at any time in the foreseeable future.

The combination of requirements just described has led many to conclude that the SDI computer system would be far more complex than any other computer system ever proposed or built. While there is no precise measure of software complexity, a crude indicator is the number of lines in the program text. The Fletcher report estimated that 6 to 10 million lines of software would be required in the SDI computer system. Officials of the Rome Air Development Center in New York have estimated 24.61 million lines.[4] This is approximately the amount of text in one thousand thick books.

Since the current state of the art makes the development of even a 1-million-line program a highly complex and risky undertaking, such estimates are quite sobering, especially since the difficulty of a software project increases more quickly than its size. This is because errors are often caused by unexpected interactions between two parts of the program, even if each would work correctly by itself. If every line interacted with every other line, the number of interactions would be proportional to the square of the program size. Such a drastic explosion of complexity would make it impossible to write programs of more than a few lines. By carefully structuring a program as a set of separate "modules," the number of interactions can be sharply reduced, but the complexity still grows faster than program size. In addition, different kinds of software display different levels of difficulty for the same total size, sometimes differing by factors of five or more.[5] The difficulty of its requirements makes it unlikely that the SDI software would fall anywhere near the low end of this scale.

The complexity of the SDI software requirements has been captured by Charles Zraket, vice president of the Mitre Corporation, which is the air force's principal "think tank" for systems analysis:

> If we make a linear extrapolation from our past experience, the overall effort needed to plan, design, and specify the performance of a comprehensive BMD system, and then to develop, implement, test, and verify the operational software code to

> meet these specifications, would be several tens of thousands of man-years. Extrapolation may be misleading, however, as the air defense, air traffic control, and ABM systems developed in the 1960s and 1970s tracked only a few hundred objects and made only tens of intercepts at a time. Furthermore, it would have to carry out these tasks while many complex, software-dependent interactions were taking place among the various layers of the defense system and with offensive and allied forces. It is possible that a team of a few thousand professionals working for up to twenty years might be needed to accomplish such a feat. This would be an undertaking unprecedented in the history of software development and implementation.[6]

The inherent complexity of the SDI software problem is not likely to be circumvented by any sudden innovations. Some tout artificial intelligence, automatic programming (derivation of the program directly from its specification), or program verification (mathematical proof that the program meets its specification) as breakthroughs that will change the nature of software engineering, but we agree with the Eastport group that these expectations are unfounded. In practice, automatic programming is just a catchphrase for higher-level programming languages. Program verification directly addresses critical problems in software engineering, but progress in the area has been slow and the prospect of formally verifying a real-time program of millions of lines is extremely remote. Progress in AI has also been slow, and the fundamental problems of cognition and inference addressed by AI researchers are not software engineering problems. It is therefore not surprising that AI has had little impact on software engineering.

Frederick P. Brooks, who led the team that produced IBM's System 360 and defends the possibility of building the SDI software, has said, "if it cannot be done with today's techniques and technologies, it cannot be done at all."[7] With this in mind, we examine the potential of three accepted software development techniques to meet the SDI's challenge.

THE LIMITATIONS OF SYSTEM REDUNDANCY

System redundancy involves using more than one independent system, meeting the same requirements but built to different specifications, in order to provide additional assurance that at least one of the systems will work.

System redundancy is different from module redundancy. Modules are the units into which large programs are usually divided, and module redundancy is a technique used at a finer level of detail than system redundancy to provide software fault tolerance (see following section). Conceptually, the difference is that redundant modules must meet the same *specification*, while redundant systems meet only the same *requirement*. The three arms of our nuclear retaliatory "triad" (bombers, land-based missiles, and sea-based missiles) provide an example of system redundancy: each meets the requirement of assuring our ability to inflict unacceptable damage on the Soviet Union in response to a nuclear attack, but the technical specifications for the systems are completely different.

A common difficulty with system redundancy is guarding against a single point of failure of all the "independent" systems—that is, if one component failed or was destroyed, the entire system might fail as well. For example, our C^3I system is a point of a common vulnerability of the three arms of the strategic triad. Another difficulty with redundancy can be unintended interactions between the components during operation, such as fratricide between warheads. It should be noted, too, that redundancy is generally the most expensive way to increase reliability.

In the case of the SDI, the possibility of using some kind of system redundancy was stressed by the Eastport group. They argued that the system outlined by the Fletcher report (and followed by the SDIO and contractors in the first two years of the program) is too centralized and monolithic, and consequently too rigid and brittle. In proposing a more loosely organized system, the Eastport study stated that "most of the architectures proposed [by SDI software contractors]—including the model architecture presented in the Fletcher Report—are sufficient in terms of sensors and weapons, [but] the panel does not regard them as feasible."[8] Instead, they see a Star Wars computing system that is highly decentralized, and one that uses system redundancy to ensure reliability.

An extreme example of such system redundancy would be the deployment of a set of completely independent orbiting battle stations. Every station would need sensors and weapons, software for aiming and control, signal processing, track formation, decoy discrimination, kill assessment, scheduling of its own weapons and sensors, and communication with the ground. Some connection with the ground is required, if only to receive weapons release codes and to report on the progress of the battle. Thus, most of the functions of the SDI system would have to be performed by each station. Even so, there appears to be no way to avoid some kind of network: to remain in contact with the ground while orbiting, each battle station would have to communicate with a number of different ground stations. And it is imprudent to depend on a single communication link through the atmosphere, where laser communication can be prevented by weather and radio is vulnerable to jamming and sabotage. As a result, independent battle stations would undoubtedly be linked into a satellite communications network. Given the existence of the network and the practical disadvantages of total independence, there would be compelling reasons to introduce some degree of cross-coupling into the system.

The main operational disadvantage of totally independent stations is the lack of coordination. With some kinds of sensors, accurate and efficient tracking requires forming a stereo image by fusing data from more than one station—somewhat akin to the triangulation method a surveyor uses to measure a land site. Decoy discrimination and kill assessment are likely to benefit from (or require) observation of specific events during a target's trajectory, including bus separation, attack results, and interactive discrimination probes. Without coordination among the battle stations, a given station would have to rely exclusively on data that it could collect during the portion of the ICBM trajectory visible to it. Since trajectories are thousands of miles long and the ranges of sensors are limited, this lack of coordination would be a serious handicap.

As a result of these difficulties, it seems impossible to build an SDI computing system from independent, simple parts. If the parts were truly independent, each would have to solve by itself so many problems that it would in fact be quite complicated, rather than simple. A communication network is required in any case. The benefits of coordination are so great that it would probably be impractical or impossible to avoid sharing information between the battle stations. Experience has shown that even modest amounts of coordination can open the door to unforeseen interactions that compromise the autonomy and robustness of supposedly independent components. Without full-scale testing, even loosely coupled SDI systems could be expected to exhibit such interactions, with potentially fatal results.

THE LIMITATIONS OF SOFTWARE-FAULT TOLERANCE

Much has been said about the possibility of software-fault tolerance for the SDI. This refers not to software that tolerates hardware faults, but to systems that tolerate software errors. Tolerance of hardware faults is a mature technology, since hardware faults are component failures and it is easier to model the effect of such failures. Unfortunately, software faults are not component failures but design errors, and the assumptions about statistical independence and probable impact that characterize hardware malfunctions do not apply. Tolerating software faults is an uncertain and not very scientific art.

As noted above, large programs are generally divided into units called modules. This suggests a fault-tolerance technique called *module redundancy*, in which two or more software modules are written to the same specification by independent programming teams. The idea is that it is unlikely that different teams will make the same error. In operation, the different programs can be run concurrently, with their results compared after each operation (concurrent redundancy). Or one of them can be used until an erroneous result is obtained, and then the other can be substituted (replacement redundancy). In the right circumstances, module redundancy can provide improvements in reliability, but it imposes such severe constraints on system structure that it can be impractical to apply.

The most obvious difficulty is the need for multiple independent programming teams to implement each software module that is to be treated in this way. The teams must be coordinated closely enough that their modules will work together, but not so closely that their independence is compromised. This problem is not as difficult, however, as the more subtle constraints concerning performance and complexity.

Concurrent module redundancy degrades performance, because of both the cost of comparing results and the need to synchronize all the versions after each operation. Each operation is as slow as the slowest version. If the module produces a large amount of information, the cost of comparisons can be prohibitive.

The second method, replacement redundancy, is attractive if erroneous results can be detected by the program that is using the replicated module. The error must be detected before any other module has committed to the use of the erroneous results. But since the error is often detected in the process of using the erroneous result, this is not always possible. In this scheme, the worst-case cost of an operation will far exceed the typical, error-free case. This can make the scheme incompatible with real-time constraints.

Another problem with module redundancy is that the software for coordinating the independent versions introduces additional complexity that can itself become a source of errors. For example, the space shuttle uses module redundancy in its computer system. The first flight of the shuttle was stopped four seconds before lift-off because the backup system failed to synchronize with the primary system.

An experimental study has shown that the assumption underlying software module redundancy—that programming teams are unlikely to make the same error—is open to question.[9] This is not surprising: a weak team may produce many errors that are all its own, but a difficult specification includes traps that may catch many or all of the teams. Finally, a crucial point discussed in the final section of this chapter is that errors in the common specification will be shared by all software writers.

In addition to module redundancy, several other fault-tolerance techniques are sometimes more practical, although they are more ad hoc and correspondingly uncertain.

In the *sanity checking* technique, the software is required periodically to send a signal indicating that it is still functioning. Failure of this signal to arrive causes the computation to be terminated. Sanity checking is an attempt to prevent one runaway computation from infecting the whole system. Of course, there is no way to know exactly what damage has been done, or where. This technique was used in the Safeguard ABM system.

Perhaps the simplest and most valuable technique for tolerating software faults is *retry*: when an error is detected, the offending computation is tried again. In a purely sequential program with no interaction with the outside world, this technique is fruitless because if the software got it wrong once, it will always get it wrong. But when many machines compute concurrently and interact with the outside world, a second try may succeed. This is not very scientific, but it often works in practice.

A final example is the technique of *dynamic resource location*. Instead of always relying on the same statically chosen component to provide some particular service—which would leave the requesting module stuck if that component failed—the dynamic resource location strategy has the requester search through the available resources until it finds one that is working. For example, to forward a message a satellite could try to send it by several routes, continuing its search until it received an acknowledgment.

These techniques are not foolproof, and when used in combination they can interact in unanticipated ways. For example, the combination of retry with dynamic resource location can actually amplify the impact of an error in the following way. If the operation that provoked a failure in one system component is subsequently retried, the retry may automatically locate another resource that is prone to the same failure, causing it to fail as well. Repetition of this pattern, if not stopped by some other mechanism, results in a wave of fatal errors that can cripple the entire system. In the SDI system, if a message being forwarded by a satellite contained an anomaly that caused its recipient to fail, then the satellite's persistent efforts could quickly bring down the whole network. This kind of global failure has been observed in existing systems and is just one example of the ways in which fault tolerance techniques, like other aspects of software complexity, can interact to cause unanticipated problems. Such problems are typically discovered only during operational use.

The inescapable conclusion is that systems cannot necessarily be made tolerant of software faults simply by investing more money and programming effort in redundancy. When used appropriately, software fault tolerance can improve system reliability, but the techniques are difficult to apply and their effectiveness is uncertain.

THE LIMITATIONS OF SIMULATION AND PARTIAL TESTING

There are two main questions to be asked about software testing: How realistic is the test—that is, to what extent is it performed under the actual conditions in which the software will be used? At what scale is the test conducted?—that is, to what extent does the testing environment test the entire system with the full load it would encounter in practice?

Although these two questions obviously interact, they are often treated as if they were independent. For example, testing a single system component under actual field conditions is very realistic, but small scale. On the other hand, simulating the operation of a complete system entirely in the laboratory represents full scale, but sacrifices much realism. Naturally, it is not feasible to perform all tests at full scale under actual operational conditions. The testing of any large software system employs a spectrum of approaches, ranging from simulation of individual components to full-scale operational use of the entire system. Especially in the early stages of a project, small-scale testing under simulated conditions can be invaluable in finding a large number of problems at reasonable cost. The important point to note, however, is that all experience with large software systems shows that full-scale testing under actual operational conditions invariably reveals flaws that would not have been uncovered by partial testing or simulation.

In the case of the SDI, full-scale operational testing would involve confronting the deployed system with an actual nuclear attack, complete with thousands of warheads, multiple nuclear explosions, and so on—in short, an actual nuclear war.

This kind of testing is clearly impossible, a point that is not in dispute. It is sometimes argued, however, that simulations and partial testing could substitute for full-scale operational testing of an SDI system. There are several reasons why this claim is implausible.

The most realistic partial testing of an SDI system would consist of having a simulated opponent (or "red team") fire actual missiles with dummy warheads at a target and seeing whether the system could shoot them down. There are several problems with this scenario. For one thing, there is no way for the red team to know what kinds of countermeasures an actual opponent would use (and indeed the actual opponent could observe the test and revise its countermeasure strategy). For another, some countermeasures, even if predictable, would not be acceptable as part of a test (for example, attacking one's own command and control system). Similarly, the surrounding environment of the test could not accurately reflect that of actual use, which would include nuclear explosions within the atmosphere and in outer space, and other disruptive effects. In addition, of course, it is inherent in the notion of partial testing that saturation problems would not be uncovered.

Simulation, on the other hand, encounters a different set of difficulties. Fundamental to the use of simulation is the ability to predict and model the parameters of the situation being simulated. To the extent that the situation is understood and controlled, the simulation can reflect it accurately. In the case of the SDI, however, the conditions of an actual attack are not well understood. Not only the countermeasures to be used by the opponent, but even some of the important physics of the situation (for example, the atmospheric effects of high-altitude nuclear detonations) are only partially understood. A further difficulty is the necessity to perform the simulation in real time. To test by simulation a real-time system as it interacts with its environment is extremely difficult. The system must be presented with a complete simulation of its environment, one that accurately reflects both the incoming missile attack and any changes in the situation due to the actions of the system itself. This requires another large computer system with complex software of its own, raising the question of how one could gain confidence in the simulation.

Aside from the SDI-specific difficulties of partial testing and simulation, there is an underlying assumption in the proposal that is extremely dubious: that full realism and full scale can be explored independently. As has been pointed out previously, the basic problem with software reliability stems from unexpected interactions. The problems of full-scale use and operational conditions can be expected to interact with unexpected events, invalidating the implicit assumption of independence lurking in the proposal to test them separately.

Simulations can be very impressive. They come out of a computer and carry the stamp of its authority; their results may be presented with great numerical precision or displayed dramatically with dynamic color graphics. But it should always be remembered that simulation can only be carried out with respect to a model, and if the model is not an accurate reflection of reality, then the simulation results may be worthless.

Even models of very simple systems often contain serious oversights. For example, what could be simpler than to model the movement of the moon around the earth, as was necessary to write the software for the Gemini 5 mission? Unfortunately, the model that was used overlooked the fact that the entire earth-moon system also moves in orbit around the sun. As a result, the spacecraft came down one hundred miles from its intended landing point.[10]

It is easy to imagine that similar blunders could be made in modeling a nuclear battle. The model for possible warhead trajectories might neglect the possibility of spinning two warheads around a connecting tether, adding a helical deviation to the ballistic trajectories. The model for determining a target's velocity using radar might ignore the possibility of attaching lightweight radar-reflecting "fronds" whose motion would jumble the signal. The model for communication node failure might accommodate failures of arbitrary patterns of nodes at arbitrary rates, but ignore the possibility that an opponent might alternately jam and unjam some communications node, instead of destroying it outright, at a frequency that would cause the network reconfiguration algorithms to thrash between different configurations (tricking the system into spending all its time computing its own "connectivity" instead of managing the battle).

These arbitrary examples are only intended as reminders of

the limitations of modeling. The actual models are likely to contain many errors that are far more mundane. In addition to simple oversights, the models will probably contain implicit assumptions to make these very difficult problems tractable. If every parameter of the possible penetration aids and penetration strategy is estimated conservatively, the problem is likely to become insoluble. If the estimates are not conservative, some of them are certain to be inaccurate.

The fact that subtle differences between testing environments and operational use can make a big difference is illustrated by the fact that the United States has never successfully test-fired a Minuteman missile from an operational silo. The air force tried four times. On the first three attempts, the missile never lifted off. On the fourth attempt, it exploded. Since then, all tests have been carried out from the special testing installation at Vandenburg Air Force Base.[11] Given the extensive experience the U.S. military has had with ballistic missile engineering, such failures are a telling commentary on the far more daunting—and less well understood—testing and operations of Star Wars.

Why is it that operational testing is required if a complex software system is to be trustworthy? One of the first truths encountered in learning to use a computer is that its main virtue is also its most infuriating difficulty: it does exactly what you tell it to. This fact lies at the root of one of the most fundamental limitations of software engineering: one can never have more confidence in a computer program than one has in the specification that the program is designed to satisfy. This truth may be obscured in cases where the specification is not cleanly separated from the program itself, but it holds nonetheless. If the directions embedded in the software are self-consistent but inappropriate to the situation at hand, the system will still carry them out mechanically and exactly. A computer cannot detect that its instructions are inappropriate.

It is vain to hope that artificial intelligence or any other development will remove this limit. Considerable research interest is now focused on the topic of formal software specification. This important area of research may, in the long run, develop powerful new methods to develop software that meets its specification, including program verification and automatic programming. These techniques are still in their infancy, however—at least compared with the state of maturity needed to tackle a system as complex as the SDI. The prospect of formally verifying or deriving a system meeting the SDI's requirements any time during the next several decades is extremely remote.

In any case, a more fundamental question remains: Is the specification itself free of errors? That is, does the specification correspond to the real-world requirements that the system must satisfy? At first glance, this problem might appear analogous to that of program correctness, suggesting the idea of automatic generation or checking of correct specifications. The problem is fundamentally different, however, since the real-world requirements that the system must satisfy are not themselves formally specifiable.

How then are errors removed from specifications? There are two ways that this is done in practice. If the requirements are sufficiently simple, the designers of the system can sometimes satisfy themselves, through a priori arguments, that the specifications fit the requirements. This typically works only when the program is small and exhibits little or no interaction with its environment. Obviously, this is not the case for the SDI system.

The only other approach is operational testing, which simultaneously ensures that the software meets its specification and that its specification is appropriate for the requirements of the actual situation in which the system will function. In practice, then, the results of operational testing cause both the program and its specification to change and evolve. Without operational testing, it is not possible to achieve confidence that the specified system will meet the requirements, even if it somehow were possible to guarantee that the program met the specification. Both fault tolerance and simulation depend on a specification of the behavior of the system and its environment; if the specification contains errors, the validity of both techniques is fundamentally undermined.

Because of the inability to perform operational testing, the confidence that anyone would have in the SDI system is inherently limited. It is limited to one's corresponding confidence in the correctness of the model of a Soviet ballistic missile attack being used in the specifications, a model necessarily speculative in many respects. Neither software-fault tolerance, nor simulation testing, nor system redundancy offers any hope of lifting this limitation.

The SDI is inherently dependent on its computer system, without which any collection of exotic weapons, sensors, and strategies would be useless. The required computer system would be far more complex than any previous computerized weapons system and would require software well beyond the current state of the art. Given the magnitude of this software engineering challenge, there is a significant chance that the development effort would simply fail to produce a deployable system at all.

It is fitting to recall the following passage from the 1980 Turing Award Lecture given by C. A. R. Hoare. "At first I hoped that such a technically unsound project would collapse," he remarked of another large software project, "but I soon realized it was doomed to success. Almost anything in software can be implemented, sold, and even used given enough determination. There is nothing a mere scientist can say that will stand against the flood of a hundred million dollars. But there is one thing that cannot be purchased in this way—and that is reliability."[12] Rather than failing to produce a deployable system, then, the SDI development effort could lead to deployment of an unreliable system, one that could fail to stop an attack or could accidentally activate itself when no attack was underway.

The techniques available for increasing the reliability of the SDI software have inherent limitations. Optimists can believe that a system could be deployed that would work if it were needed. Because operational testing is impossible, however, the issue could never be settled with certainty. The reliability of the system would always be in doubt.

5
Lethal Paradox: The ASAT-SDI Link

JOHN TIRMAN AND PETER DIDISHEIM

The element of the president's Star Wars vision that immediately sets it apart from all other ballistic missile defense concepts is its location: it would be space based. Defense in the high frontier would involve satellites—orbiting weapons platforms, "fighting" mirrors, bundles of sensors, on-board computers. In what numbers and combinations, no one can say with assurance, but it is obvious that satellites would be pivotal. The reason follows a simple progression: destroying the Soviet ICBMs in boost phase, before each released its ten or more warheads and its many decoys, is essential; and the only "line of sight" that permits boost-phase interception is from outer space.

The need for space-based weapons and sensors is fundamental regardless of the particular weapons employed, though each technique might alter the exact positioning of defense satellites. Kinetic energy weapons would have to be in low orbits—probably between 200 km and 1,000 km altitude—as close to the rising boosters as possible to shorten the time their projectiles would fly to their targets. Similarly, most lasers need to be in low orbits because the maximum intensity of the beam on the target decreases as the square of the distance; for example, from geosynchronous orbit (40,000 km), a beam is 1,600 times less powerful than from low earth orbits of 1,000 km, and 100 times weaker than at 4,000 km distance.

Some weapon components, such as one set of mirrors for the free-electron laser system, might be in geosynchronous altitudes, 40,000 km above the equator. But it was soon clear that low-orbit satellites are the likely configuration for many, if not most, of Star Wars' space assets.

The president's men know, however, that this seemingly inevitable "look" for boost-phase defense contains a serious—and possibly fatal—defect. That problem can be summed up in one word: *vulnerability*. The space assets, particularly those in the predictable low orbits, would be like sitting ducks on a pond—easy targets for Soviet antisatellite weapons. Edward Teller had long eschewed the idea of space-*based* defense, touting his "pop-up" concept instead. Two days after the president's March 23 speech, science adviser George Keyworth told a reporter that he too favored pop-up systems, precisely because satellites "could be knocked out in advance" by Soviet ASATs.[1] Early reports of the Fletcher group and independent analysts readily pointed out the same flaw.

The Strategic Defense Initiative nonetheless envisages the missile defense to be significantly space based: for example, the leading SDI "architecture" study, released in October 1985, foresees thousands of satellites in seven layers. The automatic answer to the question about the vulnerability of these many space assets has been that the SDI is exploring "survivability" measures, ways to protect satellites from ASAT attacks, though the case for such measures (and the claim that they have a high priority in the SDI) is far from convincing. The program has retreated from its early optimism about using, among others, chemical lasers in low orbits to intercept boosters, tending rather to emphasize midcourse interception; but there is universal agreement that an effective defense *requires* boost-phase interceptors, and thus the vulnerability problem is every bit as urgent.

There is another dimension to this satellites-as-sitting-ducks quandary. For many of the weapons being nurtured in the SDI will make excellent ASATs, even if they are never used for missile defense. Assuming the Soviets pursue similar lines of development, they too will possess powerful space- and ground-based lasers, kinetic energy weapons, and the like. The result of this technology push will be high-quality satellite killers that will threaten any space-based components of Star Wars.

Thus, the two kinds of space weapons—missile defense and antisatellite devices—are locked in a lethal paradox. The continuously evolving ASAT capability will loom as a greater and greater threat to the boost-phase and midcourse elements of the SDI. But the program itself is frenetically inventing the very techniques that will result in more sophisticated ASATs—thus sowing the seeds of its own destruction. The nature of the new antisatellite threat does not stop here, however, for the early result of the SDI will be the heightened jeopardy of *current* military satellites. These vital space assets—used for early warning of nuclear attack, command and control of forces, intelligence gathering, and so on—will be vulnerable to devastating attacks from the SDI-spurred ASATs.

So the Star Wars effort, even if it is a failure on its own terms, will degrade U.S. security as a consequence of the ASAT-SDI link—a bitterly ironic legacy for the president's quixotic vision.

The link between antisatellite and missile-defense technologies goes back to the beginning of the space age. Just like strategic defenses, antisatellite weapons were being contemplated very early on. "Men began thinking about disabling satellites," one historian notes, "well before there were any spacecraft to disable."[2] The first operational U.S. ASATs were spun from the Nike Zeus BMD system of the late 1950s and early 1960s, itself derived from the Nike Hercules air defense system. The nuclear-tipped Nike Zeus missiles were meant to intercept Soviet warheads as they descended outside the atmosphere. This gave the missile an inherent ASAT capability, although the adaptation from its BMD role to the ASAT role, begun in 1962, included extending the device's range from 100 to 150 miles altitude. The new nuclear-tipped satellite killer was ready for use in 1963, but was abandoned in 1967 in favor of newer "Thor" technology, a decision that followed the junking of Nike Zeus for BMD missions in favor of the Nike X and Spartan missiles.

Thor—in mythology the Norse god of thunder—was a booster developed for intermediate-range ballistic missiles;

like Nike Zeus, it was forged into its antisatellite mission from another program. Also like Nike Zeus, it was initially, and urgently, adapted to combat a perceived Soviet threat from orbital nuclear bombs, a threat that never really materialized and, in any case, was soon constrained by a United Nations "statement" that later evolved into the U.S.-USSR Outer Space Treaty of 1967. Thor had somewhat greater range than Nike Zeus and became the U.S. ASAT until it was phased out by the Ford administration in 1975. Soon after, in response to what was then believed to be a greater Soviet emphasis on space weapons, Ford initiated the F-15 ASAT program, which continues to this day. The current ASAT is a two-stage rocket propelled from the belly of the F-15 fighter jet and able to destroy Soviet satellites in low orbits by direct impact. A similar design was actually tested in 1959 under code name Bold Orion, using a B-47 aircraft and a nuclear-tipped rocket developed by the Martin Company. The F-15 version has had its troubles, but the air force is committed to the program, despite technical difficulties, cost overruns, and congressional restrictions that have put it far behind schedule and raise doubts that it can fulfill its mission.

With the surge in research resulting from President Reagan's Star Wars speech, attention given to ASAT techniques has grown considerably. The similarity of the hardware and the missions persists into the new realms of directed energy, electromagnetic rail guns, and particle beams. Technological parallels and reciprocal threats are not the only basis for the ASAT-BMD symbiosis, however. The Reagan administration has resisted ASAT arms control furiously, in part because sanctions would seriously hamper SDI demonstrations of technology—what is not permitted under the ABM Treaty is permitted in the unrestricted realm of antisatellite technology. A space-based laser ready for testing can be legally demonstrated in an "ASAT mode," whereas testing the same technology in an "ABM mode" would violate the proscriptions of the ABM Treaty.

The refusal of the U.S. government to negotiate an ASAT ban will rebound against American security and, most ironically, against the SDI's mission itself. Nearly every technology being contemplated for missile defense is applicable to an antisatellite role—chemical lasers, free-electron lasers, particle beams, X-ray lasers, and a variety of kinetic energy devices. Not all of these would, in practice, be developed as ASATs, for there are "survivability" measures available to the Star Wars defense that would vitiate some more than others. The high cost of these R&D efforts will also retard their progress as space weapons of any kind, though the demands on these techniques as ASATs are far less than as BMD interceptors.

Perhaps more important, some of the exotics will not be pursued because anti-BMD ASATs in much simpler incarnations are immediately available. This is true whether the emphasis of the SDI remains on boost-phase interception or shifts toward midcourse interception. But the present orientation of the Reagan administration is to pursue a variety of BMD weapons techniques that also are envisaged as satellite killers.

SATELLITE VULNERABILITY

The vulnerability of Star Wars' components in space derives from the nature of orbits. There are several different ways a satellite can revolve around the earth. At low altitudes, some 200 km to 5,000 km, a satellite can move in polar orbits (north-south, if tracing its direction along the earth's surface), equatorial orbits, or "inclined" orbits (at an angle to the plane formed by the equator). Some orbits—particularly those used by Soviet Molniya satellites—are highly elliptical, not always at the same altitude, ranging from very low perigee (500 km) to very high apogee (40,000 km).

At 36,000 km—one-tenth of the way to the moon—a satellite is in a geosynchronous orbit, that is, it is stationary relative to a point on the globe, revolving around exactly in sync with the rotation of the earth. There are also semisynchronous orbits at about 20,000 km, and supersynchronous orbits half way to the moon. For the most part, however, satellites are deployed in the variety of low, elliptical, or geosynchronous orbits.

A satellite is launched into specific orbits according to its mission. For example, satellites in very low orbits—200 km or about 120 miles up, just outside the atmosphere—complete a revolution quickly, in about ninety minutes. Only a relatively small area of the earth is visible from such a low-altitude orbit, however. The higher the orbit, the slower the revolution; from higher orbits, more surface of the earth is visible. At geosynchronous altitude, almost the entire hemisphere is visible. Military satellites of the United States and the USSR are scattered among these different orbits, according to the requirements of their purpose, their capability, and their importance (see fig. 5.1). Photoreconnaissance, which uses visible light and infrared cameras, must be in low orbit to get good-quality, detailed photographs. Many communications satellites are in geosynchronous orbits due to their ability to transmit radio waves to the 80 percent of the hemisphere they "see."

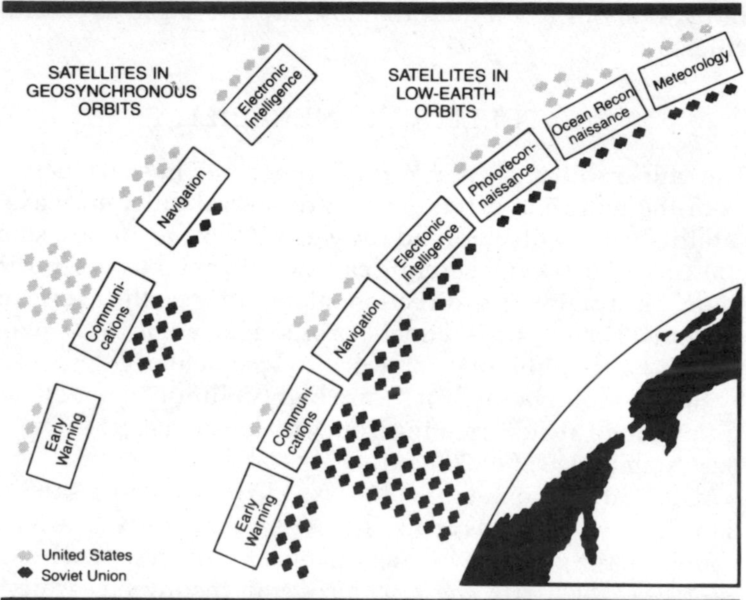

FIG. 5.1. The typical distribution of U.S. (gray) and Soviet (black) satellites currently used for military tasks includes a high number of U.S. satellites in geosynchronous orbits (40,000 km altitude) and larger numbers of Soviet satellites in low earth orbits (200–5,000 km). Although low-orbit satellites could be vulnerable to the current generation of ASATs, the geosynchronous space assets could also be jeopardized by the development of speed-of-light weapons and other techniques being pursued in missile-defense R&D.

In a Star Wars defense, a large fraction of the satellites bearing weapons would be placed in low, polar orbits to give the defense its optimal line of sight to Soviet ICBM fields. The trade-offs available to SDI planners include very low orbits that enable kinetic energy weapons, for example, to reach their targets more quickly, but then sacrifice the amount of surface area covered, thereby also sacrificing the number of Soviet missiles within range. Higher altitudes (but still in the 200 to 5,000 km of low orbits) permit a better range, but are farther from targets. The trade-offs are important: shorter range means the defense will need more satellites to attack the entire fleet of ICBMs; but the increased distance of higher orbits means that the technical demands on the weapons (flight time for kinetic energy weapons, brightness for directed-energy weapons) will be greater.

Another consideration is the chronic "absenteeism" of low-orbit satellites. Unlike those in geosynchronous orbits, which hover over the same spot along the equator, satellites in low orbits revolve around the earth, constantly moving relative to the earth's surface. As a result, a large number of defense satellites will be entirely out of range of the Soviet missiles at any one time. This absentee ratio has been estimated at between 6:1 and 10:1, meaning that for every defense satellite "on station" over Siberia, at least six will be entirely out of range.

The most salient fact about low orbits, however, is that they are fully predictable. Once a satellite is deployed into an orbit, that orbit becomes a consistent path. It is quite possible to maneuver a satellite, but that takes fuel, and, unless maneuvering is also constant, a new, predictable orbit will eventually be established. Geosynchronous orbits are also predictable, of course, because they remain stationary relative to the earth. It is this fact, perhaps more than any other, that renders defense satellites vulnerable to attacks from antisatellite weapons. Knowing the exact—or probable—path of an orbiter (and its velocity) is a tremendous advantage to the attacker.

The Star Wars armada would include weapons-bearing battle stations, and separate satellites used for command, control, communications, and intelligence (C^3I); battle management (BM); and sensing, acquisition, tracking, and kill assessment

(SATKA). The BM/C³I and SATKA satellites will be arrayed in many different locations, but most will be in low orbits in the "field of battle," while others may be in geosynchronous orbits. The Soviet offense will have many targets to attack and will be able to choose the time and method of attack. Moreover, due to the defense's "absentee" problem, the offense gains a great advantage in terms of cost. That is, the offense need only "punch a hole" through the Star Wars low-orbit satellite cover—destroying the fraction of the defense satellites "on station" over Siberia—to launch its ICBMs through to attack the United States.

How would such attacks *against* the Star Wars system be engineered? Remarkably, two candidate systems are readily available, years or decades before any Star Wars system itself. One is a direct-ascent missile, the second an astonishingly simple—yet lethal—device known as a space mine.

The first is the Galosh ABM interceptor missile, which has been deployed for fifteen years around Moscow (as allowed under the ABM Treaty). The Galosh system is a "terminal" missile defense complex, comprised of approximately sixty-four fast-ascent, three-stage rockets intended to destroy incoming nuclear warheads. It is similar to the U.S. counterpart (SPARTAN) missile deployed in North Dakota, which was intended to protect Minuteman ICBM silos but was abandoned in 1975 because it could have been easily overwhelmed. The Russian version, which might also be useless against nuclear attack, is nonetheless adaptable to become a devastating antisatellite weapon. Galosh missiles are nuclear-tipped and ascend rapidly toward the target. There exist no reliable means either to protect the BMD satellites of the Star Wars fleet or to attack the Galosh as it homes in on its targets.

A key advantage for this satellite killer is that the targeting accuracy for the Galosh is not demanding. Since the position of a satellite that is not maneuvering can be predicted with perfect accuracy, each Galosh could be preprogrammed to intercept a given defense satellite. If the satellite did not maneuver, no further targeting would be required. Powerful ground-based radars, of the type already deployed in the Moscow ABM system, could detect any evasive maneuvers by the BMD satellite and command the Galosh to change its course accordingly. The Galosh could also be designed to home in on the radar waves reflected from the BMD satellite. Since all defense satellites would be carrying sophisticated optics and electronics that are highly vulnerable to the thermal and electrical shocks produced by the intense X-ray pulse emitted from a nuclear explosion, the Galosh can be set to detonate at a very considerable distance from its prey—a satellite hardened against such attacks could still be damaged by a one-megaton explosion 100 km away. It has been suggested that this "electromagnetic" pulse would also impair the functioning of the Soviets' command and control facilities on the ground. But that is improbable if the Galosh's warhead is of relatively low yield, and the earthbound ABM stations—which, after all, must function in the presence of friendly as well as enemy nuclear explosions—will be hardened against such effects. Nearby Russian satellites would be in jeopardy, however.

The Galosh is being modernized with new Soviet missiles already in development, notably, the SH-04 and the SH-08, which now have BMD missions but might be adapted to antisatellite missions. It is telling that these already available technologies can be improved for the antisatellite role, with better targeting mechanisms, higher resistance to defensive counterattacks, and so on, because they are relatively mature at present.

The second candidate for near-term deployment is the space mine. Space mines are small, maneuverable satellites that can use either conventional (e.g., shrapnel) or nuclear explosives to destroy nearby prey. They can be launched into the same orbit as the target satellites, maneuvering to stay close if necessary, and explode instantly upon a command from the ground during or in advance of an ICBM launch. Cheap to build and cheap to launch, they can be readily proliferated. (There is, perhaps, no finer illustration of the "cost-exchange ratio" than that of space mines versus a Star Wars battle station: a $3 million space mine could destroy a BMD satellite worth $2 billion to $5 billion.) Space mines can also be placed in geosynchronous orbits to attack early warning satellites, the mirrors used in the free-electron laser BMD scheme, SATKA satellites, and other vital space assets of the defense.

Some pro-SDI analysts claim that the deployment of space

mines would be a "provocation," that large "keep-out" zones around defense satellites would be implied, negotiated, or unilaterally declared, and that space mines violating a zone would constitute a hostile act. There is, however, already a contrary precedent: nuclear submarines and surface ships are routinely trailed by their adversary's subs. Indeed, the United States has always maintained that space has the same inherent freedom of access as the "high seas" under international law—an argument used to justify U.S. reconnaissance satellites when the Soviets protested them in the early 1960s. Yet the lethality of space mines is forcing analysts to reconsider the "open skies" policy established by President Eisenhower. "Without agreed or tacitly accepted keep-out zones, space mines could easily develop into the single most pernicious threat to a stable military regime in space," observes Ashton Carter, a Harvard physicist and a leading expert on space weapons. "Simply attacking and destroying overt space mines positioned near one's satellites is a policy option without legal warrant, at least as provocative as the deployment of the minefield, and possibly impractical if the mine-layer persists in launching new and better mines." Even Colin Gray, a strategic theorist close to the Reagan administration, acknowledges that keep-out zones have no precedent and violate the Outer Space Treaty. Moreover, during periods of superpower tension, trying to enforce a keep-out zone by destroying the space mine could itself precipitate war. As Gray puts it: "given that direct action against a spacecraft believed to be a space mine would be an act of war . . . , the political incentive to delay such action would be at its strongest precisely when the action might be most needed on prudential military grounds."[3] As Carter, Gray, and others who have studied the matter agree, space mines—by their sheer simplicity—present a seemingly irresolvable threat to space-based defense.

Space mines and the Galosh missiles are *immediate* threats to space-based assets. New technologies will give an offense additional options for attacking satellites, some of which will be quite devastating indeed. For the most part, these emerging techniques are kinetic energy and directed energy weapons that can be deployed in a variety of ways. Here we see the crushing irony of the SDI's relentless technology push, for on these very frontiers of ballistic missile defense extremely versatile ASATs may be born.

Consider, for example, ground-based lasers. Powerful lasers, which have the advantage of large power plants or other fuel storage nearby, can be focused to hit low-orbit defense satellites. Under ideal conditions, these lasers could dwell at length on a low-orbit satellite whose instrumentation (e.g., infrared sensors that can be "blinded" by infrared lasers) is highly sensitive. The technology faces at least two potential impediments: cloud cover and maneuvering satellites, both actually drawbacks of a fixed, ground-based site. All high-energy lasers face beam absorption and scattering by clouds, although the devices would be constructed in deserts, mountaintops, or other low-cloud areas. The second problem with fixed sites arises because satellites need not pass over precisely the same point if they are equipped to maneuver. As a result, a ground-based laser may not be within range of its low-altitude space targets at the crucial time—during a severe U.S.-USSR crisis, when nuclear war is most likely.

The cost of ground-based lasers is not insignificant (a U.S. test facility in New Mexico will cost $1 billion), but they are garnering high acclaim by the United States and, apparently, the Soviet Union. The U.S. Department of Defense has warned that the Soviets could deploy ground-based ASAT lasers within the decade. And SDI chief Abrahamson told a congressional panel in early 1986, "Work with atmosphere compensation and free electron laser technologies has progressed to the point where it appears that the potential for large, effective ground-based laser systems is very real."[4]

A number of exotic ASAT technologies hold some promise as well. An outstanding example of a cutting-edge device being nurtured in the SDI is the nuclear-pumped X-ray laser. Even a very powerful X-ray laser can penetrate only a tiny fraction of the atmosphere; its prospects for boost-phase BMD, therefore, appear to be nil if fast-burn boosters can be developed that burn out within the atmosphere. The X-ray laser *is* a rather promising candidate for an ASAT, however. And officials at the Livermore lab now see this as one of the principal objectives of the program. It is potentially lightweight, which makes it suitable to the "pop-up" BMD scheme—launching it from a submarine into space—favored by Edward Teller. But even Teller's protégé Lowell Wood now admits that not enough time would be available to launch the weapon for interception of Soviet ICBMs.[5] But pop-up does hold some promise for utilizing the X-ray laser as an ASAT, particularly one aimed at the enemy's midcourse Star Wars satellites.

Chemical lasers, excimer lasers, free-electron lasers—all of which have been contemplated for Star Wars weapons—could be prime antisatellite devices as well. Neutral particle beams, which offer little for boost-phase defense due to atmospheric interference, are more amenable to the ASAT role in the unrestricted physical environment of outer space. Each has some cost and technical restrictions, but these limitations are less severe for the antisatellite mission than they are for the antimissile mission. The U.S. Department of Defense claims that the Soviets are working on a space-based laser ASAT that could be operational in the 1990s; a particle beam ASAT has also been explored that could destroy satellites or disrupt their electronic equipment and might be tested in space in the mid-1990s. Such weapons could potentially be used to attack geosynchronous satellites from low orbits.

The specific links between the Strategic Defense Initiative and such advanced weapons as ASATs can be clearly seen in the SDI's own comments. The chemical laser is an excellent example. This weapon, which "lases" hydrogen fluoride, has never been thought of as a promising Star Wars weapon by experts. But its ASAT potential is far more obvious. The chemical laser has always been viewed by its program managers as proceeding along a path of evolutionary development: first for ASAT use, then for antiaircraft purposes, then possibly for missile defense. Maj. Gen. Donald Lamberson, former director of the chemical laser program, explained to Congress this stepping-stone approach: "It is much easier to kill a satellite than it is a strategic aircraft, and doing that is much easier than killing a ballistic missile." In a similar vein, former DARPA director Robert Cooper, when asked in early 1983 whether the Pentagon's laser effort could render nuclear weapons obsolete, told Congress: "It is certainly a worthy objective, but a very difficult one . . . an antisatellite system based on space-based laser weaponry could be a near term, less stressing possible goal." In contrast to the BMD goal, which Cooper called "the most ambitious goal that could be undertaken," the ASAT objective was, in his view, "highly predictable and we think we can do it." A space-based laser weapon would be a "devastating ASAT," according to Cooper. "The firepower and the flexibility of such a laser weapon," he has said, "would be very difficult to defend against."[6] The principal hydrogen fluoride laser currently under development, called ALPHA, is expected to undergo tests by 1988 at a power level of two megawatts. While these tests would show no direct application for missile defense, they could well demonstrate an ASAT capability.

Finally, a variety of kinetic energy weapons under development are dedicated or potential ASATs. The Soviets have for several years tested a ground-launched ASAT that goes into orbit before attacking its target by direct impact. This device, labeled a "blunderbuss" by one observer, is certainly not an adequate anti-BMD weapon, given the length of time it takes to stalk its quarry, which allows the defense ample opportunity to counterattack. The U.S. ASAT launched from an F-15, also a kinetic energy device, is far more sophisticated, being a direct-ascent weapon that has high-quality homing capability. Its SDI counterpart—called the space-based kinetic kill vehicle—is scheduled for space tests in the early 1990s.

Of the other techniques being pursued in the SDI, electromagnetic "railguns"—which propel small homing vehicles at hypervelocity rates—are, theoretically, adaptable to the work of antisatellite weapons. But why go high tech when low tech will suffice? Not only are space mines a far cheaper and thoroughly reliable kinetic energy weapon, but other, similar mechanisms are available as well. The most ingenious proposal of this sort envisages the launching of steel pellets in a "cloud" that would collide with BMD orbiters. Such a nonexplosive, direct-ascent "warhead" would impact with a geosynchronous satellite at its orbital speed of 3.6 km per second, much higher velocity than current antitank guns; in low orbits, orbital velocity is 8 km per second. As a result, even very small pellets of one gram, optimally shaped for penetration through shielding, could destroy a multi–billion dollar Star Wars battle station.[7]

Whether the offense uses sophisticated ASATs such as orbiting lasers or the relatively primitive but efficient space mines, the options to attack decisively the space-based assets of a defense are plentiful. Given what we know, these attacks can be engineered in a way that maintains the offense's cost advantages over the defense, as well as the tactical edge of surprise attack. In short, the range and efficacy of antisatellite threats seem utterly lethal to Star Wars.

SATELLITE SURVIVABILITY

The SDIO acknowledges the significance of improving the survivability of its would-be space assets and is studying methods of protecting BMD satellites. The subject is not new. Concern for the safety of satellites has long informed the U.S. military space program: during much of the 1970s, in fact, satellite survival methods were considered as an alternative to the supposed "deterrent" effect of developing a U.S. ASAT to match the nascent Soviet capability. Now the emerging threats to satellites of all kinds are so sophisticated that incumbent survivability R&D faces a severe—perhaps inconquerable—challenge.

Indeed, the issue of survivability has emerged as a dominant concern, so much so that, according to a widely discussed 1986 Senate staff report, the "overall assessment on survivability . . . appears bleak." The report, which was written after extensive interviews with SDI and weapons lab staff, notes that even some of the optimistic SDI managers "admit . . . that solutions to certain aspects of the survivability dilemma (for example, protecting transition-phase deployment) will have to be legislated through arms control," certainly a poor prospect. Such assessments reflect accurately an emerging consensus among independent experts that survivability for a space-based system is either too difficult technically, too costly, or both.[8]

In any case, the new "counter-countermeasures" being researched by the SDIO fall into five categories: ablatives, maneuvering, concealment, redundancy, and shooting back.

Ablatives

An important means of protecting satellites, and one of the most rapidly developing R&D efforts, is the creation of new ablative materials intended to harden space vehicles against laser attack. The Defense Advanced Research Projects Agency (DARPA) has reportedly developed "special graphite derivatives that can withstand laser energy 'an order of magnitude or two greater than can typical aerospace materials.' These laser-resistant graphite compounds are effective against laser weapons operating in the infrared as well as the visible light bandwidths and impose only modest weight penalties."[9] If battle stations are coated with these compounds, goes the theory, the utility of laser ASATs—ground or space based—would be greatly diminished.

Such ablatives, however, are no panacea. It is doubtful whether such hardening could protect against lasers if important components such as large mirrors, which must be kept scrupulously clean, or fragile sensor arrays were exposed for several minutes during battle. Nor would ablatives protect against the disruptive effects of kinetic energy weapons; that would more likely require armor plating, with considerable weight penalties (and higher launch costs) and potential complications with the actual functioning of the satellite. And the destructive power of space mines, among other ASATs, could be increased more cheaply than commensurate upgrading of satellite survivability. Ablatives also will not protect against nuclear attacks.

There is, above all, an irony about ablatives. As with so many aspects of strategic defense, technological advances benefiting the defense can benefit the offense as well. The high-quality ablatives applied to U.S. defense satellites can be applied to Soviet boosters with considerably greater effect. The laser attack of the offense can afford lengthy "dwell times" against satellites that may vitiate hardening, whereas increasing dwell times of the BMD lasers against boosters penalizes the defense, for the longer the dwell time, the more BMD satellites are required to attack all ICBMs.

Anything heavier than ablatives—steel armor, for example—used to protect satellites would be prohibitively expensive. A Livermore lab paper, for example, estimates that 1 million tons of armor would be required to be "even transiently effective against credible threats." At $1000/lb. boost cost, such armor would require $1 *trillion* to lift alone.[10]

Maneuvering

Attention is being invested in the potential for maneuvering satellites to avoid the offense's attack. Against certain kinds of ASATs, such as the current Soviet system, maneuvering might very well succeed, even with the weight penalty of increased fuel. Overall, however, maneuvering has limited promise: it has no usefulness against speed-of-light interceptors such as directed energy or nuclear weapons and is of limited utility against space mines. The last can be made to maneuver themselves to follow a maneuvering BMD satellite. And maneuvering during battle to avoid offensive countermeasures will complicate the already challenging tasks of precision targeting.

Concealment

Satellites can be made more difficult to detect. "Stealth" techniques, jamming, and spoofing may be available to block or confuse an ASAT's terminal guidance system, for example. Some of these survival methods, which have been under study to protect communications satellites, could complicate the offense's task. When applied to a large, complex BMD system, however, the possibilities for concealment are not great. The offense need "find" only a few of the defense's satellites, which will be deployed for months or years, whereas the defense must conceal all of its space assets, once again bringing the cost-exchange ratio decisively into play. The predictability of orbits, the size and technical complexity of BMD satellites, and the offense's ability to adapt and present new technical means more readily than the defense can respond all benefit the offense.

Redundancy

A simple response to vulnerability is to replicate the systems to assure the survival of enough weaponry and SATKA capability to attack the boosters adequately. This is less a technical problem than one of economics and of command and control. The required size of the Star Wars fleet is already dependent on the Soviet configuration of forces, booster hardening, and other factors, at a cost-exchange ratio that now favors the offense, and this ratio is likely to favor the offense in these trade-offs in the future. Most ASATs, given lower sophistication, would cost less, inherently, than any BMD system satellites. This difference is particularly stark in the case of space mines. So replicating the weapons-bearing and support satellites does not appear to be a prudent option for the defense, given the already enormous costs of the system before replication.

Shooting Back

For battle stations transporting weapons, the option to attack the offense's ASATs is an obvious response. Laser weapons, in particular, would probably have this capability against direct-ascent missiles and offensive space assets. They could also be deployed on convoys of additional satellites. Once an anti-satellite attack commenced, or an ICBM launch began, the defense convoys could attack the space mines, lasers, and so forth to protect the battle stations that must concentrate on destroying the Soviet missiles and warheads aimed at the United States.

Such counterattacks are limited in at least two ways. First, infrared chemical lasers do not have unlimited capacity for attack since they must be fueled, and this fuel storage has severe physical constraints. The same factor limits kinetic energy weapons and all space-based weapon systems. Even ground-based alternatives (the free-electron laser) may not be sufficient if the offense's attack is unexpectedly large. Second, the offense can generally choose the time and method of its assault; when coordinated with an ICBM launch, attacks against the Star Wars satellites could place intolerable strains on the BMD system. In other words, it is unreasonable to expect that the defense can both fend off direct attacks and destroy a high percentage of protected ICBM boosters. Convoys deployed specifically to protect the space-based BMD system can be attacked by the same means; again, cost considerations will tend to favor the offense.

The shoot-back strategy also suggests an ongoing measure-for-measure competition in space weapons. One can imagine

Soviet ASATs providing the impetus for U.S. anti-ASAT development, which would give rise to Soviet anti-anti-ASATs, which would demand a U.S. response. This is the scenario that President Reagan's program dictates, one in which the superpowers deploy growing armadas in space not unlike naval aircraft carriers and their carrier battle groups. The analogy of defending an aircraft carrier is a pertinent one; U.S. aircraft carriers now require enormous task forces for self-defense. Concentric rings of destroyers, attack subs, early warning aircraft, and other vessels form the layers of defense *essential* to a carrier's survival. A $3 billion to $4 billion carrier requires $17 billion worth of accompanying ships and aircraft, 70 to 90 percent of which are for self-defense. All orbiting BMD platforms could well require similar investments in defensive layers. Each introduction of a fresh ASAT threat would demand a response.

Perhaps most important in countering "shoot back" are the single-shot, expendable weapons available to the offense. For example, X-ray laser ASATs, if proven feasible, could destroy BMD satellites before a convoy ASAT could prevent them from doing so. The same applies to near-term technologies. Overt space mines would normally accompany BMD satellites within lethal distance, and a counterattack from a Star Wars weapon would be foiled by salvage fusing—that is, the space mine woud explode anyway, destroying its nearby quarry. The Galosh warheads can be protected from laser attack by shrouds (protective, ablative covering) and could be equipped with tethered decoys to confuse the sensors and homing devices employed in a counterattack. Galosh and space mines can also be proliferated more cheaply than BMD satellites.

The timing is essential to recall here as well: space mines would be detonated before there would be an opportunity to counterattack in most cases; indeed, space mine explosions or other ASAT attacks could be the first act of war. It is difficult to imagine a way to foil such single-shot expendable weapons, particularly given their cost advantages. In any case, engaging in a shoot-out with ASATs would be a losing exercise for a defense whose mission is to shoot at boosters instead.

Consider the problems the Star Wars defense would have in stopping a Galosh missile attack. The currently deployed

Galosh missile burns out in about twenty seconds, well within the atmosphere, and only during this very brief interval is it vulnerable to counterattack techniques that rely on its bright booster flame for infrared siting or homing devices. Consequently, the Galosh in boost phase cannot be destroyed by homing kill vehicles, since such kinetic weapons would be far too slow to reach it. Only speed-of-light weapons could attack it, but because of the very short burn time they would have to be considerably more powerful and responsive than ICBM interceptors and would require levels of technical performance surpassing the already daunting BMD task. After the Galosh engines stop burning, it would be a much dimmer object, but it would still be heated by air friction until it reached the top of the atmosphere some thirty seconds after launch. To impede its detection above the atmosphere by infrared sensors, the Galosh could be covered by the type of heat-absorbing shroud that is always used to protect satellites. The shroud is shed on leaving the atmosphere; the warhead would then be at room temperature (or could even be cooled) and exceedingly difficult to detect against the warm background of the earth. Further protection of the weapon could be provided by one or more of the following: maneuvering, tethered decoys, and an ablative shield if the BMD satellite carried laser weapons. (Maneuvering and ablatives work in favor of the Galosh and not the defense satellites due to the time needed for targeting and laser dwelling.) Finally, the Galosh is so much cheaper than its quarry that each BMD satellite could be attacked by a salvo of Galosh missiles.

The full impact of this scenario can only be grasped when one imagines *many* different and separate antisatellite attacks commencing in tandem with an ICBM launch, whose own missiles are equipped with clever countermeasures to fool or disrupt the space-based defense systems. One must assume, too, that once deployed in space—recalling that the launch costs alone are very high—a BMD system is somewhat static: changes, repairs, and the like are possible in orbit with the aid of the space shuttle or its successor, but the possibilities for rapid alterations to meet new ASAT threats are obviously limited. As a result, the Soviets can optimally tailor their ASAT complex to challenge the Star Wars fleet, whereas the

SDI's managers must anticipate in advance, perhaps years in advance, what ASAT threats they must counter. This is a tall order.

THE DANGEROUS LEGACY OF SDI

An advocate of missile defense might retort: Of course there will be countermeasures, ASATs, shoot back, convoys, ASATs to attack convoys, and so forth—that is one of the goals! Complicate the Soviets' mission, make it more difficult and expensive to accomplish, and one has effectively enhanced deterrence by making the results of a nuclear strike less certain, more risky. If Star Wars accomplishes that, they say, then we will have taken a great stride forward in protecting our homeland.

It may be true that today it is "easier" for the Soviet Union to attack the United States with nuclear weapons than it would be if a missile defense (of any kind) were in place. But the price of an added measure of risk, since attacking the United States is already a suicidal act, is extremely high—high not merely in dollars or rubles, but in strategic stability. The advent of sophisticated ASATs starkly illustrates this cost of Star Wars, even if some future administration declares SDI a failure and does not attempt to deploy a space-based missile defense.

One can readily see the hair-trigger qualities of ASATs in a U.S.-USSR confrontation that included space-based defenses. Already mentioned is the vexing problem of keep-out zones around BMD satellites. In periods of tension, a space mine "violating" the unilaterally declared zone could spark shooting that would precipitate further hostilities, even nuclear war. Or what if one of the thousands of BMD sensors gave a false alert of an ICBM launch? It is often alleged that Star Wars weapons, if mistakenly fired, would hurt nothing, zipping harmlessly through space. But a false alert instigates more than the weapons dedicated to the ICBMs. In a space environment loaded with ASATs and anti-ASATs, preemptive attacks might commence instantly as an automated response to the false alert. The convoys protecting Star Wars battle stations would probably begin to attack Soviet ASATs within range. American submarines might also be commanded to initiate nuclear attacks against Soviet ground-based lasers, Galosh launch sites, and so on. Or what if a space mine wandered unintentionally into a keep-out zone, possibly triggering the entire BMD system, even nuclear war? Particularly stark is the realization that the action of a U.S. space defense (triggered by accident) destroying the Soviet space defense is identical to the behavior that the Soviets would anticipate at the launching of a U.S. first strike. In short, the complexity of a space weapons regime, quite contrary to adding a layer of deterrence, breeds mischief of the most consequential kind.

Advanced antisatellite techniques in the absence of missile defenses are not as precipitously catastrophic, but nonetheless could degrade security and stability. Some analysts suggest that several military satellites, such as those used for navigation or nuclear targeting, present hostile threats that should not be protected from attack. "ASATs challenge the rather paradoxical proposition that space—alone among earth, sea, and air—should be a sanctuary in which satellites can conduct a wide range of military activities, such as surveillance and navigation, free from the fear of destruction," writes Ashton Carter, a vocal skeptic of the SDI.[11] Along with other analysts, he suggests that the superpowers may want to develop ASATs not only to threaten satellites used in non-nuclear conflicts, but to threaten BMD systems as well—an ironic twist on the notion of the "lethal paradox" of the ASAT-SDI link.

Neither of these points is decisive, however. Countering the hostile operations of targeting satellites may not require antisatellite attacks: electronic countermeasures, for example, could accomplish virtually the same purposes without initiating a shoot-out in space. The latter course, moreover, would likely invite an in-kind response from the Soviet Union, with U.S. satellites—every bit, if not more, crucial to U.S. operations in the same land or sea conflict at issue—thereby jeopardized or destroyed. Such a competition typically leaves the United States at a disadvantage compared with an ASAT-free regime.[12] The second rationale for ASATs (that they present a convincing hedge against deployment of space-based defenses) has so far failed to deter the SDIO. In any case, as we have seen, very advanced ASATs would *result* from BMD research, and simpler, wholly sufficient ASATs are near term, though not yet tested. If there is an anti-BMD deterrent effect, it should already be operative and would remain so even with tight new restrictions on ASAT testing. There will always remain a U.S. (and Soviet) nuclear-armed ASAT capability inherent in the existence of ICBMs.

In fact, unrestricted ASAT competition, fueled by its Star Wars parent, will bring new and deeply provocative weapons to the superpower confrontation with no compensating virtues. The enhanced antisatellite capability of laser weapons in particular is a quantum leap over the crude Soviet ASAT of today, not to mention the advances in tracking, targeting, and so on that will accompany the development of the kill mechanisms. Such instantaneous lethality will inexorably contribute to the tenseness of crises, providing one more steppingstone to higher levels of conflict and danger.

This is the fundamental paradox—and irony—of the Strategic Defense Initiative. Not only do antisatellite weapons, those of today and those that will be created within the SDI, fatally threaten the Star Wars armada of the twenty-first century, but they will threaten the vital military satellites of the twentieth. This is, indeed, a real and perilous "window of vulnerability" that, once opened, will be extremely difficult to close.

6
The Soviet Response: New Missiles and Countermeasures

RICHARD L. GARWIN

One of the persistent illusions about Star Wars is the idea that only the United States is capable of technological innovation, that somehow SDI can proceed without a commensurate effort by the Soviets to defeat space-based missile defenses. In fact, the Soviets will probably transform their offensive nuclear arsenal in several different ways to aid penetration of the strategic defenses: they could expand the size of their nuclear arsenal as well as develop fast-burn boosters, "passive" measures such as hardening boosters, deceptive measures for preventing accurate aiming of lasers against boosters, decoys for boost phase and midcourse, and close-spaced objects to counter kinetic kill vehicles in midcourse, and so on. Consider, for example, the relatively simple expedient of doubling the numbers of ICBMs. If the Soviets did so, holding the destruction from nuclear war to a certain "acceptable" level would require that the Star Wars defense permit only half as many of the original weapons to penetrate, and half as many of the added weapons as well. For the offense, then, the options are obviously plentiful.

Few of these options would be necessary unless the space-based defense could be made survivable against general ASAT threats and especially against space mines, as explained in the previous chapter. Such attacks are probably the preferred approach for the offense. Other responsive actions by the offense include jamming communications links, dazzling sensors, or detonating nuclear explosives above the atmosphere to create a hot and mottled background. Nonetheless, the changes in missiles and the inclusion of an array of decoys also promise to seriously impede the defense's mission. Provisions designed into the defense system to handle these countermeasures will greatly increase its cost and reduce its performance.

In this chapter, a few innovations available to the offense will be briefly assessed, demonstrating how readily technology can be applied to foil Star Wars while maintaining a relative cost advantage.

TRANSFORMING MISSILES

Many tools are available to the offense to counter the defense by overwhelming it, underflying it, or outfoxing it.

Fast-Burn Boosters

The fast-burn booster in particular has broad utility. Given the many statements by SDI leaders and industry experts that a highly capable defense must have the "leverage" of boost-phase interception of boosters, it is of interest that the fast-burn booster would prevent boost-phase interception by several of the most technically demanding defensive technologies and would considerably reduce the effectiveness of others. This technique of fast-burn boosters was identified by the Fletcher panel and assessed by preliminary contractor studies first reported in July 1983. Simply put, a fast-burn booster is a two- or three-stage solid-fuel booster with a rocket-nozzle "throat area" approximately five times larger than in a normal rocket. The rocket fuel is arranged to burn at a similarly greater rate. As a result, an ICBM can achieve its speed of 7 km per second, while reducing boost time from the usual 180 to 300 seconds to some 40 to 50 seconds. Under these assumptions, the payload of warheads and decoys achieves its final speed at an altitude of some 80 to 90 km, well within the shielding layers of the atmosphere. That is low enough to allow the covering air to strip the electrons from the hydrogen atoms of a neutral particle beam weapon or to strongly absorb the soft X rays in an X-ray laser beam. The fast-burn booster totally defeats boost-phase kill by homing kill vehicles (HKVs), since orbiting HKVs cannot descend to 90 km altitude in the available time; in any case, an orbital speed HKV would have great trouble in homing at 90 km altitude because the very hot air produced by air friction at that altitude would interfere with its infrared homing mechanism.

Ordinary visible or infrared lasers could penetrate to these altitudes of 80 to 90 km, or even right to the ground. Under the assumption of a 40-second engagement time, however, the lasers have much less time to kill a particular booster or the entire set of boosters. By comparison with a 200-second engagement time for the current generation of Soviet ICBMs, such as the liquid-fueled SS-18s, a 40-second engagement time would, under likely circumstances, require five times the number of laser battle stations of a given capability to be operating. The impact of shortening boost time and a modest increase in number of boosters are shown in figure 6.1. Thus, 3,000 small single-warhead ICBMs with 40-second engagement time cannot be killed by fewer than 1,000 orbiting laser battle stations of the assumed characteristics, and granting for this example the SDI goal of being able to repoint the laser mirror in 0.1 second.

The fast-burn booster is old technology. Far more stringent requirements were met by the technology of the rocket motors in the Sprint ABM interceptor missile of the 1960s. Dozens of the Sprint missiles were manufactured by the United States, and eighty were deployed and operational in the Safeguard system in 1975.

Single-Warhead missiles

The Soviet Union can nullify most weapons thus far proposed for boost-phase interception (and seriously stress those few that would still be capable) by moving some fraction of its current warheads onto, or augmenting its strategic force with, single-warhead ICBMs based in small silos and clustered in a region about 1,000 km across. The costs of such changes are certainly not prohibitive. An early preliminary design of a fast-burn booster capable of carrying a standard Mark-21

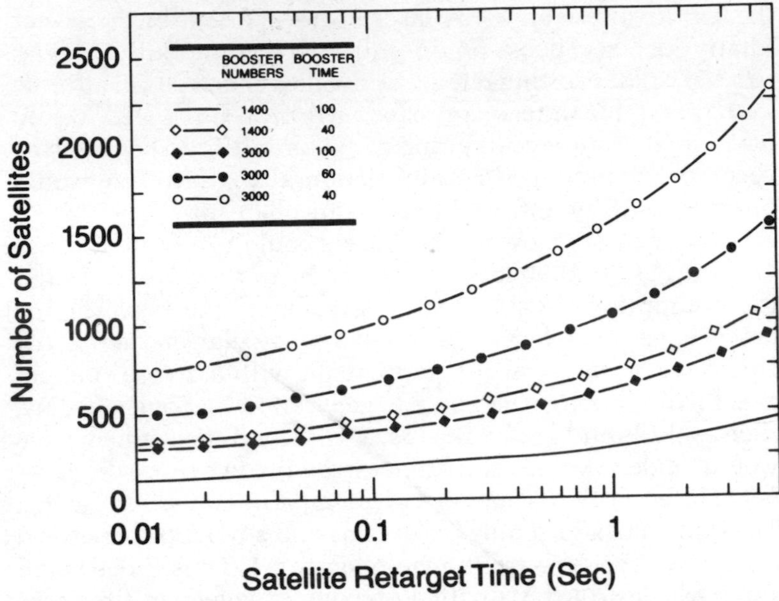

FIG. 6.1. The number of defense satellites required to intercept clustered Soviet ICBMs is dependent on several factors. In this graph, the numbers of boosters and the boost time are variables. Other factors, here held constant, include laser brightness (perfect mirror 10 meters in diameter, 25 megawatts of perfect laser light from hydrogen fluoride) and hardness of the booster (200 megajoules per square meter). As the graph shows, longer laser retargeting time (horizontal axis) requires more defense satellites (vertical axis) to "cover" the entire ICBM force. The different lines also show that more boosters and shorter boost time drive the number of defense satellites higher. For example, against 3,000 fast-burn boosters and with 0.5 seconds of retargeting time from one booster to the next, and with everything else working perfectly, the defense would need 1,344 satellites to destroy all the boosters.

(MX) warhead to intercontinental range was provided by the McDonnell-Douglas Corporation in letters to the Fletcher committee in July 1983. In particular, two examples in their design series (numbers 16 and 22) would burn out in 40 seconds at an altitude of 80 km, launching a warhead and decoys toward targets in the United States. The contractor estimate for ten-year cost (including research, development, procurement, and operation of the missile and its basing system) amounts to $11.1 million each for a deployment of 1,000 warheads. This $11 billion investment would seriously stress a space-based defense. Moreover, it would force the laser defense to fail Ambassador Nitze's criterion of "cost-effectiveness at the margin" against expansion of the offensive force. For if laser battle stations could be bought for $2 billion each, as some of their proponents indicate, 3,000 single-warhead, fast-burn boosters costing $33 billion would then require 1,000 laser battle stations working perfectly and costing $2 *trillion*.

The single-warhead ICBM system has great flexibility, since warheads from different silos could, if desired, be sent to the same point, could be scheduled to arrive in any sequence, and the like. The extra cost of one guidance system per warhead is not excessive for modern guidance systems, and the single-warhead missile saves about 50 percent in overall system weight because it does not need the postboost deployment vehicle (bus) for sending the warheads to individual targets. Furthermore, with burnout at 80 km altitude and a normal reentry angle (and thus launch angle) of 22 degrees, the single-warhead ICBM need sacrifice neither accuracy nor the ability to carry decoys or countermeasures to defeat later phases of the defense. This will be discussed later in connection with decoys of various kinds.

The SDIO has unfortunately made contradictory statements regarding the feasibility, cost, and penalties of the fast-burn booster.[1] Of the single-warhead missile, the U.S. variant being the "Midgetman" ICBM, all Department of Defense and air force public comment has been directed to a gold-plated Midgetman system, incorporating both high accuracy and mobility; the air force attaches a $44 billion price tag to a 500-warhead force. But that high cost is not necessary for the kind of silo-based force the Soviet Union could build in order to maintain a nuclear offensive capability in the face of what might otherwise be projected to be a substantial boost-phase interception system. At times it is suggested that forcing the Soviets to replace their "monster 10-warhead SS-18 missiles" by small single-warhead Midgetmen would be worth the cost of a Star Wars defense, but it is pure sophistry to suggest that the threat to U.S. security is greater from ten warheads on a single SS-18 than it is from ten of the same warheads on ten small single-warhead, fast-burn boosters.

Hardening Missiles

If the "skin" of a booster can be made more resistant to the heat of a laser beam, the laser will have to dwell longer on the booster in order to destroy the skin and disrupt the missile's flight. Such "hardening" will penalize the defense because the number of laser satellites must increase dramatically.

Robert Cooper, as assistant secretary of defense and head of the Defense Advanced Research Projects Agency, revealed an air force program for providing hardening against laser heat to a previously unstated degree. Although no details of the performance of that material have been revealed, an indication of the capability of "ablative" materials (which protect the object they are covering by vaporizing, and thus absorbing large amounts of heat in the process, which keeps the underlying material cool) can be obtained from the heat of vaporization of carbon—the principal component of ablative material on many U.S. warheads. The amount of heat that must be supplied to destroy the boosters used as the example in calculating the results of figure 6.1 is 20 kilojoules (kJ) per square centimeter. (One kilojoule is the energy delivered by one kilowatt in one second, e.g., a hundred-watt light bulb produces 1 kJ of heat in ten seconds.) What does it take to absorb this heat, delivered anywhere or everywhere on the skin of the booster? This 20 kJ/cm^2 is just enough to vaporize a layer of graphite about 2–3 mm thick, weighing only 0.4–0.6 g/cm^2. As a result, effective hardening can be achieved by the application of a relatively thin layer of carbon graphite (or some better material) to the booster skin.

The weight of the laser hardening material used on the ICBM will reduce its ability to carry weapons, but this weight penalty can be small. The first and sometimes the second stage of an ICBM need not be propelled to full speed but is dropped or "staged" to eliminate the heavy tankage and engines (and now the ablative coat that would be "protecting" empty tankage). Accordingly, the mass of shielding applied to the first stage and sometimes the second stage can be compensated by a decrease in overall payload that is considerably less than the shielding mass applied while still maintaining the same final speed of the warhead, and hence the missile range. For instance, on the large Soviet SS-18 with an overall launch mass of 220 tons and an 8-ton payload, the assumed 0.4–0.6 g/cm^2 of ablative coating on the first stage would weigh some 1.32 tons. But 1.32 tons of hardening on the first stage can be compensated by a payload reduction of 0.22 tons. An actual design, of course, will have to provide hardening for the second stage and for the postboost vehicle (or bus) and thus pay a larger penalty, but about 0.88 tons total. Even with a greater amount of ablative material—for example, 2 g/cm^2 over the entire vehicle (perhaps necessary if the ablative material is less efficient or if a correspondingly greater hardness is desired)—the overall payload penalty would be about 2.9 tons. A 2.9-ton payload reduction need *not* require the offload of nine warheads of 350 kilograms each; eliminating bus fuel for those warheads eliminated and reconfiguring the bus would provide 2.9 tons of payload reduction with the loss of only four to five warheads.[2]

If the weight of the hardening threatens to cut substantially the number of warheads the Soviet force can be expected to deliver, there are still options to reduce the burden. For example, the offense would be able to take advantage of the fact that the effectiveness of the defense (and, conversely, the vulnerability of the boosters) is greatly dependent on the moment-to-moment positioning of the laser battle stations. In simulations at Lawrence Livermore National Laboratory, it was confirmed that particular laser battle stations (especially the closest ones) can kill boosters much more effectively than others. A laser battle station at 500 km can kill sixteen boosters (if retargetable instantly) in the time that a laser battle station at 2,000 km can kill one booster. As a result, the offense can save money (and thereby impose costs on the defense) by more heavily hardening one side of the booster and flying with that side rotated toward the closest laser battle stations at the time of launch. Furthermore, since lasers work by concentrating their heat onto a relatively small spot (typically 1 m diameter or less in this case), it is wasteful to harden equally the entire surface of the booster. When a laser spot is sensed on the booster, the booster could quickly rotate a bit in order to present the thicker shield to the blowtorchlike heat. Indeed, only the ablative material need be moved, and a thick shielding patch could be moved axially as well as circumferentially, thereby greatly reducing the mass of hardening required. This is speculation, of course, particularly in the absence of laser boost-phase defenses, but the ingenuity and investment required to achieve such hardening seems small compared with the technology and the cost of the defense itself.

It is essential to recall that innovation applied to ICBMs not only permits greater penetration, but drives up the expense of Star Wars. Hardening the offense and transforming the Soviet ICBM force to single-warhead boosters involves a modest addition in cost for the offense, but a large multiplication in cost for the defense. A combination of such alterations is even more decisive.

Deploying 10,000 additional warheads on single-warhead missiles of burn time comparable to that of the 1,400 existing ICBMs (but clustered in a region 1000 km across) would increase the size of the required laser force by at least a factor of 7. If the burn time of the boosters was then shortened by a factor of 5, the required laser force would be increased by a further factor of 5—a factor of 35 altogether. Fast-burning and single-warheading reinforce one another. In the computer simulation mentioned earlier, C.T. Cunningham of the Livermore Lab found that some fifty-five idealized laser battle stations could destroy the entire current Soviet ICBM force in boost phase (ignoring, of course, the anachronism of assuming a current Soviet force opposed by a set of fifty-five laser battle stations that could be available only beyond the year 2000). But he found that hardening, or changing to fast burn, or silo clustering reduced the number that could be killed by those laser battle stations to about 20 to 30 percent. With all three—hardened, fast burned, and clustered—no boosters could be killed by the assumed force of laser battle stations.[3]

Even considered in isolation from other countermeasures, these cost-effective changes in the ICBM force would seriously impair the functioning of the space-based defense and escalate the defense's costs precipitously.

Modified Trajectories

New defenses can be countered by old responses. In the 1960s, the Soviets tested a fractional-orbit bombardment system

(FOBS), the nominal reason for the deployment of the U.S. nuclear-armed ASAT systems of that era. At that time, the worry was that a standard U.S. ABM system looking north toward the Soviet ICBM fields could be destroyed by a FOBS attack in which the Soviets launched south from their silos, attacking the U.S. defensive radars from their southern "blind" side—about a 70-minute flight in comparison with the nominal 30-minute flight of the ICBMs. The warheads would be launched into a low circular orbit just above the atmosphere and "de-orbited" by retrorockets to drop onto their targets. But facing an SDI—particularly one that could involve homing kill vehicles, neutral particle beams, and X-ray lasers—one might wish for the protective shield of the atmosphere at every point in the path of the missile from launch to impact. This can be achieved by FOBS flight at 90 km altitude, this time on the direct low-orbit path that will need only 20 minutes; free-flying decoys need not then be used. Of course not all warheads need be transferred to FOBS to complicate the problem of the defense.

Another modified trajectory would be useful for attack on coastal cities and installations farther inland. The depressed-trajectory submarine-launched ballistic missile, apparently never tested thus far, would give less warning than other missile attacks and would provide its warheads the protection of the deeper atmosphere.

Nonballistic Nuclear Threats

Even a highly effective defense against strategic ballistic missiles would be of little benefit if the offense supplemented its ICBMs and SLBMs with strategic cruise missiles carrying nuclear warheads. Former secretary of defense James Schlesinger pointed out the necessity of countering all forms of nuclear weapons delivery and suggested that to add effective air defense to an effective BMD would cost an additional $50 billion annually.

An example of what can be done with 1970s technology is the U.S. strategic cruise missile, either in the air-launched version or in similar missiles launched from submarines or the ground. The primary penetration aid of this cruise missile through air defenses is its flight close to the ground, invisible to radar unless that radar is on an aircraft or a satellite. Even looking down in this way, normal radar would not be able to see objects as small as cruise missiles against the ground, which scatters radar waves (the so-called ground clutter problem). But "Doppler radar" does have this potential. "Coherent" Doppler radar, like that of the U.S. airborne warning-and-control-system (AWACS) aircraft, can "filter out" the ground reflection by taking advantage of the Doppler shift in the frequency of an oncoming target—the same phenomenon that accounts for the drop in pitch of a train whistle as it passes the observer. The simpler "incoherent" Doppler radar can be used to detect cruise missiles above the ground by detecting those patches of "ground" at a given range and angle from the radar where the total radar reflection is changing with time. It does this by comparing the reflection pattern of two successive radar pulses and detects a moving object like a cruise missile by the comparison of these pulses. The aim of the radar designer is to reduce as far as possible the size of the patch of ground that can be distinguished by the radar, in order to detect the smallest possible moving object. The aim of the cruise missile designer is to reduce its radar reflection ("cross-section") so as to make the radar designer's job more difficult. The U.S. Advanced Cruise Missile, now in development, presumably will have a much smaller radar cross-section than the air-launched cruise missiles deployed since 1983 on B-52 bombers.

Radar has a large and hence highly directional antenna (reflector), which ensures that only a small patch of ground is illuminated at one time and that the reflected energy from that same small patch is received as efficiently as possible at the radar. But the collocation of the receiver with the transmitter is a liability for the radar; the transmitter cannot conceal itself, and hence the receiver is subject to jamming by the offense. This requires the defense to counter the jamming—either by destroying the jammers, by adding anti-jam capability to the receivers, or the like.

As for detection by sensors of infrared (heat) energy, the very small engine of the cruise missile, with a thrust on the order of 200 pounds as compared with missile engine thrusts in the range of 2 million pounds, can have its hot metal parts hidden from observation from above. With such shielding, it would be extremely difficult even with a perfectly operating infrared sensor system to detect the cruise missiles. The warm wake of air left by the cruise missile exhaust cannot be detected through the atmosphere.

Even if cruise missiles could be detected reliably, killing them in a cost-effective manner would remain a problem. Decoy cruise missiles need not have nuclear warheads and could be very small, but would appear larger because their radar reflectivity (detectability) would be enhanced by corner reflectors or by a lesser application of "stealth" technology. If the cruise missiles are attacked by homing missiles in the atmosphere, the cost of a decoy may be less than that of a homing missile; this comparison is made more striking by the necessity to have defensive missiles everywhere, while the attacking cruise missiles may be clustered in arbitrary attack corridors. In any case, if one compares the detectability and the vulnerability of a large number of stealthy cruise missiles and decoys penetrating U.S. territory with the vulnerability and detectability of a much smaller number of high-cost AWACS aircraft in the United States, it is clear that the AWACS will have to be protected as aircraft carriers are today, and probably with the same likelihood of total loss in case of nuclear war.

As a result of these technical and economic trade-offs, cruise missiles present an additional option to the offense, one that will again compound the already complex tasks of the defense at costs that continually favor the offense.

DECOYS

In developing new ICBMs, the Soviets will consider methods to confuse and mislead the defense's sensors. The most readily available way to create confusion is to develop and deploy a variety of decoys in boost phase and midcourse.

Boost-Phase Decoys

In his testimony of November 10, 1983, before the House Armed Services Committee, then under secretary of defense Richard DeLauer emphasized that the best countermeasures to a defense are "decoys, decoys, decoys, decoys." The SDIO, however, has denigrated the effectiveness of boost-phase decoys with the observation that the defense can simply ignore boosters fired from cheap launch pads or that do not have the precise boost trajectory typical of high-class guidance systems.

Such decoys are quite possible, however, and their cost can be reduced and their effectiveness increased by the general tool of antisimulation. For example, consider a defense that is programmed to ignore boosters that are not "real." A surface-launched booster decoy might be passed over by the defense because—unlike normally functioning ICBMs—it staggers during launch. Offensive planners, however, could base some ICBMs on the surface next to the ICBM silos, with accurate guidance systems programmed to "stagger" during boost, which in no way affects the ultimate accuracy of the ICBM. Rather than simulating real boosters by basing the decoy boosters in silos and giving the decoys an excellent guidance system, the offense will build decoys as cheaply as possible and modify the real boosters to appear like the decoys (hence the term *antisimulation*). Current-generation ICBMs could have boost-phase decoys supplied in this way, but future single-warhead missiles would be even more adaptable to the role. The multiplicative costs imposed by certain countermeasures are easily seen in this case—a fast-burn small missile is as costly to kill as a fast-burn large missile (and a lot cheaper to make), and a fast-burn decoy for a small missile is also a lot cheaper than one for a large missile.

Postboost Vehicles

The SDI as defined by the Fletcher committee depends crucially on birth-to-death tracking. (The Eastport study later criticized any "architecture" using an interdependent system of birth-to-death tracking, since that would build into the system a potential single-point failure.) In their enthusiasm for technology, at least as it aids the defense, the Fletcher committee apparently assumed that such tracking would enable the detailed observation of the deployment of warheads and decoys from the postboost vehicle (bus) by laser radar, imaging systems, and the like. The decoys could then be ignored by the rest of the system, and firepower concentrated on the warheads in midcourse. Of course, permanently registering any object as "harmless" is fatal to the defense, given the opportunities for antisimulation.

My earliest comments on this system noted that it would be simple to erect an umbrella or other "modesty shield" around the bus so that the decoys and warheads would be first observed fully formed rather than in the process of birth. Such accoutrements are still possible, but an offense designed to operate in the presence of an otherwise effective defense would likely depend upon fast-burn boosters carrying individual warheads and decoys. It would add unnecessary vulnerability to include a bus in such a system, and it would also add to the cost and weight of the system.

Instead, boosters can dispense credible decoys, and indeed this can be done by a fast-burn booster—despite comments to the contrary by SDIO. Consider a booster that burns out at 80 km altitude, speeding at 7 km/second toward its target 10,000 km away. Gaining altitude at about 2 km/second, it has 5 additional seconds before the warhead and decoys reach 90 km altitude. During this period, the second-stage engine would be shut off, and the warhead and its associated guidance and decoys, constituting a "microbus," would be liberated to fall toward the target. The act of "staging" (the separation of the warhead from the empty rocket case and engine) might push the warhead and the attached guidance system, giving it a velocity on the order of 0.5 m/second different from the precise velocity planned to bring it onto its target.[4] To correct the speed by 0.5 m/second in 4 seconds can be achieved with a maximum thrust on the warhead of 1/80 the force of gravity—a rocket engine providing 5 kg of force or less. The amount of fuel burned during this velocity adjustment period would be only about 70 grams (less than 3 ounces).

Decoys and warheads together would have their speed adjusted precisely as indicated above, before the warhead rises to 90 km altitude and before decoys are dispensed. Some 10 decoy packages, each weighing 5 percent as much as the warhead, would be separated within 1 second from the warhead. These "5 percent" decoys would be shaped like the warhead or reentry vehicle (which is in the form of an ice cream cone of length 1.75 m and maximum diameter 0.55 m) and would lose about 4 m/second speed in traversing the entire atmosphere above 90 km altitude at a usual launch and reentry angle of 22 degrees.[5] Putting a tiny rocket nozzle on each decoy, which burns no more than 35 grams of fuel in 4 seconds, will prevent any such observable loss of speed, and a similar rocket on the warhead itself will eliminate any possible discrimination of the warhead from the decoys, and will maintain warhead accuracy. After 10 seconds (above the atmosphere), each of the 5 percent decoys and the warhead will envelop itself in a light aluminized plastic balloon, splitting off 9 such balloons each weighing 0.5 percent as much as a warhead, to provide some 100 objects that in midcourse look identical to radar and infrared sensors.

Midcourse Decoys

The booster made to look like a cheap decoy was only one example of antisimulation. In general, even if there is a possibility of defeating the defense system or increasing its cost by providing a decoy that looks exactly like the booster or reentry vehicle, the cost of that decoy is increased by the requirement to make it simulate the real thing in all observable aspects. A reentry vehicle that is stabilized as it flies through space, as a finely machined or molded cone, could be observed by radar or by infrared: its shape and surface features could be characterized, as could some aspects of its size and surface temperature. Extremely light and cheap decoys could be provided by the thousands to mimic certain aspects of radar cross-section, but to mimic all of the observable aspects of the warhead would be difficult to achieve and to validate.

Fortunately for the offense, such expensive mimicry is not necessary. Antisimulation comes to the rescue of the offense. Again, one chooses a convenient, cheap decoy; in this case it would be a roughly spherical balloon large enough to enclose the warhead. A balloon of aluminized plastic would appear the same to radar whether it enclosed a warhead or not. Because of the possibility of observation by infrared telescopes, the balloon must be made of multilayer aluminized plastic, used for "superinsulation" of liquefied-gas storage systems on Earth. Such a balloon that is empty could not be distinguished by radar or infrared from a similar balloon surrounding a warhead because the warm warhead inside is shielded, by the multiple layers of reflective insulation, from radiating through the outside of the balloon.[6] This was the nemesis of the army's Homing Overlay Experiment, which included the investigation of various types of decoys; but only late in the program did the army face forthrightly the multilayer aluminized plastic balloon that had been proposed to them at the beginning of the program as a sure way to counter the infrared discrimination being tested.

In any case, the aluminized balloons would provide excellent covering for warheads through the twenty-minute journey through outer space—the midcourse of ballistic flight. This phase has gained particular attention since satellites intended for boost-phase interception are now believed to be fatally vulnerable to Soviet attack. Indeed, SDIO appears to be considering the deployment of defense systems before the year 2000 with no space-based lasers, probably no ground based lasers with relay mirrors, but largely depending instead on traditional terminal defenses (with or without nuclear warheads) and space-based homing kill vehicles.[7]

Destroying warheads in midcourse by HKVs is enormously complicated by the availability to the offense of the option of close-spaced objects. Each of the warheads can be accompanied by a number of decoys tethered at a distance of twenty meters or so, the job of the decoys being made easier by enclosing the warhead in a balloon to resemble a decoy. A HKV with infrared homing would have great difficulty selecting one of the targets from the complex, but even a very smart HKV would not be able to *distinguish*, on its own, between the warhead and the decoy. If HKVs were launched against warheads initially bare, but that "grew" such tethered decoys during the ten- or twenty-minute HKV flight time, almost all of the warheads would survive.

The relative ease of deploying effective decoys (combined with the offense's ASAT capability) raises a difficult question for SDI: how much will it cost to deploy the additional space assets needed to cope with this enormous and baffling "threat cloud"? Visions of a defensive system based on a small number of satellites carrying large numbers of HKVs have been demonstrated to be vulnerable to Galosh nuclear-armed interceptors, space mines, and the like,[8] and SDI studies have apparently rejected such options in favor of very large numbers of satellites, each having one or a few HKVs. Indeed, the SDIO's John Gardner, describing in October 1985 the leading candidate SDI architecture, sketched a system that uses some 7,000 satellites, many of which would be deployed for mid-course interception. It should be noted that this increase in survivability, with its greater cost to the offense to destroy each HKV satellite, does not come free to the defense. In particular, system overhead such as station keeping, communication, telemetry, and the like must be done once per satellite. With a move toward individual rockets in orbit, the systems must be proliferated. In addition, since SDI has primarily discussed homing by long-wave infrared telescopes, the refrigerators for helium-temperature cooling of the sensors must be replicated as well. In short, the costs of proliferating space assets are high.

Interactive Discrimination

In the minutes of free flight, the path of a light decoy could in principle be perturbed by the impulse provided from a short-pulse laser evaporating a thin layer from the surface of the decoy balloon; the balloon surrounding the warhead would also be "pushed" in the same way, but it would eventually be restrained by its heavy contents. This "interactive discrimination" might be attempted where passive discrimination with infrared sensing or "active discrimination" by measuring radar reflection would be defeated. Nevertheless, the size of the laser required to discriminate one hundred or one thousand decoys per booster is comparable with the size required to *destroy* a booster in boost phase.

"Weighing" decoys and warheads by laser pushes could be countered by attack on the space-based lasers or mirrors required to produce such pushes, but the offense has other options.[9] These include arranging decoys so that some move toward the laser, while some move away, and others do not move at all. This can be achieved by coating wings or fronds on the decoys (and on the balloons enclosing the warheads) with metal film to reduce the evaporation of plastic from one side or the other. The fronds (if arranged to wave in space) would also require that the defensive system observe each decoy for a long time in order to get a good measure of its velocity or its velocity change. Finally, decoys could be equipped with a small sensor of sudden velocity change, connected to a gas cell or a set of firecrackers, which would compensate the laser push; such a sensor need have no electronics, but could be built entirely of "fluidic" technology—cheap, robust, and effective. Do these decoys exist now? No, but they would if the defensive laser threat emerged.

Another approach discussed for interactive discrimination is the use of neutral particle beams (hydrogen atom beams of 200 million electron volts of energy), reaching thousands of kilometers through space at half the speed of light, undisturbed by the magnetic field of the earth, and provoking the emission of neutrons or gamma rays from the fission components of the warhead or from its structure. The magnitude of the emitted radiation (and perhaps its details) could distinguish a warhead from a light decoy. Indeed it could, but the physical requirements are daunting. Added to the physical needs is the primary requirement for *survival* of the neutral particle beam accelerator, which is of substantial size and value and must withstand ASAT attacks. The detector of the scattered radiation could be located at the accelerator itself, but it could be used more effectively if it were closer to the individual decoys and warheads; many detectors on individual satellites would thus be needed. However, with even a small fraction of the defense's neutral particle beam capability, the offense could use a neutral particle beam machine to overwhelm the detectors with stray particles and signals, and thus render it impossible for the defense to detect or discriminate warheads from decoys.

The vulnerability of space-deployed defenses, combined with the utility of fast-burn single-warhead boosters in nullifying "pop-up" interceptors for boost phase, has forced SDI to retreat to midcourse interception. Arguments that the offense is still vulnerable in the "minutes-long post-boost phase" ring hollow in view of the countermeasures. The difficulties to be faced by the defense in midcourse include confronting an attack of a hundred credible decoys per small booster (a million in all), plus an untold number of dazzling corner reflectors and the like. In these twenty minutes, too, the detonation of a few percent of the warheads would create a never-before-experienced environment for the defense. But the defense faces an additional, and ultimate, asymmetry: 1 percent of the nuclear warheads would suffice to destroy a nation.

Although modifications and supplementations of the offensive force probably take second place in cost-effectiveness to attack on the defensive system, enough can be done by offensive modifications alone to arouse the enthusiasm of technologists and industry in defeating defenses. In general, this seems to ensure that a Star Wars defense will be mimicked by those interested in defensive technology, destroyed by those interested in countermeasures, and overwhelmed and bypassed by those interested in modernizing offensive forces.

7
Limited Defense: The Unspoken Goal

PETER A. CLAUSEN

As originally proposed by President Reagan, the goal of the Strategic Defense Initiative is to provide an effective defense of American society against Soviet nuclear attack. Such a defense, Reagan stated on March 23, 1983, would permit the United States to replace the strategy of deterrence (the threat of retaliation in response to Soviet attack) as the basis of American security and, by rendering nuclear weapons "impotent and obsolete," would open the way to nuclear disarmament. It is now apparent, however, that this radical vision contrasts sharply with the technical and strategic objectives that actually guide the SDI program. Although the president continues to invoke the image of an invulnerable America—and this image clearly forms the basis of public support for the program—in practice the SDI's goals are much more modest.

This gap between public rhetoric and actual policy is due largely to the widespread recognition among experts, both within and out of government, that the president's original vision is unlikely ever to be realized. It is therefore not surprising that rationales for partially effective defenses, whose technical prospects are more promising, should be put forward to justify the SDI. Moreover, even those who remain optimistic about the eventual development of highly effective population defenses have argued that the deployment of limited, interim systems during the long transition to a defense-dominant world would benefit American security. Increasingly, the distinction is drawn between "first-generation" SDI technologies that might be deployed within the next ten years or so and the more distant "Star Wars" weapons that have dominated the program's public image. Whether seen as a fallback position or as a transitional step, limited defenses have become the practical focus of the SDI program.[1]

Several possible roles, none of them new, have been proposed for partially effective U.S. missile defenses. All have in common the fact that they would supplement rather than replace offensive nuclear forces and would not fundamentally alter the existing condition of mutual U.S. and Soviet vulnerability to nuclear devastation in the event of war. The most prominent objective ascribed to such defenses is to strengthen deterrence by adding to the uncertainties Soviet planners would face when contemplating a first strike. A limited defense in this case would be built to protect American retaliatory capabilities—particularly land-based missiles and command and control centers—against preemptive attack. It is also argued that partial defenses could deter limited nuclear strikes by the Soviet Union by raising the threshold for effective attacks, and protect against small nuclear powers such as a nuclear-armed Libya or against an accidental launch of a few Soviet missiles. (An additional mission, defense against short-range ballistic missiles in Europe, is discussed in chap. 8.)

Despite the central importance of these objectives in the administration's thinking, the technological, strategic, and arms control issues raised by limited defenses have not received the detailed scrutiny they deserve. The various arguments for intermediate or first-generation SDI systems are unconvincing when the strategic costs and side effects of deployment are taken into account. The push for limited defenses is likely both to accelerate the arms race as offensive measures are taken in response to defenses, and to strip away the protection afforded by the Antiballistic Missile Treaty. The deployment of partial defenses by the United States would in most cases require a relaxation or abandonment of the ABM Treaty's constraints and would thus invite the extension and upgrading of Soviet missile defenses. These consequences would more than outweigh the purported benefits of limited defenses for U.S. security and could well result in an overall weakening of deterrence.

SDI AND LIMITED DEFENSE TECHNOLOGIES

The term *limited defense* can be applied to a range of different approaches to ballistic missile defense. It is sometimes used to describe a territorial or nationwide defense of limited effectiveness—a so-called thin area defense. At other times, it refers to localized defenses whose coverage is limited to particular geographical areas or to specific targets such as missile fields, command and control systems, or other military facilities. At the extremes, limited defenses could range from partially effective space-based weapons designed to intercept Soviet missiles during their initial boost phase of flight to land-based terminal defenses of ICBM silos. These systems would differ greatly not only in their technology but also in their strategic implications.

Given the current technological thrust of the program, a first-generation SDI system would fall somewhere between these extremes. It is unlikely to include boost-phase weapons, which are still in the early stages of research and development and whose feasibility even in the long term is highly questionable. Instead, the emphasis is likely to be on terminal defenses designed to intercept incoming missiles toward the end of their passage through space (the late midcourse phase of the trajectory) and as they reenter the atmosphere.

On the other hand, the most mature terminal technologies—those for localized defense of hardened military targets—have been downgraded by the SDIO, in keeping with the administration's insistence that the goal of the program is to shield the nation as a whole. This downgrading represents a major shift of emphasis from the U.S. missile defense program of the 1970s, which was tailored to the protection of Minuteman and, subsequently, MX missile installations. SDI, in contrast, is aiming to develop the higher-risk but potentially more powerful technologies needed for the protection of population centers and other "soft" targets. As the administration reported to Congress in 1985, "The driving requirements for the terminal tier are survivable defense of targets that are easily damaged by nuclear weapons or soft targets (i.e., cities, industry, etc.) and an affordable system that can defend the entire United States."[2] This same point was emphasized by James Fletcher, who chaired the technical panel that prepared the ground for SDI: "The terminal defense now envisioned could be used to protect wider areas. . . . The goal of near-term limited defense is *not* 'hard point' defense. Rather, it represents a completely different (and broader) way of defending our strategic assets."[3]

Two consequences of this technology approach are notable. First, SDI is not optimized to produce the earliest deployable missile defense, despite the fact that the administration often describes the program as a hedge against the threat of an early Soviet breakout from the ABM Treaty. Second, a gap exists between the technical emphasis of the program and the limited defense roles, particularly the defense of retaliatory forces, increasingly invoked on its behalf.

The probable technologies for a first-generation SDI deployment would provide a late-midcourse and reentry phase defense using ground-based interceptors and radar assisted by air-based and perhaps space-based sensors for early identification and tracking of incoming missiles. A key program is the Exoatmospheric Reentry Vehicle Interceptor Subsystem (ERIS), a non-nuclear homing vehicle under development by Lockheed that would destroy incoming missiles by collision outside the atmosphere. This program is the successor to the Homing Overlay Experiment conducted in the Pacific in June 1984, in which a Minuteman missile launched from Vandenburg Air Force Base was intercepted at an altitude of over one hundred miles before it reentered the atmosphere. ERIS is based on technology similar to the U.S. antisatellite weapon tested in 1984 and 1985.

ERIS would be supplemented by shorter-range interceptors designed to destroy those missiles leaking through the midcourse defense. Current programs in this area are the High Endoatmospheric Defense Interceptor (HEDI), which would operate at the upper reaches of the atmosphere, possibly with a nuclear warhead, and the Low Endoatmospheric Defense Interceptor (LEDI), which would provide a "last-ditch" defense (at a range of a few miles) of hardened military targets. Target acquisition and tracking would be provided by the

Airborne Optical System (AOS), an infrared sensing system to be based on a Boeing 767 aircraft, and the Terminal Imaging Radar (TIR), a ground-based and possibly mobile radar for atmospheric tracking and warhead-decoy discrimination. These systems are scheduled first for individual and then integrated demonstrations during the late 1980s and early 1990s.[4]

If deployed, these technologies would, like the Safeguard ABM briefly deployed by the United States in the 1970s, provide a defense with a broad "footprint," the coverage area protected from nuclear warheads. Indeed, SDI director Abrahamson has testified that the ERIS system, deployed in North Dakota, could provide coverage of all of Canada and the United States.[5] Such a defense could potentially serve a number of strategic roles—as a defense of hardened military targets, as a thin area defense of soft military, industrial, or urban targets, or as the terminal layer and first installment of the full-fledged, highly effective population defense to which the SDI ultimately aspires.

The defensive system that the Soviets might deploy in the near term could also serve multiple roles. The Soviet Union already has an operational missile defense—the Galosh system deployed around Moscow in conformity with the ABM treaty—and has been developing the components of an improved system that U.S. analysts have designated as the ABM-X-3. The latter includes two new nuclear-tipped missiles for endoatmospheric and exoatmospheric interception (the SH-08 and SH-04) and new transportable radar for tracking and guidance (the Flat Twin and Pawn Shop). Though well behind emerging U.S. BMD technologies in such areas as non-nuclear kill devices and infrared sensors, the Soviets could deploy the ABM-X-3 system widely and could do so more rapidly than the United States could deploy a first-generation SDI. Like the U.S. system described earlier, the Soviet defense could provide broad area coverage suitable either for a limited defense of military targets or as the base for a more comprehensive territorial defense. The most likely role for a limited Soviet defense is generally considered to be the protection of command and control, leadership, and other military targets rather than missile silos.[6]

These characteristics of the defenses the United States and

the Soviet Union might deploy in the near term suggest that such defenses would be limited in their capabilities but not in their potential applications. This fact has important implications for the stability of a regime of limited defenses, whether such ABM systems are deployed independently or as the initial phase of a negotiated "defensive transition." In particular, the superpowers would confront a very slippery slope if they attempted to amend the ABM Treaty to permit the deployment of limited defenses. In practice, it may prove impossible to open the treaty up only part way while holding the line against unrestricted territorial defenses. This risk is crucial in assessing the merits of the various rationales for American deployment of limited defenses.

DETERRENCE OF PREEMPTIVE ATTACK

The administration's most prominent rationale for a partially effective missile defense is that it would strengthen deterrence by adding uncertainty to a Soviet preemptive nuclear strike meant to disarm the United States by destroying U.S. nuclear forces. A defense would thus protect U.S. retaliatory forces rather than the American population, since the former would be the targets of a such a strike. Accordingly, the deterrence argument for SDI represents no basic change in current strategy: U.S. security would continue to be based on the capability to inflict devastating offensive retaliation on the Soviet Union. The role of defenses would be no different in principle from other means of protecting that capability against preemptive Soviet attack, such as the basing of missiles in hardened silos or on invulnerable submarines.

The protection of U.S. retaliatory forces is an obvious role for imperfect defenses because it is technically much less demanding than comprehensive population defense. Nothing approaching a perfect or leakproof defense is needed since the objective is simply to assure the survival of a fraction of U.S. nuclear forces sufficient to threaten the Soviet Union with unacceptable retaliation. As a result, these forces can be defended preferentially—that is, the defense can concentrate its efforts on saving selected targets while allowing others to be destroyed. Moreover, because the defended targets are hardened, the defense could intercept warheads at shorter range than in the case of soft targets such as cities, which can be destroyed by nuclear explosions even at a great distance.

The deployment of strategic defenses to protect U.S. retaliatory forces raises two questions. First, how urgent is the problem of preemptive attack against these forces? Second, would defenses, and SDI-type defenses in particular, actually strengthen U.S. retaliatory capabilities when Soviet offensive and defensive responses are taken into account? An examination of these issues suggests that for the purpose of deterring preemptive attack, SDI is at best redundant and at worst counterproductive.[7]

On the first question, the Reagan administration's policy has been contradictory. The President's Commission on Strategic Forces (the Scowcroft commission) reported in 1983 that while U.S. silo-based missiles are theoretically vulnerable to destruction by accurate Soviet ICBMs, this does not constitute a critical weakness in American deterrence. Since the majority of United States strategic warheads are based on submarines and bombers that would escape preemption, the ability of the United States to deliver devastating retaliation is not in doubt even if land-based missiles are destroyed in a Soviet strike.[8] Accordingly, the commission proposed to base the MX missile in existing Minuteman silos in preference to the Carter administration plan for shuttling the missile among a large number of shelters (which President Reagan had rejected on political grounds). In accepting this proposal for MX basing, the Reagan administration seemingly put to rest the "window of vulnerability" theme that had previously been so prominent in its rhetoric about U.S. military weakness. But in arguing for the SDI on the grounds of deterrence, the administration and its supporters have reverted to that theme, implying that the threat to U.S. ICBMs is a fatal deficiency that invites Soviet nuclear blackmail if not an actual disarming first strike.[9]

If one accepts the Scowcroft analysis, there is little justification for defenses to increase the survivability of American land-based missiles. But even taking a more alarmist view of the problem of missile vulnerability, it is far from clear that SDI defenses, matched by Soviet deployments, would strengthen deterrence. On the contrary, there is a serious risk that mutual deployments of such defenses would reduce U.S.-Soviet deterrent stability in general and U.S. retaliatory capabilities in particular.

The potentially adverse impact of territorial defenses on nuclear stability has long been a key argument against their deployment and is one of the basic premises underlying the ABM Treaty. The problem stems from the inherently two-sided character of such defenses. On the one hand, they may help protect retaliatory forces against a first strike and thus strengthen deterrence. On the other hand, they may help shield an aggressor against retaliation following an attack on the adversary's nuclear forces and thus help magnify the effectiveness of a first strike. In a context of U.S.-Soviet rivalry and suspicion, it is the second, aggressive role that is most likely to dominate each superpower's perception of the other's defense. Indeed, imperfect defenses may appear all the more threatening in this respect because they might be expected to perform better against "ragged" retaliation than against an all-out, well-coordinated first strike. As a result, mutual U.S. and Soviet deployments of imperfect defenses would undermine deterrent stability, especially during a crisis, by increasing both countries' incentive to inflict the first blow if conflict seemed imminent. In other words, these defenses would aggravate the very problem they are ostensibly intended to solve.

In addition to this weakening of crisis stability, mutual defenses would have specific implications for overall U.S. retaliatory strength. Those who advocate the SDI as a means of protecting U.S. retaliatory forces have consistently ignored the critical role that the ABM treaty itself plays in protecting the effectiveness of these forces by blocking the deployment of Soviet defenses. A relaxation or abandonment of the treaty to deploy defenses would sacrifice this protection. More American missiles might survive a Soviet attack (assuming the Soviet Union does not expand its offensive forces to offset U.S. defenses), but fewer would reach their targets in the Soviet Union. Any gain in ICBM survivability achieved by SDI must be balanced against this loss in target penetration due to Soviet defenses.

The net impact of this trade-off on U.S. retaliatory capability would depend on the relative effectiveness and coverage of the two defensive systems and on the specifics of U.S. and Soviet offensive forces. On a priori grounds, however, the United States would seem to have more to lose than to gain since the majority of U.S. warheads are already invulnerable: In exchange for protecting *fewer than half* its warheads from preemptive attack, the United States would be subjecting *all* of them to the attrition that would be imposed by the Soviet defense.

A simple example illustrates this problem. The United States currently has about 5,000 ballistic missile warheads available for retaliation at any given time—about 2,000 on vulnerable silo-based missiles and about 3,000 on invulnerable submarines at sea. SDI could protect some fraction of the land-based warheads that might otherwise be destroyed preemptively, but Soviet defenses would in turn intercept a fraction of both land- and sea-based U.S. missiles that would otherwise reach their targets. Even in the unlikely event that the United States were completely successful in defending its land-based missiles, a Soviet defense of only 50 percent effectiveness would cause the United States to suffer a net loss in retaliatory capability: such a Soviet defense would intercept 2,500 of the 5,000 U.S. warheads, whereas without defenses the United States would at worst lose its 2,000 land-based warheads and still have its 3,000 sea-based missiles available.

In theory, these problems could be minimized if the United States and the Soviet Union were to deploy localized defenses, unambiguously dedicated to defending missile silos, rather than the broader area defenses they are currently developing. Such "point" defenses could protect each country's nuclear forces against preemption without eroding the other's retaliatory capability against urban-industrial targets, and as such might help strengthen and stabilize deterrence. In addition, point defenses would draw upon more mature ABM technologies than those pursued by the SDI, and thus give the United States an earlier deployment option.[10] But there are several practical problems with this approach.

First, as noted earlier, a silos-only defense is inconsistent with U.S. policy, which requires that even first-generation terminal defenses provide nationwide coverage consistent with the eventual goal of effective population defenses. President Reagan has repeatedly disavowed any intention of confining SDI to the defense of retaliatory forces, stating that the goal of the program is to "destroy missiles, not protect them." At this point, a defense tailored to the protection of U.S. nuclear forces would require a fundamental change in the public rationale for SDI (and might well jeopardize public support for the program).

Second, even if U.S. policy on this issue were to change, it would be very difficult to amend the ABM Treaty to permit extensive deployment of point defenses without severely eroding the effectiveness of the treaty's ban on nationwide defense. This is why the treaty restricts even silo defenses to a single site in each country. If the treaty were so amended, each superpower would be able to deploy a significant part of the technical base for a territorial defense, and neither could be confident that the other would not attempt to quickly expand and upgrade its system. Moreover, the Soviet system would lend itself more readily than the U.S. system to such expansion because of the relative proximity of Soviet missile fields to urban areas. The risk of a Soviet breakout would thus be far greater than under the existing treaty, which, ironically, many SDI advocates believe already allows the Soviets too much leeway.[11]

Finally, it is doubtful that point defenses would be effective against unconstrained offensive proliferation and other countermeasures. While such defenses might require the Soviets to allocate up to several additional warheads to each target, they could be overwhelmed if the Soviets were willing to pay that price in order to maintain the ability to attack U.S. missile silos. In order to strengthen deterrence, then, point defenses would have to be accompanied by arms control limits on offensive warheads.

Yet such limits could be very difficult to negotiate unless two conditions were met. First, the superpowers would have to perceive each other's defenses as unequivocally dedicated to the protection of missile silos, rather than as possessing a latent potential for upgrading to a territorial defense. As noted above, this condition would be hard to meet in practice.

Second, the superpowers would have to agree to reverse the trend toward the targeting of each other's nuclear forces, which has been central to both countries' strategies over the past decade. However, if they were really willing to shift away from countersilo targeting strategies, they could move in this direction through offensive arms control alone (in particular, by reducing the ratio of warheads to targets through a phasing out of highly accurate, multiple-warhead missiles), without the deployment of point defenses and the revision of the ABM Treaty that that would require. Thus, the same arms control that would allow limited defenses to be effective in stabilizing deterrence would also make them unnecessary for that role.

OTHER RATIONALES FOR LIMITED DEFENSE

Deterrence of Limited Soviet Attacks

In addition to deterring an all-out disarming strike against U.S. retaliatory forces, SDI advocates argue, partially effective defenses could deter "selective" Soviet attacks against specific targets—for example, a limited strike against U.S. military facilities for the resupply of NATO forces during a European conflict. Partial defense could raise the threshold for such strikes, making it impossible to accomplish their objectives using only a few warheads. Instead, a much larger attack would be necessary to destroy the target, increasing the prospect of widespread collateral damage and hence, the argument goes, the likelihood of U.S. retaliation. This rationale is stressed by the Hoffman report on the strategic implications of U.S. defenses, prepared for the administration in 1983.

The argument is flawed in several respects. It assumes that in the absence of defenses the Soviets may be tempted to conduct selective nuclear strikes in the belief that damage could be so well contained that the United States would choose not to retaliate. This is a highly unlikely scenario—inconsistent with the Soviet view that a nuclear war could not be limited and with the Soviet aversion to high-risk strategic and foreign policy actions.

In addition, this role for defenses directly contradicts the goal of damage limitation in the event deterrence fails, which is frequently cited as one of the benefits of SDI. In effect, limited defenses would be used to raise the expected level of damage caused by a nuclear attack, thus strengthening the very logic of mutual assured destruction that the SDI is ostensibly designed to escape. As the Hoffman report notes, such defenses "could force the Soviets to increase their attack size radically" in a way that would be "inconsistent with limiting the level of violence."[12]

Finally, SDI proponents again fail to consider the reverse side of their arguments—the implications of Soviet defensive systems for U.S. strategy. If, as claimed, limited defenses can foil selective nuclear options, they would raise serious doubts about the NATO strategy of "flexible response" for deterring a Soviet conventional attack on Europe. In response to criticism of the flexible response strategy by advocates of a nuclear no-first-use policy, the Reagan administration has argued that NATO cannot dispense with nuclear options and that a purely conventional deterrent would invite Soviet aggression. However, as NATO leaders have been quick to grasp, the SDI implicitly contradicts this argument and suggests a weakening of the U.S. commitment to a nuclear deterrence strategy in Europe. Resulting fears of a decoupling of U.S. and European security have been a major source of allied apprehension about SDI. Indeed, superpower defenses could present the alliance with the worst of both worlds—undermining the flexible response strategy on which it currently depends, while draining resources away from the conventional force improvements that would make possible a less-nuclear-dependent NATO strategy. These issues are taken up in detail in the next chapter.

Defense against an Accidental Soviet Launch

Even a very imperfect defense might be capable of intercepting one or a small number of missiles launched accidentally against the United States, and this possibility is sometimes raised in support of the SDI. This is clearly a fallback position, designed to salvage some population-defense role for SDI, despite the negligible prospect that the United States could ever be protected from a determined large-scale Soviet attack.

Even this seemingly modest objective would require a nationwide defense since all urban areas would have to be covered. As such, it would carry the same costs as a defense against deliberate Soviet attack. The ABM Treaty would have to be radically amended, allowing both superpowers to deploy systems that would unavoidably increase their potential for full-scale breakout. Each would fear a threat to its retaliatory capability and would feel strong pressure to undertake offensive countermeasures accordingly.

These negative effects could be avoided only if defenses were deployed under conditions of close superpower cooperation. Under these ideal conditions, however, it would be possible to take other measures, far simpler and less costly, to reduce the risks of inadvertent nuclear war and even to deal with accidental launches. For example, U.S. and Soviet missiles could be equipped with command-destruct links, such as are already used in flight tests, that would permit the destruction of a missile by remote control after launching.

Defense against Third-Party or Terrorist Nuclear Attacks

Protection against attack from a small nuclear power or terrorist group is another fallback role for SDI. It suffers from the same defects as the accidental-launch rationale. Like the latter, it calls for a nationwide defensive system that would gut the ABM Treaty. Even if ostensibly aimed at third-party attacks, such defenses would inevitably be perceived by the superpowers as mutually threatening and would thus have adverse consequences for crisis stability and offensive arms control. The experience of the U.S. Sentinel ABM program is relevant here. As announced by Defense Secretary McNamara in 1967, the Sentinel system was nominally a thin defense directed against the incipient nuclear capability of China. Nevertheless, it was clearly in large part a response to the Soviet Galosh deployment and was regarded by U.S. advocates of defenses as the initial phase of an anti-Soviet system. There is little doubt that the Soviets viewed it as such.

One must also question the relevance of missile defenses to the kinds of nuclear threats that third parties might potentially pose. While the threat of nuclear terrorism is real, a ballistic missile attack against the United States is undoubtedly among the least plausible forms it would take. It is far more likely that nuclear weapons would be introduced clandestinely into U.S. territory or delivered by aircraft. Moreover, any program to develop and test an intercontinental missile by a country such as Libya would certainly be detected in time for appropriate countermeasures to be taken—possibly jointly by the two superpowers.

The SDI confronts an awkward dilemma. Its desirable goal of effective population defense is not feasible, while its more modest, feasible goals are not desirable. None of the limited defense roles proposed for SDI would offer the United States benefits at all commensurate with the costs to American security interests of a weakening or scrapping of the ABM Treaty and the acceleration of the arms race that would result.

In each case, the advantages claimed for limited defenses are overshadowed by the adverse consequences of ABM deployments. In particular, there are no foreseeable circumstances in which the United States would gain by trading existing ABM treaty restrictions for a regime that would sanction extensive Soviet defenses or increase Soviet capabilities to deploy such defenses rapidly. Soviet defenses could erode U.S. and NATO deterrence, require new U.S. investments in offensive nuclear weapons, and create a less stable strategic relationship—negating the apparent benefits of U.S. limited defenses when the latter are considered in isolation.

In the final analysis, the arguments for limited defenses used to support SDI are artificial and strained. They represent an after-the-fact attempt to find a mission for a program whose original goal, however attractive and idealistic, is unattainable and understood to be so by those responsible for the program. The result is an almost surely unprecedented gap between policy rhetoric and reality—between the vision used to gain public support for the SDI and the actual objectives that guide it.

8
Europe in the Shadow of Star Wars

JONATHAN DEAN

Not unnaturally, the first reaction of European NATO governments and public opinion to important new developments from the United States and the Soviet Union is to ask what effect these developments will have on the security of Europe. In the spring of 1986, for example, Western European countries reacted in a highly negative way to the U.S. antiterrorist bombing of Libya because they feared for the security of their own citizens.

Europeans were also wary when, in March 1983, the U.S. administration suddenly converted a modest research program on ballistic missile defense—designed to provide a reasonable degree of insurance against possible long-term Soviet advances—into the basis of a fundamental change in the strategy of defending the United States and its allies against Soviet nuclear attack. The immediate European reaction, which continues to prevail, was that the possible negative consequences of this sudden reversal of strategy outweighed the potential benefits.

The European assessment of the Strategic Defense Initiative was not greatly affected by the belief that the SDI would provide effective defense of the European population against Soviet nuclear attack. Europeans were too realistic, and too scarred by two cataclysmic world wars, to believe in any such nostrums. In the interval since President Reagan's original announcement, however, European opinion on SDI has become confused by two factors: the belief that Europe has been left behind in the field of electronic high technology, and the increasingly insistent arguments of a number of European defense experts that defense of Europe requires protection against shorter-range Soviet cruise and ballistic missiles.

The central interests of Europeans remain as follows: that the strategy of nuclear retaliation remain unweakened as the best way to deter any Soviet attack on Europe; that U.S.-Soviet nuclear arms negotiation result in a stable, lower level of weapons; and that an arms race in space be prevented. European political and public opinion does not consider SDI worth the collapse of U.S.-Soviet relations. It wants the issue negotiated between the two superpowers, either through maintaining the ABM Treaty or revising it by agreement. Majority European opinion will support some level of SDI research. But whether or not this research is genuinely promising—not now the case regarding comprehensive defense—Western Europe will remain apprehensive over SDI as long as the superpowers fail to reach agreement on strategic defenses. And Western Europe will oppose American or European actions on testing and development that place at risk existing or possible U.S.-Soviet arms control agreements. If there is no U.S.-Soviet agreement on the subject and no change in administration policy, this resistance from our allies will be an obstacle to SDI deployment. It will also be an important source of U.S.-European friction, which can deeply erode the alliance.

THE DEVELOPMENT OF EUROPEAN VIEWS

When President Reagan suddenly revived the theme of protecting the American population against Soviet missiles, European leaders objected immediately to the lack of prior consultation. After the first detailed presentation of the SDI by Secretary of Defense Weinberger in April 1984 to NATO defense ministers, they went public with their disapproval of the plan. Federal German defense minister Manfred Woerner declared that deployment of a U.S. defense against ballistic missiles could destroy the NATO alliance. French foreign minister Claude Cheysson urged the United States to drop the mistaken idea of a "Maginot Line in space."

Several factors caused European leaders to react so adversely to the notion of a U.S. space-based BMD. Most important, the proposed system aroused new fears about the reliability of the American nuclear guarantee for the security of Western Europe; in addition, Europeans anticipated both increased U.S.-Soviet tensions and renewed public controversy over defense in their own countries, which in turn could cause more U.S.-European friction and thus erosion of the NATO alliance.

At the time of President Reagan's announcement, European leaders were still engaged in a difficult struggle with their own domestic opinion to preserve the credibility and effectiveness of the American nuclear deterrent—credibility both for the Soviet leadership and for their own public opinion—in the face of Soviet achievement of equality with the United States in all types of nuclear weapons. By the beginning of 1984, NATO countries had finally succeeded in starting to deploy the new U.S. intermediate-range missiles. But now, after this hard-won victory, the end of extended deterrence and the American nuclear umbrella was suddenly in sight. In European eyes, this U.S. guarantee of nuclear retaliation had for decades provided the main reassurance against Soviet attack. With an effective missile defense, Europeans feared, the United States might withdraw to a Fortress America concept. Or the United States might become more willing to confront the Soviet Union militarily in developing countries, with heightened risk that conflicts of this kind would spread to Europe.

The new system of missile defense, however effective for the United States, was not likely to help much in defending the populations of Western Europe. In theory, it would be possible to erect a layered defense, of the type projected for the United States, to protect Western Europe against Soviet missiles. But space-orbiting weapons designed to destroy Soviet ballistic missiles in the boost phase—if they should in fact prove feasible—would have little value against the short-range tactical ballistic missiles the Soviets have deployed in Eastern Europe. The boost phase of such missiles is short, and their trajectory remains in the atmosphere, which blunts most of the weapons now under consideration. Because of the short flight times of these missiles, the second, midcourse layer planned for missile defense of the United States would not have great effect. Terminal defense of military installations could destroy some ballistic missiles in their reentry phase. But space-mounted defense could not protect the dense population of Western Europe from Soviet nuclear missiles, nor military targets and population from attack by cruise missiles and fighter bombers. And, of course, possible missile defense could be overwhelmed by an increase in the number of offensive weapons. Clearly, the chances for effective protection of Western European populations from Soviet nuclear attack are even smaller than the prospects for protection of the more distant, less densely populated United States. There is no feasible way to establish equal vulnerability of alliance partners through missile defense.

Beyond this, European leaders anticipated that a U.S. missile defense program, if successful, would eventually be replicated by the Soviet Union. A Soviet Union safe from American nuclear retaliation and possessing conventional forces superior to those of NATO might become more willing to contemplate political pressure on, or even conventional attack of, Western Europe; it might become more adventuresome in developing countries, too. The British and French nuclear forces would also lose their capability as deterrents to Soviet expansionism.

During the many years before BMD systems could actually be deployed, Europeans anticipated a dangerous increase in U.S.-Soviet tensions, the collapse of existing arms control agreements, and all-out competition between the United States and the Soviet Union in both offensive and defensive weapons. In particular, European leaders early voiced their concern about SDI as a threat to the ABM Treaty. In sum, then, Europeans anticipated that, with BMD systems emplaced in one or both superpowers, their own situation would become far more dangerous; Europe's requirements for stronger conventional defenses would increase dramatically, and with them, the costs of defense.

The SDI project also posed a more immediate problem of domestic politics for the European governments. Having just come through a period of acute political controversy over the deployment of intermediate-range U.S. missiles, European leaders were worried that a major new dispute over defense could have a negative impact on public support for defense budgets. Moreover, new public demonstrations of opposition to U.S. defense programs could have serious adverse effects on Atlantic relations.

Finally, the U.S. SDI program tapped into a new wave of "Europessimism" over the technological backwardness of Europe seen against American and Japanese advances in microchips and computers. West European economies are still in a phase of relatively low growth and high unemployment, the latter over 10 percent. Only the United States and the Soviet Union have the scientific and economic resources to mount a large-scale missile defense; in this respect, too, these "superpowers" are in a special class, separate from the European NATO states. The possibility of U.S. implementation of a missile defense program on the edge of new technology not only aroused fears of a permanently backward condition for Western Europe, but also enhanced already increasing European resentment at being a plaything of the superpowers.

As time passed, telling technical criticism of ballistic missile defense made it clear that the possibility of fully effective defense for the American or Soviet populations was remote. Instead, what was involved was a long-term possibility of partially effective defense, a possibility with many complex implications. Some European political leaders began to see, in missile defense, access to the most advanced American technology—a reflection of energetic and effective lobbying by administration officials. The deep personal commitment of President Reagan, reelected for another term in 1984, to ending reliance on the strategy of nuclear retaliation became ever more entrenched. As these aspects of missile defense emerged, West European opinion became more muted, more differentiated—in a word, more divided. For a better understanding of the evolution and probable future course of European opinion, we look more closely at the reaction of the governments of France, Great Britain, and Federal Germany.

FRANCE

France openly opposed the missile defense project from the outset, for reasons both doctrinal and practical. The doctrinal basis for French opposition is clear: the French believe that the only reliable dissuasion of Soviet attack on Europe is the conviction of Soviet leaders, based on firm prior Western decisions and deployments, that Soviet attack of any kind would elicit a Western nuclear response. In the 1960s, American resistance to this approach, and American insistence on what later became the NATO strategy of flexible response, fortified French determination to have the only truly reliable nuclear deterrent, one under their own direct control.

Now the SDI concept undermined the whole French approach: even an imperfect ballistic missile defense deployed by the Soviet Union could drastically reduce the deterrent capability of the French nuclear force. On the practical side, the high cost of maintaining their own nuclear force—some 20 percent of the French military budget—has for years caused the French to run down their conventional forces. In recent years, political controversy with domestic supporters of stronger conventional forces has caused the French government to adhere even more firmly to its concept of nuclear deterrence. Thus the American project for ballistic missile defense represented a double disaster: it would make ineffective France's own expensive nuclear force, and it would make inoperative the strategy of nuclear deterrence—in the French view, the most reliable guarantee against Soviet attack on Western Europe. Both the international standing of France and its national security, inextricably combined in French thinking, would be severely damaged.

In June 1984, France submitted to the United Nations Disarmament Commission a draft agreement against testing or deploying missile defenses. In introducing his text, the French representative said his government attached major importance to preventing a significant new arms race in space and argued that Soviet and U.S. programs for BMD and antisatellite weapons would undermine nuclear deterrence, a vital factor in maintaining peace in Europe. In other words, this NATO ally of the United States was so apprehensive over the effect of the U.S. ballistic missile defense program that it sought to ban it by international agreement.

In his pre-Christmas 1984 televised review of French foreign policy, Pres. François Mitterand once again urged the United States and the Soviet Union to agree to prohibit all weapons in space. And in early 1985, French defense minister Charles Hernu argued that deployment of missile defense systems by the United States and the Soviet Union would result in tacit complicity between the two superpowers to treat each other's territory as a sanctuary while pursuing their differences elsewhere. In the Bonn economic summit meeting of leaders of the major Western industrial countries in May 1985, President Mitterand bluntly refused official French participation in the SDI project.

However, in January 1986 the French government made clear that it did not oppose participation of individual French firms in the U.S. SDI research program. The conservative parties headed by Prime Minister Jacques Chirac, which gained a slim majority in the French Parliament in the March 1986 elections, are more supportive of the participation of French firms in SDI research on the grounds that it would benefit France's independent nuclear deterrent to keep abreast of developments in defense technology that the Soviets might deploy in decades to come. Nonetheless, a January 1986 report by French scientists and defense experts concluded that the French nuclear deterrent would continue to be significant for the next twenty-five years because it would take at least that time to deploy a partially effective defense, which, in the event, could still be penetrated by French ballistic missiles.

GREAT BRITAIN

The British reaction to SDI has been more circumspect from the outset. The original reaction of Defense Minister Michael Heseltine to Secretary Weinberger's April 1984 presentation of American plans for ballistic missile defense paralleled the negative reaction of Federal German defense minister Woerner. But the close relations between the Reagan and Thatcher governments brought rapid realization of President Reagan's seriousness of purpose in pursuing the aim of missile defense and a consequent muting of hostile commentary in the British government.

Despite this caution regarding public comment, the prime minister's office early saw that even the distant prospect of missile defense could place in question the rationale for Britain having its own nuclear forces, a rationale already under attack by the Labor and Liberal parties. The missile defense project also posed a threat to the economic viability of the British nuclear force. As with the French government, the timing of the American initiative was politically inconvenient for the Thatcher government, which has been involved in a hotly debated $15 billion project to modernize its nuclear forces through the purchase of U.S. Trident II D-5 missiles, again at the cost of running down its conventional forces.

In November 1984, Prime Minister Thatcher expressed exasperation over the American program; she forecast that the long-term net result of the U.S. missile defense effort would be a new East-West military balance at a higher level and higher cost. But during her brief visit to Washington in December 1984, the prime minister took a more productive and diplomatic approach—in return for her support of laboratory research on missile defense, she secured President Reagan's agreement to a public statement that the United States would adhere to the ABM Treaty and that it would negotiate on the issue with the Soviet Union before deploying defense systems.

Both sides were delighted with the outcome of the Thatcher-Reagan discussion. Administration officials were pleased that the prime minister had relinquished public criticism of strategic defense. British and European opinion seemed pleased that the administration, which had not previously made such an explicit public commitment, had drawn back from the possibility of future unilateral U.S. deployment of defensive weapons, with its potential for eliciting a drastic Soviet counterreaction. As part of this understanding and as a move toward the American position, Prime Minister Thatcher made clear that the British government did not oppose research on missile defense within the limits of the ABM Treaty. Mindful of the need to defend the rationale for the British Trident purchase and British nuclear capability generally, however, she also insisted on the validity of the Western strategy of nuclear deterrence and pointed out that there would be no alternative to deterrence for many years. The underlying point—and an important one—was that, in pursuing the distant and quite possibly unattainable goal of effective missile defense, the Western alliance should not neglect or jeopardize its main defense, nuclear deterrence both American and British. Prime Minister Thatcher made this point specific in her speech to the U.S. Congress in February 1985.

In March 1985, Foreign Secretary Sir Geoffrey Howe, in a major policy address, reiterated British concerns about the SDI's impact on extended deterrence, the impact of partially effective strategic defenses, and the possibility that the SDI would stimulate rather than curb the offensive arms race. While reaffirming Britain's support for SDI research within the terms of the ABM Treaty, Howe also noted the danger that the momentum generated by the research could itself become a force toward eventual deployment. The timing of the speech within a few days of the opening of the Geneva talks indicated the importance Britain attaches to the issue.

FEDERAL GERMANY

As a non-nuclear country, Federal Germany is even more dependent on the U.S. nuclear deterrent than Britain and France, but also even more interested than those countries in avoiding increased U.S.-Soviet tensions. This is because of its more exposed geographic position in the front line of the huge NATO–Warsaw Pact military confrontation, its own active policy toward East Germany and Eastern Europe, and the strong antinuclear sentiments of the German public.

In his sharply negative initial reaction to the April 1984 briefing by Secretary of Defense Weinberger on American plans for strategic defense, German defense minister Woerner argued that a perfect defense against ballistic missiles could not be achieved and that partially effective defenses would increase tension and instability between the superpowers, driving an expanded arms race. In the longer run, as defenses were improved, the United States and the Soviet Union would become more secure and Western Europe would become less secure. The binding glue of the alliance—the sharing of equal risk by its members—would be dissolved.

This concept of equal security of members of the alliance, and the related concept of equal vulnerability and shared risk, is an expression of the basic German fear of desertion by the United States. This was the motivation behind German desire to have the United States deploy in Europe a new generation of intermediate-range missiles at a time when Soviet parity with the United States in nuclear weapons cast into increasing doubt American willingness to risk an all-out strategic nuclear exchange in order to protect Germany from Soviet attack.

Despite these initial German worries, concern over possible damage to German-American relations through a new Euromissiles-style debate in the German public brought greater restraint. In October 1984 the Bundestag Caucus of Chancellor Helmut Kohl's Christian Democratic Party issued a position paper on ballistic missile defense that reflected a deliberately more balanced and cautious position. Official German statements in early 1985 echoed this position, noting that BMD research did not violate the ABM Treaty and was a powerful incentive to the Soviets to negotiate arms control, and that Western Europe should not be "technologically decoupled" from the research phase of the program. But the Bundestag statement emphasized that nuclear deterrence must be maintained—that there should be no zones of lesser and greater security in the alliance and no decoupling of the U.S. security umbrella in Europe.

After President Reagan's reelection in November 1984, most European leaders reluctantly relinquished their original hope that the United States would trade off its entire missile defense program against large Soviet reductions of nuclear missiles and thus eliminate the entire headache. European NATO governments realized that, whether or not any missile defenses were ever deployed, the U.S. missile defense program was here to stay. As a result, closer attention has been paid to the implications for Europe of the missile defense program's research phase.

EUROPEAN INVOLVEMENT IN SDI RESEARCH

The strongest attraction of the U.S. missile defense program for Europeans has been the possibility of European participation in an important new technological development from the early stages. To many, the possibility of participating in research on the forward edge of American defense technology appears as a sudden cure for Europe's economic ills. The Reagan administration has repeatedly emphasized its desire to share the new technology with Europe and, indeed, ultimately to engage in the maximum possible coproduction.

On March 26, 1985, Defense Secretary Weinberger, addressing NATO's Nuclear Planning Group in Luxembourg, explicitly invited the NATO nations, as well as Australia, Israel, and Japan, to participate in the SDI research program. At the conclusion of their meeting, the NATO defense ministers issued a declaration of support for SDI research, but coupled this with characteristic European insistence that the research be conducted within the terms of the ABM Treaty. The administration's 1985 report to Congress on the SDI, which opens the door to treaty violations by actively preparing for a number of tests in space of potential BMD components, did not allay European concerns in this regard. And, in the fall of 1985, just as the November summit meeting with Soviet leader Mikhail Gorbachev was approaching, President Reagan's national security adviser, Robert McFarlane, publicly stated that the administration had decided on a new "broad" interpretation of the ABM Treaty that would permit testing in space of the new weapons technology planned for the SDI program; in this farfetched view, only deployment of new systems was limited by the treaty. European leaders considered that adherence to this interpretation would lead directly to collapse of ABM restraints on both the United States and the Soviet Union, end any possibility of summit agreement on reductions of offensive weapons, and lead to all-out competition in both defensive and offensive weapons. The European protests streamed into Washington. They brought administration retreat to the lame position that its new legal view was correct but would not for the present be implemented for political reasons.

France has urged that the European allies develop a joint approach to SDI in order to have more say in future decisions. The seven nations of the Western European Union—a thirty-year-old organization that has been dormant for most of that time and is now being revived to strengthen Europe's role in NATO security matters—met in Bonn in late April 1985 to consider such a common front. However, the defense and foreign ministers of Great Britain, Federal Germany, France, Italy, Belgium, the Netherlands, and Luxembourg failed to agree on a joint response, announcing instead that their governments would continue to "coordinate" their responses. The socialist parties of the NATO countries held their first meeting in Lisbon at the end of March 1985 and agreed to refuse to participate in the U.S. research program and to back the French program, but the subsequent withdrawal of Italy made the agreement inoperative.

All this activity indicates serious doubts about the SDI project. The French, Canadian, Netherlands, Danish, and Norwegian governments have decided not to participate in research for the missile defense program as governments, although they will permit individual firms to participate. With difficulty and hesitation, and mainly as a gesture of political solidarity with the United States—and a sop to their own industry—Great Britain and Federal Germany had, by the beginning of 1986, concluded agreements with the United States establishing conditions under which individual enterprises in their countries could participate in SDI research. Internal differences between Chancellor Kohl's Christian Democrats and Foreign Minister Genscher's Free Democrats, who were far more negative about the implications of SDI, caused long delays in concluding the German agreement. These two were the only NATO governments, by the spring of 1986, prepared to enter official agreements with the United States enabling their private companies to participate in SDI research under agreed rules. *None of the agreements commits the signing government to support the SDI project itself.*

The American record on cooperation in production and research with Europe in the defense field is very poor. Project after project has been scuttled by service representatives in the Pentagon, by competing American firms, or by members of Congress whose constituencies house American competitors.

Moreover, the problem of sharing new technology with European countries poses some risk of security penetration by Warsaw Pact agents or of resale to Pact countries. The Reagan administration has taken an even more restrictive position on this topic than its predecessors. These factors underlie the attack by the Social Democratic opposition on the agreement concluded by the Kohl government with the United States, whose text was leaked to the German press in April 1986. The Social Democrats criticized the Bonn government for having committed itself, as a condition of the SDI research agreement with the United States, to tighten its own controls on export of sensitive technology to Warsaw Pact countries and to cooperate in expanding the list of items whose export was prohibited. They argued that these commitments, if realized, would damage present and future export possibilities to Eastern Europe and elsewhere. They pointed out that the text of the German-American agreement reveals that the United States retains all rights of ownership to the results and applications of new technology developed under SDI research contracts as well as the right to classify the results as secret and to prohibit their use in the civilian sector. Both rights, the critics pointed out, could be invoked to prevent German companies from gaining any benefit whatever from their participation in SDI research.

Short-term gains for Western European companies participating in SDI research, whether or not on the basis of official agreements between their governments and the United States, are not likely to be great. It is doubtful that the SDI research budget will exceed a total of 20 billion dollars over the next five years or that European companies will receive more than 5 percent of this sum, a total of 200 million dollars a year spread among many companies. Great Britain, a major participant, expects less than $40 million in contracts for British firms during 1986–1988. Nonetheless, on the smaller scale of European research, these sums may, as in the United States, create long-term institutionalized support for continuing the program.

THE EUROPEAN DEFENSE INITIATIVE

Meanwhile, a European stepchild of SDI has made its appearance. In late 1985, Federal German defense minister Manfred

Woerner began to argue publicly that European countries should consider what he called the European Defense Initiative (EDI), a system of antimissile defenses designed to deal with shorter-range Soviet delivery systems—SS-21, SS-22 and SS-23 ballistic missiles, some aircraft missiles, and cruise missiles—for which the SDI could provide no effective answer. The genesis of this scheme was manifold: the fact that SDI could not cope with this wide range of Soviet threats to NATO forces; the desire to define an area in which possible European contributions to SDI research might find application in a way that would directly benefit the defense of Europe; and the prospect of a direct way of overcoming European technological backwardness by deploying a demanding—and lucrative—new generation of weapons.

There were other important progenitors for EDI: In seeking to convert the antinuclear sentiment of European public opinion into budgetary support for improvement of European conventional defense, NATO leaders had launched the Emerging Technology or ET concept—the idea of combining aircraft-mounted sensors, ground computers to convert their findings to targeting information, and "smart" munitions self-guided by radar or infrared sensors in the last stage of their trajectory, into a program that could deal with the Warsaw Pact's reinforcing echelons in a conventional attack. In particular, aided by aircraft-mounted radar and infrared sensors, NATO could deploy thousands of ballistic or cruise missiles with conventional warheads or "standoff" missiles (with a range permitting launch from allied air space) mounted on NATO fighter-bombers to strike targets such as bridges and railheads deep in Warsaw Pact territory, break up airfield runways, and even, it was hoped, strike mobile Pact armored columns on the move.

Study of this possibility by NATO military experts resulted in the dismaying conclusion that Warsaw Pact forces could deploy the same weapons systems. In particular, the traditional NATO scenario of rapid Warsaw Pact attack with limited four-to-five-day preparation was amplified to include prior attack on the same type of installations that NATO intended to attack with its new Emerging Technology—command posts, airfields, nuclear storage sites, or storage depots for prepositioned equipment—but on the NATO side of the dividing line. It was believed that, through still further improvement of their accuracy, Soviet SS-23s could be adapted for use with conventional or chemical warheads. Although even the new model SS-23s are not capable of the necessary accuracy, some NATO experts promptly wrote them into the Pact attack scenario and a new version of the Soviet threat to NATO came into existence.

In other words, it is now realized that if NATO deploys in Europe large numbers of missiles armed with conventional warheads, the Soviet Union will do the same, with the result of an increased threat to NATO fixed installations now under some jeopardy from increasingly capable Pact aircraft. A large-scale NATO deployment of missiles with conventional warheads, therefore, might have to be accompanied by improvement of NATO defenses against a comparable deployment on the Warsaw Pact side. These possible deployment decisions, which could accelerate military developments, might otherwise have taken place, but far more slowly and less intensively.

In coming years, then, NATO may begin to consider acquiring and deploying not only the ET technology, but also what is being called extended air defense—a system perhaps consisting of improved Hawk air defense missiles directed against Soviet cruise missiles as well as a system of defenses against tactical ballistic missiles possibly modeled after an advanced version of the U.S. Patriot antiaircraft missile or a European equivalent. A large portion of these expensive new weapons would be produced in Europe. If deployed, however, these new defenses would protect NATO command and control, nuclear missile and storage sites, and airbases, not the civilian population.

The first thing to note about this project is its enormous cost. The ET program is modestly estimated to cost around $40 billion to $50 billion, and the air defense component the same amount. NATO projects of this kind, like SDI itself in the United States, can only be pursued at the cost of diverting funds from far more urgent NATO programs of conventional defense, like increasing ammunition stocks. At a time when European assessment of the threat of direct attack from the Soviet Union is at an all time low, major increases in the defense budgets of European NATO countries seem excluded for years to come.

These new NATO antimissile defenses would consist mainly of a class of weapons called ATMs, or antitactical missile defenses: souped-up, more rapid, longer-range antiaircraft missiles that can intercept ballistic missile warheads or cruise missiles in their final phase. Such defenses could reduce to some extent the number of warheads striking fixed military sites, perhaps against an efficiency of up to 50 percent. The answer for the attacker, as with SDI, is to increase the number of offensive delivery systems and to use penetration aids. ATMs are not forbidden in the ABM Treaty, which prohibits only defenses against "strategic" missiles, but the technology is similar to SDI technology for the terminal phase. Specifically, testing ATMs in the air or space may violate and undermine the 1978 agreement by the United States and the Soviet Union in the Standing Consultative Committee (set up by the ABM agreement to arbitrate disputes), which defines testing in the "ABM mode." ATMs would have to be tested against warheads of velocity and trajectory similar to that of submarine-launched ballistic missiles (SLBMs). The United States has already accused the Soviet Union of violating the ABM Treaty, claiming that the USSR's SAX-12 antiaircraft missile has a built-in antimissile capability. European development of an ATM system would raise the same issues of compliance and would contribute to eroding the ABM agreement from below, like antisatellite weapons at the other end of the scale. Deployment of ATM systems in Europe would provide a further target and incentive for preemptive attack, thus contributing to crisis instability as well as to intensifying the arms race. The United States is also prohibited under the ABM Treaty from transferring ABM technology to other states, including allied states; such activity might occur either in the context of collaboration with NATO Europe on SDI or ATM research.

If a European Defense Initiative proceeds and the Soviet Union mounts an extensive public diplomacy campaign warning the Western Europeans against actions that would violate the ABM agreement, European public opinion may oppose further activity on the European Defense Initiative. Moreover,

Western European governments, however concerned they might be about the effects of U.S. SDI tests on maintaining the ABM agreement, would no longer be in a position to raise effective objections in Washington against these SDI tests.

The answer to this complex of problems is not two new waves of expensive new weapons in both NATO and the Warsaw pact. It is arms control: In the U.S.-Soviet talks in Geneva on intermediate-range nuclear missiles—the INF talks—both countries have in the past suggested what amounts to a freeze on deployment of shorter-range nuclear delivery systems as part of a first agreement on reduction of INF missiles. The wording of this first INF agreement should be so formulated that it limits all ballistic and cruise missiles of both INF and shorter range, regardless of whether they are equipped with nuclear, conventional or chemical warheads (a difference that, in any event, cannot be verified). Such a step would prevent large-scale deployment of new missiles with conventional warheads and make development of new defensive systems against these missiles far less compelling.

THE MORE IMMEDIATE CONSEQUENCES

As the report by the French scientists again confirms, actual realization of any SDI or EDI is decades away. Other problems are more immediate. In the next several years, if the Geneva talks proceed and do not give way to a breakdown of arms control restraints on both superpowers, the major problem for Western European governments posed by the U.S. ballistic missile defense program is likely to be a political one: its negative impact on basic European attitudes toward the alliance with the United States and toward defense. The missile defense issue has not yet become an issue of broad public interest, but its potential for arousing widespread negative reaction among the European public is great, largely because of the political heritage of the INF controversy.

Conservative governments successfully deployed the INF missiles and continue to dominate the Western coalition. The European antinuclear movement is now weaker in areas where it was strongest, in Federal Germany and the Netherlands. The concepts of the peace movement, however, have been institutionalized through their adoption by the European political Left. Sharply decreased faith in the capacity of the arms control process to control or even affect the East-West military relationship has accompanied the growing disaffection with the strategy of nuclear deterrence. In the view of large segments of the European public, the arms control process has proved powerless to stop enormous increases in nuclear capability on both sides. For many, including most opposition parties in Western Europe, this conclusion leads to support for unilateral measures of disarmament by the West as the only action likely to stop the spiral.

Most of the skepticism and worry about ballistic missile defense both in Europe and in the United States is connected with fears of adverse Soviet reaction and resulting all-out competition between the Soviet Union and the United States. Consequently, the critical variable that will determine the degree of activation of Western European public opinion on the issue of missile defense is the degree of Soviet opposition to the missile defense project and the Soviet Union's ability to make a compelling case for its position to political opinion in Europe and the United States.

Already, Soviet public information output to Western Europe focuses strongly on Soviet opposition to the SDI, which is portrayed both as a threat to peace and as a direct obstacle to arms control agreements. Soviet statements, among them General Secretary Gorbachev's arms control program of January 15, 1985, make it appear that the Soviet Union is prepared to move toward an interim agreement on intermediate-range nuclear forces, without linking this to U.S.-Soviet agreement on SDI. Whether, if a partial agreement on Euromissiles is actually in sight, Soviet leaders will then eliminate any connection to progress on space weapons is open to question. In any event, the Soviet public diplomacy will give continued prominence to Soviet opposition to SDI. For a time, the mere fact that the United States and the Soviet Union are negotiating on the subject will assuage European concerns about the possible negative effects of disputes over missile defense. But as shown in the disappointingly meager arms control results of the November 1985 Geneva summit, progress in Geneva is likely to be very slow. Both sides are increasingly likely to publicize their positions and to appeal for public support.

Western European political leaders, however loyal to the alliance with the United States, are in general agreement with the substance of the Soviet position on two central issues. First (and despite the progressive weakening of the credibility of this concept among Western European leaders) is the desirability of maintaining nuclear deterrence as the primary element in maintaining stability between the superpowers. Second is the desirability of heading off, through U.S.-Soviet agreement, an all-out competition in missile defense and offensive weapons. Advocacy of these two concepts by European leaders under pressure from their own domestic opinion for a negotiated outcome in Geneva could make it increasingly difficult over the next several years for the U.S. administration to maintain allied support for its negotiating position, unless it is prepared to move in the direction of these allied—and Soviet—views.

If the United States and the Soviet Union were to agree on some way to handle the missile defense issue, most of the grounds for opposition to missile defense both in Europe and the United States would be eliminated. On the other hand, if the two countries do not succeed in finding some formula on SDI that at least avoids a rupture in their dialogue, then it appears possible that, in the next four to five years, first one superpower and then the other will gradually slip out of the restraints of the ABM Treaty and move into a competitive situation both on defensive and offensive weapons from which it will become increasingly difficult to draw back through new agreements. In 1989 the United States plans to begin a series of demonstration projects beginning with the Airborne Optical System, a targeting and ranging system mounted on an aircraft, which the Soviet Union will almost certainly consider a violation of the prohibition in the ABM Treaty against testing components of the ABM system in the atmosphere or in space. In such circumstances, the SDI project will in all likelihood be a source of serious progressive alienation between Europe and the United States, alienation that will erode the political substance of NATO awareness of common goals and willingness to cooperate to achieve them.

This risk is not theoretical: if present opinion trends continue, sometime in the next decade a government committed to unilateral arms reduction to brake the upward spiral of U.S.-Soviet arms competition will come to power in a NATO European country. Already, strong opposition parties in NATO's Northern Tier—Great Britain, Federal Germany, Belgium, and the Netherlands—urge policies that move in this direction. When one or more of these governments comes to power, NATO will be exposed to a serious and deeply divisive challenge—and concern over SDI and its consequences will have been a major driving force in this development.

9
Transition Improbable: Arms Control and SDI

PETER A. CLAUSEN

The Strategic Defense Initiative has dominated and deadlocked the U.S.-Soviet arms talks since the current negotiations began in early 1985. President Reagan has held resolutely to the position that the program is not subject to negotiation, belying speculation that the administration might use SDI as a "bargaining chip." The Soviet Union, meanwhile, has demanded the curtailment of SDI as a precondition of reductions in nuclear weapons. The resulting stalemate reflects more than the clash of superpower interests, however. Behind the impasse in Geneva lies policy disarray in Washington. The United States has failed to articulate a consistent statement of the SDI's arms control goals or a coherent strategy for implementing them. This failure, in turn, reflects basic and still unresolved questions about the purpose of Star Wars and its wider consequences for U.S.-Soviet relations.

Two conflicting visions of SDI confound the effort to unravel its arms control dimension. The first assumes an unprecedented level of strategic reconciliation and cooperation between the superpowers. It is the notion of a defensive transition, jointly managed by the two countries, with arms control an indispensable element. An entirely new arms control framework would be negotiated in which offensive forces would be reduced and defenses phased in, perhaps even with technology sharing at some point in the future.

The second vision assumes a continuing adversarial relationship, with competition extended to the "new high ground" of space. Here, SDI is seen as a way to reverse the alleged U.S. strategic decline of the 1970s and to restore U.S. nuclear superiority. The program's arms control function is to serve as a lever for agreement on U.S. terms, but its value does not stand or fall on the success of this tactic. In the absence of Soviet agreement, the United States would deploy missile defenses unilaterally and force the Soviets into a new arms race that would play to the American technological edge.

The idea of a cooperative transition has dominated the president's public rhetoric on SDI, and has been put forward as the motivating strategic concept underlying U.S. policy in the Geneva arms talks. According to Ambassador Paul Nitze, the administration's senior arms adviser and the chief articulator of the concept, "we would see the transition period as a cooperative endeavor with the Soviets. Arms control would play a critical role."[1]

The key U.S. objective in the arms talks, from this standpoint, is to engage the Soviets in a dialogue on the merits of defenses in hopes of converting them to support a mutual shift from offense-based deterrence—resting on the threat of nuclear retaliation—to a defense-based relationship in which nuclear forces can be progressively reduced and ultimately phased out. As described by then national security advisor Robert McFarlane in March 1985, "our policy must be to first establish agreement between ourselves and the Russians on the value of defensive systems. Once we have reached agreement on that, then we must establish a path for the integration of these defensive systems into the force structure that will be stable."[2] Reviewing the status of the Geneva talks following the November 1985 summit, Nitze reiterated that "we are calling for a cooperative approach to the deployment of defensive systems—as opposed to a 'race.' "[3]

Nitze has described the defensive transition as a three-stage process occurring over a long period of time.[4] During Phase I, lasting perhaps ten years, the United States and the Soviet Union would negotiate deep reductions in their offensive nuclear forces, emphasizing the most destabilizing systems such as large multiple-warhead missiles. Research on strategic defenses would continue within the confines of the Antiballistic Missile (ABM) Treaty, and the "erosion" of that treaty would be reversed. If research indicated the feasibility of effective, survivable, and cost-effective defenses, the ABM Treaty would give way in Phase II to a staged deployment of defenses, while offensive reductions continued. This transition stage might continue for several decades. Finally, in Phase III highly effective defenses would be deployed and nuclear weapons reduced to near zero.

In contrast to this vision, there is ample evidence that the adversarial approach plays a key role in administration thinking about defenses. This theme is especially evident in the frequent alarms sounded about Soviet defensive programs and the growing administration tendency to invoke an alleged "ABM gap" to justify the SDI. Here the prospect of a Soviet SDI is seen not as a development to be welcomed but as a profound threat to U.S. security requiring both offensive and defensive responses. Secretary of Defense Weinberger clearly reflected this view in his letter to the president prior to the 1985 summit: "Even a *probable* [Soviet] territorial defense would require us to increase the number of our offensive forces and their ability to penetrate Soviet defenses to assure that our operational plans could be executed."[5]

The competitive model of SDI reflects more than specific concerns about the threat of a Soviet ABM, however. The administration has portrayed the SDI as a way of redressing broader, adverse strategic trends that would otherwise lead to Soviet superiority. "The nature of the military threat has changed and will continue to change in very fundamental ways in the next decade," states an authoritative U.S. policy report on SDI that was released in June 1985. "Unless we adapt our response . . . our susceptibility to coercion will increase dramatically. . . . The trends in the development of Soviet strategic offensive and defensive forces, as well as the growing pattern of Soviet deception and noncompliance with existing agreements, if permitted to continue unchecked over the long term, will undermine the essential military balance and mutuality of vulnerability on which deterrence theory has rested."[6]

In this light, SDI represents a way not of ending the superpower arms competition but of shifting it to a different plane where Soviet advantages would be blunted and American advantages maximized. This expectation helps explain the administration's insistence that the Soviets will not be given a "veto" over the ultimate fate of SDI. Should the Soviets reject a negotiated transition, the United States reserves the right to abrogate the ABM Treaty unilaterally and proceed with Star Wars deployment.

If the Soviets do not have a veto over SDI deployment, however, they nonetheless can block the cooperative defensive transition the United States has proposed. By declining the invitation to construct a new defense-dominant relationship, and choosing instead to offset and counter U.S. defenses, they can foreclose the new arms framework sought by the United States. The result would be a two-front arms race and a radically changed strategic environment—a prospect that might be welcomed by proponents of the competitive version of SDI, but that hardly resembles the vision held out by President Reagan and Ambassador Nitze.

All indications to date are that the Soviets find the U.S. invitation easy to refuse. There is little doubt that their own perceptions of the SDI are dominated by the adversarial model. The program is viewed in conjunction with U.S. offensive force modernization (especially the MX and Trident II missiles) as a determined bid for American strategic advantage.[7] The Soviets' top priority at the Geneva talks has been to block SDI, and they have insisted that cuts in strategic offensive forces be preceded by a commitment to strict limitations on defenses. In this, they are reaffirming the underlying formula of the SALT agreements and ABM Treaty, while the United States wants to replace that formula with a defensive transition. This fundamental contradiction was papered over when the two countries agreed in January 1985 that the arms talks would address the "linkage" between offenses and defenses, but it has deadlocked the negotiations since.

The prospects for breaking this deadlock on American terms are negligible. The defensive transition concept is plagued with logical contradictions and practical obstacles that would make it difficult to negotiate even under ideal circumstances and that virtually rule it out in the present atmosphere of U.S.

ambivalence and Soviet suspicion. Accordingly, the arms control impasse is likely to persist until the SDI is placed on the bargaining table or until the momentum of both U.S. and Soviet programs reduces the ABM agreement to a dead letter, which would inaugurate a new offense-defense arms race between the superpowers.

The discussion that follows examines the first two phases of Nitze's scheme: the initial phase of offensive arms cuts and the transition phase itself, in which defenses would be progressively deployed and offenses reduced further to produce a defense-dominant strategic equation. Unless these stages can be successfully navigated, the third and final phase becomes moot. In any case, the merits of the plan presumably do not depend on achieving total nuclear disarmament in the third phase. If this were the only arms control outcome that could justify embarking on a transition to defenses, the policy would appeal only to the naïve.

PHASE I: THE ACTION-REACTION PROCESS

The Reagan administration plan significantly calls for large offensive reductions prior to the deployment of missile defenses. Although administration officials frequently have spoken of SDI as a catalyst for arms control, the sequence outlined by Nitze suggests that this formulation is misleading and even backward. Instead, restrictions on offensive arms are to precede the defensive transition.

This sequence has the virtue of realism in two respects. First, it corresponds to the great disparity in maturity between offensive and defensive technologies. Since the effective defensive weapons envisioned for SDI may not exist for decades, a scheme placing defenses first would require that arms control be deferred indefinitely. Second, putting arms reductions ahead of the transition acknowledges the close relation between limits on offensive forces and the potential performance of defenses: the latter are much more likely to be effective if offensive responses to them are constrained.

The potential for a rapid buildup of U.S. and Soviet strategic forces over the next ten years illustrates this second issue (see table 9.1). By the mid-1990s, nuclear warheads could, with aggressive modernization, be double the level they would reach if current SALT constraints remain in force. Especially significant is the scope for a very large increase in Soviet ballistic missile warheads over the next several years. As a result, a U.S. missile defense deployed in the mid-1990s would need to be capable of intercepting 10,000 Soviet warheads—more than the entire current Soviet force—simply to keep pace with the growth of Soviet forces that could occur in the interim if compliance with SALT ends.

Here, as on many key SDI issues, conflicting administration viewpoints can be cited, and U.S. officials have sometimes predicted that layered defenses will ultimately enjoy technical leverage even against unrestricted offensive proliferation. Nevertheless, the idea that arms control plays a crucial role in giving defenses a chance is a basic element of the transition strategy. According to a Senate staff report based on interviews with SDI officials, "it is generally agreed within SDI that a U.S. defensive deployment would have to proceed hand-

TABLE 9.1 Potential Growth of Nuclear Forces

	1985[a]	*1994 SALT*[b]	*1994 No SALT*[c]
United States			
ICBM warheads	2124	2800	5430
SLBM warheads	5760	5248	6976
Total missile warheads	7884	8048	12406
Bomber weapons	3276	5708	13788
Total warheads	11160	13756	26194
Soviet Union			
ICBM warheads	6420	7320	16032
SLBM warheads	2844	3954	5362
Total missile warheads	9264	11274	21394
Bomber weapons	820	2940	6404
Total warheads	10084	14214	27798

[a] Arms Control Association, *Countdown on SALT II* (Washington, D.C.: Arms Control Association, 1985), p. 40.

[b] Congressional Research Service, *US/Soviet Strategic Nuclear Forces: Potential Trends with or without SALT* (Washington, D.C.: Library of Congress, 1984), pp. 48, 50.

[c] Ibid., pp. 66, 68. Assumes "aggressive modernization."

in-hand with deep reductions in Soviet offensive nuclear forces for the defense to be truly effective."[8]

Notably, both the Fletcher and Hoffman panels drew attention to this relationship, despite their quite different tones (the former optimistic and the latter pessimistic) regarding the technical potential of advanced defenses. The Fletcher report noted that "the ultimate utility, effectiveness, cost, complexity, and degree of technical risk in this system will depend not only on the technology itself, but also on the extent to which the Soviet Union either agrees to mutual defense arrangements or offense limitations."[9] Similarly, the Hoffman report stated that, if current Soviet policy toward SDI were to change, "it might also be possible to reach agreements restricting offensive forces *so as to permit* defensive systems to diminish the nuclear threat."[10]

Such statements imply that effective defenses are more accurately viewed as the beneficiary of offensive arms control than as a stimulus to it. If so, then effective defenses depend at least in part on a superpower agreement to allow—and even encourage—them to emerge by not undertaking offsetting arms buildups and other countermeasures. This is the logic of Phase I offensive reductions.

Here a central contradiction of the defense transition appears, however. While the shift to a defense regime assumes prior agreement to restrict offenses, the very anticipation of defenses creates new incentives for offensive expansion. The process thus threatens to become a self-defeating prophesy, undercutting the conditions of its own success. The arms reductions posited in Phase I require the suspension of the "action-reaction" process whereby each superpower would normally increase its offensive forces in the face of prospective defensive systems on the other side. Unless a plausible basis for such a suspension can be found—allowing the United States and Soviet Union to agree to reduce arms while simultaneously encouraging the development of missile defenses—the transition will never get off the ground.

Technical expectations about future defenses do not offer an adequate basis for such an agreement. In theory, the superpowers might forego offensive buildups and embark on Phase I arms reductions if they held either highly pessimistic or highly optimistic views of the technical potential of defensive systems. In the former case, they would see no need to compensate for the effects of defenses and could agree to reductions without putting their nuclear capabilities at risk of future erosion. In the latter, they might agree to anticipatory cuts in ballistic missiles on the grounds that these weapons are destined to become wasting assets in any case.

Both of these scenarios are farfetched. There is actually great uncertainty about the technical prospects of advanced defenses, and this makes offensive expansion a compelling response. Given current political and technological realities, a prudent U.S. or Soviet planner will regard the prospect of the adversary's missile defense as neither unthreatening enough to be ignored nor so intimidating that efforts to defeat it are futile. Instead, defenses will be seen as posing an incalculable but potentially critical threat requiring offsetting reactions. These responses would be discouraged only if defenses were to assume a decisive cost-exchange advantage over offenses—a possibility that cannot be excluded over the very long term but that will certainly not shape strategic and arms control decisions of the next decade or so. For the foreseeable future, in other words, these decisions will be guided on both sides by the assumption that the nuclear world remains offense-dominant. That this is the guiding premise of U.S. policy is clear from the Weinberger letter cited earlier.

The Reagan administration has conceded that the initial Soviet reaction to SDI is most likely to take the form of offensive measures intended to saturate or otherwise overcome any U.S. defense.[11] The desired shift in Soviet policy has been portrayed as a gradual, long-term process contingent on the United States demonstrating both the feasibility of highly effective defenses and a commitment to deploy them. For example, the Hoffman report predicted a Soviet offensive buildup in response to SDI, but speculated that "if the new defensive technologies offer sufficient leverage against the offense and they cannot prevent the West from deploying defensive systems, the Soviets may accept a reduction in their long-range offensive threat against the West, which might be reflected in arms control agreements."[12] With greater bravado, some officials (such as former science adviser George Keyworth) have flatly asserted that the U.S. technological prowess demonstrated by SDI will transform Soviet arms control incentives.

But where does this leave Phase I? If Soviet conversion to the U.S. plan must await the demonstration of SDI feasibility, then offensive cuts cannot precede the defense transition, as called for by the plan. Moreover, insofar as SDI feasibility depends on previous offensive cuts, that demonstration then becomes impossible. The whole scheme reduces to a vicious circle that could only be broken by a prior consensus between the superpowers on the merits of a shift from offense to defense. The political incentives that might foster such a consensus, however, are no more in evidence than the technical breakthroughs that might dictate it.

In these circumstances, any prospect of blocking the action-reaction process to allow near-term arms reductions requires that the U.S. and Soviet Union each be reassured against the threat of a defensive breakthrough by the other. Only constraints on missile-defense development can create the breathing space necessary for Phase I offensive reductions. Such constraints would maintain a long lead time for the deployment of defensive systems, relative to the time required to take offensive countermeasures. In this way, each side would be protected from a sudden erosion of its nuclear capability if cooperation broke down and an offense-defense competition, rather than a jointly managed transition, was the result.

PHASE I: THE ABM TREATY AND THE PROBLEM OF BREAKOUT

The need for mutual protection against a defensive "breakout"—a sudden, rapid deployment of a strategic defense—during the initial stage of offensive reductions underscores the critical role of the ABM Treaty. It also points to another great contradiction in the administration's strategy, which requires the treaty to serve two incompatible functions—providing a buffer against breakout while simultaneously accommodating the development of ABM technologies to the point where a defensive transition could be initiated.

The contradiction is clearly evident in the disjunction between the schedules of Nitze's transition scheme on the one hand and the SDI program plan on the other. While the transition scenario calls for a ten-year period of defense research during which the "erosion" of the ABM treaty would be arrested, the SDI program is aimed at supporting a decision by the early 1990s on the feasibility of proceeding with full-scale development and deployment. According to 1985 testimony by General Abrahamson, adherence to this schedule would require amendments to the ABM Treaty by around 1991—that is, at a point when Nitze's first phase would be barely half over, even in the event of a superpower arms agreement in the immediate future.[13]

Within a few years, then, the United States will face a choice between maintaining the ABM Treaty and proceeding with the SDI as now constituted. While this situation is inconvenient for U.S. policy, it reflects faithfully the intent of the ABM Treaty. The accord's provisions were purposely crafted to preserve an effective margin against breakout by preventing either the United States or the Soviet Union from getting close to the point of being able to deploy a nationwide defense.

Article I of the treaty states: "Each party undertakes not to deploy ABM systems for a defense of its country and not to provide a base for such a defense." To increase mutual confidence in this undertaking, the treaty places severe restrictions on ABM development. Specifically, Article V prohibits the development, testing, or deployment of ABM systems or components that are space based, air based, sea based, or mobile land-based. In other words, only fixed, land-based systems may be developed and tested. Deployment is permitted only at a single site—centered either on the national capital or on an ICBM field—and is restricted to one hundred interceptor missiles.

"Agreed Statement D" appended to the treaty states that ABM systems and components based on other physical principles (e.g., directed-energy weapons or nonradar sensors) are subject to specific limitations by agreement when such systems are "created." Under the historic, and until recently undisputed, interpretation of Statement D, this provision forbids the deployment of these "exotic" systems and allows their development and testing only under the same limitations—in a fixed, land-based mode—that apply to conventional ABM technologies.

The U.S. effort to fit SDI within these provisions contains two strands. The first strains to justify the program's near-term activities under what the administration now calls a "restrictive" interpretation of the ABM Treaty. The second consists of an egregious new reading of Agreed Statement D under which full development and testing of "exotic" defenses, up to the point of actual deployment, would be permitted. At the same time, the administration invokes a strict interpretation of treaty constraints on conventional ABM development as a lever against the Soviet program. Taken together, these positions constitute an elastic and self-serving use of the treaty that belies a serious interest in reversing its erosion.

The first policy line is contained in the administration's 1985 report to Congress on the SDI, which tries to reconcile what are in effect early field tests of spaced-based and air-based ABM sensors and weapons with the ABM Treaty's constraints on development and testing.[14] In doing so, the report leans on loopholes and ambiguities in the text that, if fully exploited, would drastically shrink the treaty's margin of protection against breakout.

For example, the administration has argued in some cases that the technologies to be tested are not full ABM components (interceptors, launchers, radars, or their functional equivalents), but rather subcomponents or "adjuncts" that could serve as ABM components only if combined with other technologies. With this arbitrary designation, the Airborne Optical Adjunct (an infrared sensor to be carried aboard an aircraft) is not a proscribed air-based ABM component because by itself it could not perform all the tracking and battle management tasks required of traditional ABM radars. Similarly, the Acquisition, Tracking and Pointing System, although it would perform several key ABM functions, is alleged to be "only part of the set of technologies ultimately required for an ABM component." Other tests—such as that of the Space Surveillance and Tracking System—are rationalized on the grounds that current technologies fall short of the power levels or other performance criteria required for an effective ABM system. Finally, a number of ABM weapons concepts, including kinetic kill vehicles and space-based rail-guns, are to be tested initially against orbiting targets—that is, under the guise of antisatellite weapons rather than in the prohibited "ABM mode."

This attempt to steer SDI through the gray areas of the ABM Treaty inherently undercuts the agreement's essential function of preserving a long lead time for the deployment of defenses. Taken to its logical extreme, the administration's report suggests that the line of forbidden activities is crossed only when mature, ABM-capable technologies are tested in an integrated fashion and in an explicit ABM mode. As described by the chief U.S. negotiator for the ABM Treaty, Gerard Smith, the U.S. argument amounts to an attempt "to prepare the ground for a breakout" and as such "constitutes anticipatory breach of contract."[15]

The second line of U.S. policy—the unilateral reinterpretation in October 1985 of the provisions on "exotic" systems—casts even more doubt on the American commitment to a robust ABM Treaty. The new reading turns the meaning of Agreed Statement D on its head, reversing the policy not only of earlier administrations but of the Reagan administration itself, as reflected in its Arms Control Impact Statements prior to 1985. Article V of the treaty, the United States now asserts, constrains the development and testing only of traditional ABM systems and components and does not apply to systems based on other physical principles. Under this interpretation, then, exotic systems may be brought to the verge of deployment, including testing in the space-based and other mobile modes prohibited for traditional systems, without violating the treaty.

In effect, the reinterpretation asserts—against common sense and the historical record—that the purpose of the ABM treaty was not to restrict ballistic missile defense per se, but only a particular technological approach to it. The view that exotic systems were covered by Article V, the administration claims, had indeed been the goal of U.S. negotiators but was not accepted by the Soviets. This revisionist reading was apparently developed by the administration without consulting either the Soviets or, except for Paul Nitze, members of the U.S. negotiating team for the ABM treaty. It was quickly repudiated by Gerard Smith, and by the team's legal advisor, John Rhinelander, who described the reinterpretation as "absurd as a matter of policy, intent, and interpretation."[16]

In response to the ensuing controversy, and in particular the protests of U.S. allies who had been assured that SDI was compliant with the ABM treaty as historically understood, the administration partially backtracked. While the new interpretation would henceforth be considered the authoritative one legally, Secretary of State Shultz announced, the SDI would continue as a matter of policy to be subjected to the more restrictive standard of the earlier interpretation. How long this voluntary policy would be followed, and the conditions under which it might be changed, were not made clear.

The U.S. reinterpretation of the ABM Treaty remains perplexing in many respects, including its timing and the possible motives underlying it. It can be variously explained as an attempt to eviscerate the treaty on the part of those who have always been hostile to it or as a bargaining ploy meant to strengthen the U.S. hand in Geneva.[17] On a less Machiavellian level, though, the revision may be seen as an attempt to resolve the contradiction—which, as noted above, will appear within five years even by the administration's own reckoning—between the SDI and the ABM Treaty's restrictions as previously interpreted.[18]

This "solution" to the SDI's legal dilemmas, however, is illusory. It reconciles the program with the ABM Treaty only by subverting the latter's essential function of mutual reassurance against breakout. If only deployment of advanced defenses is barred, then the treaty's breakout margin disappears altogether. Equally important, by asserting a radical reinterpretation of the treaty's meaning unilaterally, the United States has set a precedent that undercuts Soviet incentives for compliance and the prospects for resolving existing compliance questions.

The new U.S. policy obviously invites the Soviet Union to adopt a more permissive standard in its own strategic defense program, and thus increases American vulnerability to a Soviet defensive breakout. In this perspective, the U.S. shift appears incongruous if one takes seriously the administration's allegations of a significant Soviet lead in directed-energy weapons and other exotic ABM systems. If the Soviets are in fact a decade ahead of the United States in these technologies, it is hard to explain the U.S. interest in relaxing treaty limits that stand in the way of bringing them to the point of deployment. It seems more likely that, rhetoric notwithstanding, the United States believes it holds the technological edge in exotic defenses and therefore has more to gain than lose by removing the legal impediments to their development.

However, the reverse is true regarding conventional ABM. Here, the Soviets have the potential to deploy a defense (albeit of limited effectiveness) considerably earlier than the United States. As the SDI has shifted the focus of U.S. missile defense work away from relatively mature defensive technologies, the Soviets have emphasized the incremental modernization of traditional ABM radars and interceptors while maintaining an operational ABM site around Moscow. As a result, they possess the components of a defense that could be deployed widely and fairly rapidly should the ABM Treaty unravel.

This asymmetry in superpower missile defense programs means that in the short term the United States needs the treaty more than the Soviets. From a purely competitive point of view, then, it would serve U.S. interests to maintain the treaty until SDI technologies mature to a point where the lead time for their deployment is comparable to the Soviets'. The United States would then not be at a disadvantage—on the contrary, it presumably would be poised to deploy a superior defense—when ABM Treaty restraints were relaxed or eliminated in the future.

This kind of reasoning would seem to underlie the administration's effort to hold the Soviets to a strict standard of compliance with ABM Treaty constraints on conventional systems, even as it tries to define away the limits on exotic defenses. This effort is reflected not only in the administration's probably valid charge that the Krasnoyarsk radar violates the treaty, but also in the broader and more dubious allegation that Soviet ABM activities as a whole suggest an attempt to prepare for a breakout.[19] But this tactic, however tempting as a means of legitimizing SDI, is not calculated to strengthen the Soviet commitment to the ABM Treaty.

The Soviets cannot be expected to subscribe to a reading of the treaty that is so clearly prejudicial to their own interests, given the different emphases of U.S. and Soviet programs. In assessing the implications of the new U.S. policy, the Soviets may more likely conclude that the eventual collapse of the treaty is inevitable and begin to prepare for the post-treaty strategic competition. While this does not necessarily mean that the Soviets themselves will abrogate the treaty in the near term, it does mean that the United States will not be free to set the terms and timing for the onset of that competition. On the contrary, the anomalous U.S. position of endorsing one standard as the legal one while claiming to follow another as a matter of policy probably reduces the ability to shape Soviet compliance incentives because it fails to link American behavior to Soviet activities.

Rather than signaling the Soviet Union that the United States will uphold the treaty as long as the Soviets do so, the present policy suggests that U.S. adherence is a matter of unilateral discretion, to be guided by technological and political convenience rather than reciprocity and mutual obligation. (In a clumsy attempt to pressure Congress, the administration went so far as to suggest in May 1986 that continued U.S. compliance with the "restrictive" treaty standard was contingent on full funding of the SDI budget request.) In effect, the United States now approaches the treaty as a tool to be manipulated to legitimize SDI and to discredit Soviet activities, rather than as a mutually beneficial arrangement and a necessary bridge to the defense transition.

In sum, the administration's transition scheme places demands on the ABM Treaty that subvert its basic purposes and pull it in contradictory directions. The treaty cannot shield the parties from breakout during the first phase of the transition while accommodating development programs that would allow a decision on the technical feasibility of defenses. Nor can it free the United States to carry exotic defenses to the point of deployment while protecting itself against the threat of a Soviet defense based on conventional ABM technologies. Attempting to use the treaty in this way can only encourage both parties to disregard it as a constraint on their strategic planning and as an element of predictability and stability in their relationship.

If this pattern persists, the next ten years are most unlikely to resemble the tidy sequence envisioned by Paul Nitze—a treaty-constrained exploration of the feasibility of defenses, to be followed by negotiations to amend the ABM Treaty and begin the defensive transition. Instead, this period would be one of increasingly lax and ill-defined constraints on the development of defenses, combined with continuing large uncertainties about their actual effectiveness—ideal conditions for an offense-defense arms race.

PHASE II: NAVIGATING THE TRANSITION

The contradictions of U.S. policy discussed earlier make it doubtful that the first phase of the U.S. arms control plan will ever occur. There is little prospect that the Soviets will find it in their interest to agree to arms reductions, or that the ABM Treaty can be saved and enlisted as a shelter for such reductions, while SDI is pursued on its present course. Even if these problems could be resolved, however, the chances of successfully navigating the long Phase II transition period would remain daunting. Given its inherent complexities and potential instabilities, it is questionable whether the mixed offense-defense arms control regime of the transition stage would prove negotiable or, if embarked upon, desirable.

Measuring Capabilities

An arms control regime in which defenses were being built up as offenses were reduced would create an unprecedented level of complexity in calculating and comparing the nuclear capabilities of the two superpowers. Both countries would have to be satisfied at each stage in the process that a rough equivalence was maintained, but the measurement of capabilities would be inherently subject to large uncertainties. Such uncertainties already plague efforts to assess the offensive strategic balance and have fueled extensive debate about the impact of existing arms control agreements on U.S. security.

The addition of defenses to the strategic equation would greatly compound the problem.

A key difficulty is the measurement and verification of ABM effectiveness. The impossibility of testing defensive systems under realistic attack conditions not only ensures that each country's defensive capability will be difficult to judge, but also injects a corresponding uncertainty into the assessment of the other's offensive strength. In these circumstances, the likelihood is that subjective, worst-case analysis would—even more than at present—distort estimates of the balance and obstruct agreement. Each superpower would tend to exaggerate the other's defensive capability while understating its own and would press to have any perceived ABM gap compensated for in the setting of offensive force levels.

This problem would be aggravated if, as is likely, the two countries were to deploy defenses with differing technological characteristics and target coverage. Unless one makes the implausible assumption that U.S. and Soviet defenses will have identical missions and capabilities and mature at the same rate, then the maintenance of strategic parity during the transition will probably be incompatible with the principle of equal offensive ceilings as embodied in the SALT II Treaty.[20] Any departure from that principle, however, invites a whole new level of controversy—not only between the superpowers but in the domestic U.S. arms control debate. (It is worth recalling the Senate debate over the SALT I agreement—which allowed the Soviets more ballistic missiles than the United States—and the resulting Jackson amendment requiring that any future agreement provide for equal ceilings.)

There is a converse problem as well. Existing asymmetries in the superpowers' offensive force structures mean that the deployment of equally capable defenses would have an unequal impact on their overall strategic capabilities. In particular, equal defenses would differentially affect—to the disadvantage of the United States—each country's retaliatory strength following an attack on its own nuclear forces by the other. For the United States, there would be a net loss in surviving and penetrating warheads, and for the Soviet Union a net gain. For the United States not to lose ground in this way, it would have to be granted roughly twice the defensive capability of the Soviet Union.[21] Again, however, departures from the principle of equality are likely to be extremely difficult to negotiate: it is hard to imagine an American demand for a two-to-one advantage in defenses—however legitimate from the perspective of a United States concerned about the erosion of its deterrent—bringing anything other than a summary Soviet rejection.

These problems are not inherently insurmountable, given sufficient political will and technical ingenuity. They are, however, inherently more difficult than the issues of strategic comparison associated with offensive arms control, as exemplified by the SALT agreements. In view of the bitter and unending controversy about the strategic impact and verifiability of these much more modest agreements (controversy to which the Reagan administration has been a key party), one cannot be sanguine about the prospects for negotiating the kind of regime envisioned for Phase II of the defensive transition.

Maintaining Stability

If, despite the odds, the superpowers were to negotiate an agreement and actually embark on the Phase II transition, an additional problem would arise that is potentially more serious than those discussed earlier. This is the strong possibility that the passage from an offense-dominated to a defense-dominated nuclear regime would be characterized by extreme instability.

The critical stage in the transition is the point at which the superpowers shift from a relationship of deterrence based on the certainty of retaliation to one in which retaliatory capabilities begin to be placed in doubt. As this cross-over point is approached, there is a danger that mutual first-strike capabilities would be increased. Defenses would not yet be capable of protecting either country against a full-scale attack by the other, but could be effective in coping with a retaliatory strike following a strike against the other's nuclear forces. In this interim period, "mutual assured destruction" would have been transcended, but "mutual assured survival" would still lie in the future. The superpowers would face a situation in which each could assure its survival at the expense of the other by attacking first. This would be the point of maximum risk in the defensive situation, and a far more dangerous situation than the current system of mutual deterrence. Crisis instability would be at its height: if a conflict were to appear imminent, there would be strong pressure on each country to launch its weapons first rather than risk being disarmed if the other did so.

Administration officials have acknowledged this risk of instability during the transition but have not indicated how the problem would be dealt with except that it would require close U.S.-Soviet cooperation. There is little indication that the United States has really come to grips with the implications of an arms control strategy that calls for the intentional erosion of mutual retaliatory capabilities (and thus of mutual deterrence) by the two superpowers. Focusing on the early stages of the transition, the administration has preferred to argue that deterrence would be strengthened, since defenses would add uncertainty to first strike calculations. Indeed,this function of defenses has been identified as a key to stability as the transition proceeds. For example, George Keyworth argued in 1984 that "while hardened military assets can be very successfully defended by these transition systems, civilian population centers will still be hostage to a determined adversary. . . . [This] is crucial to stability during those transition years because as long as there is some leakage in those transition defense technologies, there remains a retaliatory deterrent against first strike."[22]

This argument begs the whole question of how we get from here to there, however. After all, the end goal of the transition requires that retaliatory capabilities in effect whither away. There is no smooth transition from a system whose stability depends on the security and effectiveness of such forces to one in which societies are protected against them. The shift from one to the other cannot be finessed even by a gradual, phased introduction of defenses as offenses are reduced. At some point, the superpowers have to decide to take the leap into the unknown, voluntarily giving up their ability to inflict nuclear destruction on each other. Whether they would actually take that leap, or pull back in the face of it, is of course impossible to know in advance. The least that can be said, however, is that an unforeseeable political transformation of superpower relations would have to occur first.

It can be argued that this moment of truth will come only in the distant future, at the end of the transition period when highly effective population defenses are available, and that the solution need not be at hand now. But well before the crossover point is actually reached, the anticipation of it would begin to dominate the strategic calculations and perceptions of the superpowers. This tendency would be strengthened by uncertainty about the actual effectiveness of defenses at any given time and by the prevalance of worst-case assessment by both superpowers. In addition, the deep offensive reductions of Phase I, and their continuation in Phase II, would accelerate the approach of defense dominance (this being, of course, part of the rationale for such reductions). Accordingly, concerns about the adequacy of retaliatory forces—and concomitant fears of first-strike vulnerability—would be likely to appear early and be a persistent threat to stability during the transition period.

These concerns would place severe pressure on the close superpower cooperation needed to navigate the transition. Cooperation would be precarious at best and subject to collapse in the event of any rise in tensions between the two countries. At such times there could be strong incentives to gain a quick strategic advantage by rebuilding offensive forces—especially since the sensitive nuclear balance of the transition stage would be more subject to rapid and significant shifts than the present one. Breakout fears and temptations would be high in this system and could easily become self-fulfilling in a crisis or period of tension.

A breakdown of the transition in midstream, it should be stressed, would strand the superpowers in a much more dangerous relationship than if they had never embarked. Crisis instability would be very high. With defenses in place and offenses at low levels, the action-reaction process would assert itself with a vengeance and an all-out arms race would inevitably result. It would almost certainly prove impossible to reestablish the constraints of the ABM Treaty once defenses had been deployed on a large scale. The lesson here is that the superpowers would be most unwise to begin the defensive transition unless they were prepared to see it through.

The defense transition scheme falls apart under the weight of its own political and logical contradictions. In its effort to reconcile opposites, it resembles an arms control version of the administration's economic plan to cut taxes, raise defense spending, and balance the budget simultaneously. In the case of the defensive transition, however, the most likely outcome is that none of the purported goals of the policy will be achieved. Instead, that policy points to an early sacrifice of the ABM Treaty and an acceleration of the offensive arms race, without offering any assurance that effective population defenses will prove feasible.

Of course, to analyze the U.S. plan in this fashion may be to take it more seriously than the administration itself does. The incoherence of U.S. arms control policy reflects above all the administration's own ambivalence and divisions on this subject. In terms of practical policy, the SDI program is driven more by the quest for competitive advantage than by the vision of a cooperative transition. The best evidence of this policy is the arbitrary goal of reaching a feasibility decision early in the 1990s—a schedule that dictates the aggressive development of technology without regard for the integrity of the ABM Treaty or the evolution of the U.S.-Soviet political relationship necessary to support a joint transition.

A serious strategy to implement a defensive transition would reverse these priorities. The establishment of a political basis for cooperation would come first. As a part of this process, the ABM Treaty would have to be reaffirmed as a mutually valuable assurance against breakout, accomplished in part by closing loopholes and clarifying the limits of permissible research. SDI goals and schedules would have to be relaxed accordingly. In this context, Soviet agreement to offensive arms reductions could become a realistic prospect. Subsequently, ABM Treaty constraints could be reassessed periodically in light of political and technological developments. Conceivably, the superpowers might someday find it both feasible and desirable to cooperate in the shift to a defense-dominant relationship.

As this chapter has emphasized, such cooperation would be tantamount to a mutual agreement to allow basic deterrent capabilities to erode and ultimately disappear. The political conditions that would support this kind of agreement, and enable it to be implemented without a sharp decline in nuclear stability, are difficult to foresee. Ironically, however, if they did exist, radical arms reductions could be carried out in a straightforward fashion without the need for a defensive transition. This process would be substantially more controllable, calculable, verifiable, and stable than an attempt to phase in defensive systems as offenses are reduced.

There is no technological shortcut to the world SDI proponents claim to see on the other side of the defensive transition. When and if the superpowers are prepared to end the obsessive role that nuclear weapons play in their relationship, they can do so directly. Until then, missile defenses cannot force them to disarm against their will.

10
Is Star Wars Dead?

JOHN TIRMAN

What we have discovered in the three-plus years of the Star Wars program is similar to what we discovered in the preceding thirty years of research into ballistic missile defenses: the notion seems good, but in reality defenses are unpromising and probably destabilizing. The problem is not merely in the way the program is designed or managed. It is, rather, in the many intrinsic weaknesses that can be fatal to the system, or can be easily exploited by an adversary. At this point it seems highly unlikely that these weaknesses can be rectified, either because there are limits to technology or because advances in technology can be used by the Soviets almost as readily as they can be used by the United States. In addition, missile defenses cannot be reconciled with a commitment to strategic stability, relations with our European allies, and nuclear arms control.

The link between technology and strategic stability cannot be overemphasized. For the price we pay for the Strategic Defense Initiative's "progress" is immense. As the program proceeds toward large-scale demonstrations of technology, the ABM Treaty will be all the more in peril. At some crucial moment, many years before any space-based BMD system could possibly be considered deployable, the ABM Treaty will be abandoned as a result of another "reinterpretation" by U.S. officials or by Soviets wary of the SDI's continuation. At that moment—perhaps only a few years away—the arms control regime that has served U.S. security interests admirably will be moribund. The ABM Treaty will not only be in ruins, but any hopes for offensive nuclear limits will be dashed as well.

The collapse of negotiated limits on strategic weapons does not improve the chances for SDI's ultimate success. To the contrary, such a collapse will merely hasten the Soviets' development of offensive countermeasures (via new ICBMs and ASATs) and the deployment of their missile defenses. Indeed, the abandonment of SALT II ceilings on ICBMs will enable—even encourage—the Russians to create the variety of missiles and decoys needed to complicate a space BMD's mission. That is hardly a prescription for enhanced U.S. security.

It is important to realize, then, that arms control does not stand in the way of strategic defenses. What truly impedes Star Wars are its own inherent difficulties: its seemingly insoluble problems of battle management, software, and vulnerability; its inability to cope with unforeseeable threats; its mind-boggling economic costs; and its absolute failure to find a justifiable rationale.

The inescapable conclusion is that Star Wars is dead. Not only is the president's utopian goal impotent and obsolete, but so are the far less noble or ambitious objectives of the SDIO. For space-based defense simply is a loser. It cannot fulfill even the constricted goal of "enhancing deterrence" without stripping away many of the stable elements that the balance of power now maintains. It is, in this sense, "dead"—a lifeless and vacuous idea. Whoever is making policy in the 1990s will have to face up to the burgeoning costs, the rupture of stable relations with foe and friend alike, the drain of resources from other national needs, including military, and the poor technological prospects the SDI can truthfully offer. They will discover that the legacy of the 1980s is an empty promise of disarmament that is incurring huge costs in stability and in dollars and cents.

This mortal prognosis does not mean that SDI will simply fade away. The momentum already created, and the premature but nonetheless vocal commitment made to it by many politicians, ensures its survival as a military bureaucracy, if not as a viable concept. Some sort of terminal defense, like the

Safeguard system of more than a decade ago, might be deployed with space-based tracking elements. Such a result would at least save face for the members of Congress who voted the program tens of billions of dollars. The SDI might prove a useful bargaining tool for a future administration that returns to the sensible and popular view that if one wishes to eliminate the threat from ballistic missiles, the easiest and surest way is to eliminate ballistic missiles.

What is at stake, however, is not just the search for a graceful way to extract the nation from this embarrassing and wasteful venture, but to do so *before* it has wreaked havoc on arms control, superpower relations, the U.S. economy, and the other elements that historically have provided peace and prosperity.

A GRACEFUL EXIT?

Regardless of the SDI's poor prospects, it exists here and now. And that very existence threatens an immediate unraveling of the ABM Treaty. The first task, therefore, may be to preserve that accord while the administration continues its fitful research program. An additional incentive for an immediate plan is to seize upon the Soviet offer of deep cuts in strategic offenses. But how can these apparently contradictory impulses be reconciled at the negotiating table? Ambassador Jonathan Dean, who has more than a decade of experience negotiating directly with the Soviets, has offered a seven-point plan to extract a positive result from the apparent superpower stalemate.

The SDI issue could be handled by a U.S.-Soviet understanding agreed to at the Geneva negotiations or at a Reagan-Gorbachev summit. This understanding would depend on entry into effect of the companion agreement on reduction of strategic nuclear armaments. In this agreement the two countries would

1. Reaffirm the ABM Treaty as having continued value and validity for both countries.
2. Express continued willingness to adhere to the administration's present "narrow" interpretation of the treaty ban

against testing or deploying new sea-based, air-based, space-based or mobile land-based ABM systems or their components.

3. Agree explicitly that the ABM Treaty permits laboratory research on ballistic missile defense and ground testing of new BMD technology at the two test sites for each country designated in the agreement.

4. Update present definitions of ABM components to conform with modern technology in the areas of target acquisition and aiming, and delivery vehicles and weapons, which would eliminate the ambiguities—including those over radar arrays—that have caused existing compliance difficulties. Alternative approaches to updating definitions of components might be (*a*) to agree that neither space- nor ground-based technology will be tested in a way that destroys or damages objects in space and that space-based weapons will not be tested against targets on the ground; or (*b*) to agree that certain specified technologies will not be tested in space, including space-based directed-energy and kinetic energy weapons, and space-based beam-reflecting mirrors.

5. Agree that, unless this understanding is violated, neither country would exercise its right of withdrawal from the ABM Treaty for a period of ten years, which would also be the duration of a companion agreement on reduction of strategic nuclear weapons of the two countries.

6. Agree that, for the duration of this understanding, neither country would test in space or in the atmosphere ASAT weapons or weapons directed against targets on the ground.

7. Agree periodically to exchange information on missile defense research and to consult on whether there is mutual agreement to field test or to deploy specified types of defense systems beyond those now permitted by the ABM Treaty, either before the ten-year period expires or after its expiration.

This compromise approach would protect the U.S. government's desire to continue BMD research. If research succeeds, and there is Soviet agreement, it could provide a basis for orderly transition to the mixed system of defense and offensive weapons that the administration seeks. If the Soviet Union does not agree, the United States can consider withdrawing from the ABM Treaty after the ten-year period expires. If, as is probable, research does not succeed in developing BMD systems that are effective, survivable, and cost-effective, the improved ABM regime could continue and could be accompanied by further significant reductions of strategic nuclear weapons. As long as this understanding is an agreed interpretation of the ABM agreement or a statement of parallel action—that the United States will follow a certain course of action as long as the Soviet Union follows the same course—then there would be no need for a new treaty to be ratified by the U.S. Senate.

A "MORAL" ALTERNATIVE?

In one of his last interviews as the president's science adviser, George Keyworth made the often-repeated charge that the scientists who oppose Star Wars are tied to the status quo of mutual assured destruction—the implication being, of course, that these SDI skeptics are smugly comfortable with the 20,000 strategic warheads deployed by the superpowers. This thoroughly disingenous remark—yet another attempt to discredit critics—has the added intention of making the Star Wars idea the only alternative to the balance of terror. In depicting the opponents of SDI as being in *favor* of the present nuclear standoff, Star Wars supposedly looks more attractive by comparison.

There is, of course, an alternative. As Keyworth knows, the SDI is by no means the only way to extract ourselves from the precariousness of the current situation. The alternative is arms control—constraints on weapons technology that can be achieved through hard bargaining with the Soviet Union or, in some cases, by unilateral action. Negotiated arms control has, for the most part, an admirable record of achievement. The Partial Test Ban Treaty of 1963, the Outer Space Treaty of 1967, the Nuclear Non-Proliferation Treaty of 1970, the SALT I and II accords in the 1970s, and, of course, the ABM Treaty have all enhanced U.S. security. They were the product of sometimes strenuous and prolonged negotiations. But they were derived from the mutual perception that it is in the security interests of *both* superpowers to constrain, through diplomacy, these lethal technologies.

Arms control has been in disfavor in official circles in the 1980s, principally for two reasons. The first is that Soviet misbehavior on nonstrategic issues—the invasion of Afghanistan, for example, or its poor record on human rights—has damaged the arms control process. In this view, the Soviets should be "punished" for such misdeeds by the United States withholding participation from the bargaining table. Given the danger such aloofness inevitably produces, this attitude is most imprudent.

The second reason is that many regard the arms control process itself as suspect. It is seen as always favoring the Soviets. SALT I, for example, did not prevent the Soviets from a "rapid" buildup of highly capable ICBMs. And, of course, arms control may impede the United States from using its technological prowess to outrace the Soviets. It is undoubtedly true that the SALT process merely set ceilings on strategic arsenals. The much ballyhooed Soviet buildup of the 1970s, however, was done within the legal limits set by SALT I and, in fact, was done alongside a very assertive U.S. buildup. From 1965 to 1980 the Soviets increased their arsenal of strategic nuclear weapons from about 600 to 6,000. The United States, in the same period, increased its arsenal from 5,550 to 10,100 warheads and bombs. The rough equivalence the SALT process allowed was done in part to stabilize deterrence; for those Americans determined to maintain U.S. superiority, however, this doubling of the U.S. arsenal was tantamount to "unilateral disarmament."

Another lesson from this period is even more instructive for the Star Wars debate. In the first SALT negotiations, which began in 1969, there was the distinct possibility that constraints on the new technology of MIRV (multiple, independently targetable reentry vehicles) could be negotiated. The United States had this multiple-warhead technology; the Soviets did not. The new technique, in fact, had been developed to penetrate strategic defenses. The U.S. military and the arms control opponents argued heatedly to forego such limits: after all, why give up such an advantage? As a result, MIRVs were not constrained. By the mid-1970s, however, the Soviets had developed their own MIRVs and deployed them legally on their ICBMs. Suddenly, many of the same people who opposed the MIRV limit cried out against this new and menacing Soviet capability, since MIRVed missiles give an offense a more effective potential for a preemptive strike against military targets. The lesson is unambiguous: arms control—the elimination of MIRVs in this case—would have greatly enhanced U.S. security.

These simple truths are now being buried under an avalanche of fear of Soviet capabilities and the misrepresentation of what arms control can and cannot accomplish. Arms control is not a panacea, but its potential is demonstrably greater than an unrestricted arms race, whether those arms are offensive or defensive. And, ironically, our ability to verify the provisions of treaties is growing daily with better-quality satellites, imaging techniques, seismology, and so on. Verification, so often raised by the administration, without explanation, as a barrier to arms control, is in fact a more exact science than ever. No informed analyst would contend that verification is a real obstacle to meaningful bilateral agreements.

What are the specific alternatives to the offensive arms race *and* Star Wars? We know that constraining emerging technologies before they are tested and deployed is particularly important; thus, high on any rational agenda is an ASAT test ban. Similarly, a comprehensive ban on underground nuclear explosives could potentially curtail new kinds of nuclear weapons. The technology used to verify a nuclear test ban, moreover, has advanced very rapidly in recent years. And, of course, concrete reductions—indeed, deep cuts—in strategic and theater nuclear forces, so long elusive, now appear more urgent and more feasible than ever. Many detailed discussions of these possibilities have been published in the extensive literature on this topic; suffice it to say here that the critics of Star Wars are anything but satisfied with the status quo. Reductions, test bans, improvements in C^3, and measures for crisis stability—a very extensive range of proposals, beginning long ago, has been offered in many forums and through many channels.

A future administration will perhaps give Star Wars the unceremonious burial it deserves. Whether that is done before the Star Wars bureaucracy has made its mischief is not yet clear. The weak links of the concept and program will eventually break, but will the victim be the American people?

Notes

Chapter 1: The Politics of Star Wars

1. Panofsky quoted in George Alexander, "Scientists Split on Feasibility of Missile Plan, *Los Angeles Times* (March 25, 1983), p. 1. Administration official quoted in Lou Cannon, "President Seeks Futuristic Defense Against Missiles," *Washington Post* (March 24, 1983), p. 1. Southern newspaper: "Down-to-earth defense," *New Orleans Times-Picayune* (March 25, 1983).
2. Patrick E. Tyler, "Study Raps Laser Arms Funding Lag," *Washington Post* (March 27, 1983); Steven J. Marcus, "Corporate Push for Space Lasers," *New York Times* (April 24, 1983); Walter Pincus, "Anti-Missile Laser Plans Accelerated," *Washington Post* (August 27, 1983); Fred Hiatt, "Military Considers Unified Space Command," *Washington Post* (August 27, 1983); Walter Pincus, "Atom Weapons' Role in Space Discounted," *Washington Post* (October 15, 1983); Fred Hiatt, " 'Staggering' Costs Predicted," *Washington Post* (November 11, 1983).
3. Donald L. Hafner, "Assessing the President's Vision: The Fletcher, Miller, and Hoffman Panels," *Daedalus* (Spring 1985), p. 97.
4. The OTA and UCS studies came in for a lashing from the right-wing press and the military. The OTA report, authored by Ashton Carter, an MIT physicist at that time, was viciously attacked by Abrahamson's office. A critique was issued by SDIO, which was easily rebutted by Carter. In the process, however, OTA was forced to set up an independent review committee to assess Carter's work; the review upheld the original report. During the imbroglio, it was widely rumored that the Pentagon attempted to strip Carter of his security clearances, a type of censure that was

undoubtedly intended to discredit his work and cast aspersions on his loyalty—a tactic that has been repeated in other arenas of the SDI debate (see chap. 2).

The UCS draft report, which was headed by Kurt Gottfried, professor of physics at Cornell University, contained an erroneous assumption in its calculation of the number of chemical laser satellites required to shoot down the *present* Soviet ICBM force (one not employing countermeasures); in a technical appendix, a second error was made in calculating the weight of a space-based accelerator that might be used for particle beam weapons. These were two of several dozens of original calculations in the report and were publicly corrected one month after the draft report had been circulated in March. Some months later, in December, UCS was taken to task for the two mistakes in an article by Robert Jastrow in the right-wing monthly *Commentary*. Several likeminded columists—William Buckley, William Safire, et alia—repeated Jastrow's allegations, which included an attempt to discredit all of UCS's findings on space-based defense. The intellectual caliber of these attacks can be discerned from one of Buckley's many columns: the UCS study, he declared, "can only be compared with past findings by scientists that the world is flat, that bees cannot fly, [etc.]". Not included in the articles, of course, was the fact that the draft report (later published as part of *The Fallacy of Star Wars*) contained many optimistic assumptions about the weapon technologies, including perfect aiming, no "slew" time from one target to another, and so on, that presented these techniques in a very favorable light. The allegations, moreover, were repeated long after they had been fully refuted by the authors (*Commentary*, April 1985), which revealed the true objective of the columnists, which was to disparage the responsible critics of the president's program. Ironically, the two errors in the draft report were remarkably insignificant since both the chemical lasers and the particle beam weapons have been dropped from serious consideration as boost-phase weapons.

5. Schlesinger: Cited in Michael Weisskopf and David B. Ottaway, "SDI Director Defends Rise in Research Funds," *Washington Post* (March 20, 1985), p. A12. Abrahamson: Speech to the National Security Issues Symposium, Mitre Corporation, Bedford, Mass., October 24, 1984. The Wall Street analyst quoted is Phillip Brannon, vice president of Merrill Lynch, from a personal interview, January 1985.

For the business response to SDI, see John Tirman, "Boosting Star Wars," *Nucleus* (Winter 1985), pp. 2ff.; Malcome W. Browne,

" 'Star Wars' Science Expected to Spawn Peaceful Inventions," *New York Times* (April 2, 1985), p. C1; "Why Star Wars Is a Shot in the Arm for Corporate R&D," *Business Week* (April 8, 1985), pp. 77–78; Michael Weisskopf, "Conflict in 'Star Wars' Work Possible," *Washington Post* (April 30, 1985), p. A5; Tim Carrington, "Star Wars Plan Spurs Defense Firms to Vie For Billions in Orders," *Wall Street Journal* (May 21, 1985), pp. 1ff.; Fred Kaplan, " 'Star Wars' spending lagging, data show," *Boston Globe* (June 2, 1985), p. 1; Tina Rosenberg, "Adventures in Inner Space: How the Reagan Administration is Selling Star Wars," *Regardie's* (September 1985), pp. 95–107; William Hartung and Rosy Nimroody, "Cutting Up the Star Wars Pie," *The Nation* (September 14, 1985), pp. 200–202, which is derived from the study *The Strategic Defense Initiative: Costs, Contractors, and Consequences* (New York: Council on Economic Priorities, 1985); Fred Hiatt and Rick Atkinson, "In Strategic Defense, the Seeds of a New Industry Are Planted," *Washington Post* (October 20, 1985), pp. A1ff, among others.

For the aerospace industry's influence on Congress, see Gordon Adams's definitive, empirical work, *The Politics of Defense Contracting: The Iron Triangle* (New Brunswick, N.J.: Transaction Books, 1982).

6. James Schlesinger, speech to the National Security Issues Symposium, Mitre Corporation, Bedford, Mass., October 25, 1984.
7. The poll showed remarkably pervasive skepticism among U.S. physicists. See Peter D. Hart Research Associates," A Survey of Physicists' Attitudes Toward the Strategic Defense Initiative" (March 1986); the results were reprinted in *Nucleus* (Summer 1986), or are available from the Union of Concerned Scientists, 26 Church St., Cambridge, Mass. 02238.
8. *Washington Post* (June 22, 1985), p. A3.
9. William Broad, "Science Showmanship: A Deep 'Star Wars' Rift," *New York Times* (December 16, 1985), pp. A1ff.; Abrahamson press conference quotation, Fred Kaplan, "Director Reports Steady Progress in Space-Based Weapons Program," *Boston Globe* (November 27, 1985), p. 3.
10. The section on the X-ray laser draws from several sources, including: William J. Broad, "Gains Reported on Use of Laser for Space Arms," *New York Times* (May 15, 1985), p. A1; R. Jeffrey Smith, "Experts Cast Doubts on X-ray Laser," *Science* (November 8, 1985), pp. 646–48; Robert Scheer, "Scientists Dispute Test of X-Ray Laser Weapon," *Los Angeles Times* (November 12, 1985), p. 1; R. Jeffrey Smith, "Lab Officials Squabble Over X-ray Laser,"

Science (November 22, 1985), p. 923; idem, "Livermore Acknowledges X-Ray Laser Problem," *Science* (November 29, 1985), p. 1023; William J. Broad, "Science Showmanship: A Deep 'Star Wars' Rift," *New York Times* (December 16, 1985), p. A1; Boyce Rensberger, "H-Bomb Blast Planned To Test 'Star Wars' Idea," *Washington Post* (December 20, 1985), p. A3; William J. Broad, "U.S. Tests Nuclear-Powered Laser Despite Objections from Congress," *New York Times* (December 29, 1985), p. 23; R. Jeffrey Smith, "X-Ray Laser Budget Grows as Public Information Declines," *Science* (April 11, 1986), pp. 152–53. The author also conducted personal interviews with subjects wishing to remain anonymous. See also William J. Broad, *Star Warriors* (New York: Simon and Schuster, 1985), an excellent treatment of the Livermore lab scientists working on the X-ray laser.

11. Douglas Waller, James Bruce, and Douglas Cook, "SDI: Progress and Challenges," Staff Report submitted to Sens. William Proxmire, J. Bennett Johnston, and Lawton Chiles (March 17, 1986), typescript, p. 22.
12. Ibid., p. 51.
13. Hafner, "Assessing the President's Vision," p. 95.
14. Sayre Stevens, "The Soviet BMD Program," in A. Carter and D. Schwartz, eds., *Ballistic Missile Defense* (Washington, D.C.: Brookings Institution, 1984), p. 189.
15. Department of State, "Soviet Strategic Defense Programs" (1985), pp. 12–13.
16. Stevens, "Soviet BMD Program," p. 215. Herbert F. York, "Strategic Defense from World War II to the Present," Paper presented to the conference "SDI and NATO," University of California, San Diego (May 4–6, 1986), typescript (draft), p. 13.
17. Robert M. Gates and Larry K. Gershwin, "Soviet Strategic Force Developments," Testimony before a joint session of the Subcommittee on Strategic and Theater Nuclear Forces, Armed Services Committee, and the Defense Subcommittee, Committee on Appropriations, U.S. Senate, 99th Cong., 1st sess. (June 26, 1985), typescript, p. 5. Gates is the deputy director for intelligence of the CIA; Gershwin is national intelligence officer of the National Intelligence Council.
18. For explanations, see E. P. Thompson, ed., *Star Wars: Science-Fiction Fantasy or Serious Probability?* (New York: Pantheon, 1986), pp. 51–67; and Statement by the U.S. Secretary of Defense, Research and Engineering, *The FY 1987 DOD Program for Research and Development*, 99th Cong., 2d sess. (February 18, 1986), p. II-11.

19. As Sayre Stevens points out: "The Soviet Union continues to fear the consequences of turning U.S. technology loose and probably finds the ABM Treaty desirable as a means of constraining the application of U.S. prowess to BMD." "Soviet BMD Program," p. 217.

    The question of strategic stability, which will be addressed repeatedly thoughout the book, is uppermost in Soviet minds as well. For example, the most detailed report on SDI to come from Soviet scientists concluded: "If a space-based BMD system is vulnerable to destruction, then it cannot provide effective defense against a first strike, since the attacking side will be able to destroy the system. But such a system might give rise to the illusion that it could provide a relatively effective defense against a strategic force that had already been weakened by attack. Its deployment would therefore be seen by the other side as a very threatening move. Under these circumstances, each side—both that which had a BMD system and that which did not—would have an incentive to strike first. The net effect of deploying a BMD system would not be to provide escape from mutual deterrence, but rather to make the relationship less stable." David Holloway, "The SDI and the Soviet Union," *Daedalus* (Summer 1985), p. 267. The explanation of the Soviet report is in Holloway's words.

20. Stephen M. Meyer, "Soviet Strategic Programmes and the US SDI," *Survival* (Nov. /Dec. 1985), p. 285. Meyer is a professor at MIT and widely recognized as a leading expert on the Soviet military.

21. Ibid. Meyer speculates (p. 289) that one of the results of this effort may be a boon to the USSR: "the mobilizing vehicle for a new industrial revolution in the USSR. Much like Stalin used preparation for war in the 1930s to develop Soviet heavy industry, the SDI challenge could become the foil for the Soviet leadership to reorient the Soviet industrial economy"—an ironic result for the Reagan administration, which has sometimes depicted SDI as a way to bankrupt the Soviets.

    See also Holloway, who writes: "The Soviet Union may well feel impelled, as it has so often in the past, to try to match the United States program. The heavy stress that the Soviet leaders lay on parity in their strategic relationship with the United States will push them in this direction." "SDI and the Soviet Union," p. 272.

22. Documents are cited in Paul B. Stares, *The Militarization of Space: U.S. Policy, 1945–84* (Ithaca, N.Y.: Cornell University Press,

1985), pp. 218–19. See also, Fred Hiatt, "Air Force Manual Seeks Space Superiority," *Washington Post* (January 15, 1985), p. A13.

23. George Ball, "The War for Star Wars," *New York Review of Books* (April 11, 1985), pp. 38ff.

Chapter 2: Scientists and Star Wars

1. Alex Beam, "Star Wars Divides a Campus," *Business Week* (March 10, 1986), p. 82.
2. "Senators and Scientists Object to SDI Costs and Uncertainties," *Physics Today* (July 1985), p. 57.
3. David Parnas, quoted in "Star Wars Research Not Up to Scratch?" *Nature* (December 12, 1985), p. 497.
4. Jack Ruina, "SDI: Peer Pressure and Politics on Campus," *Technology Review* (February–March 1986), p. 13.
5. "Senators and Scientists Object," pp. 55–56.
6. Philip J. Klass, "SDI Office Pushes Innovative Science, Technology Research," *Aviation Week & Space Technology* (April 29, 1985), p. 227.
7. R. Jeffrey Smith, "Star Wars Grants Attract Universities," *Science* (April 19, 1985), p. 304.
8. David E. Sanger, "Campuses' Role in Arms Debated as 'Star Wars' Funds Are Sought," *New York Times* (July 22, 1985), p. A1.
9. Smith, "Star Wars Grants," p. 304.
10. Memo cited in "SDIO Discusses Research Disclosure Policy," *Aviation Week & Space Technology* (August 26, 1985), p. 59. Prepublication review option not imposed retroactively: see Colin Norman, "Memo Sets Policy for 'Star Wars' Publications," *Science* (August 30, 1985), p. 843.
11. "Senators and Scientists Object," p. 56.
12. Personal interview with Kenneth A. Smith, April 17, 1986. Additional Smith quotations are from this interview.
13. Telephone interview with Sheldon Krimsky, April 16, 1986. Additional Krimsky quotations are from this interview.
14. Colin Norman, "Pentagon Seeks to Build Bridges to Academe," *Science* (April 19, 1985), p. 303; idem, "Security Problems Plague Scientific Meeting," *Science* (April 26, 1985), p. 471; Philip M. Boffey, "U.S. Relaxes Scientific Data Policy," *New York Times* (September 28, 1985), p. 7.
15. Keith B. Richburg, "U.S. Finds Plenty of Takers for 'Star Wars' Study Funds," *Washington Post* (October 18, 1985), p. A34.
16. On military R&D as a percentage of total federal R&D: Vera Kistiakowsky, "Should University Researchers Accept SDI Funding?" *Technology Review* (January 1986), p. 10; Civilian R&D as a

Percentage of GNP: Sen. John Kerry, "U.S. Science and Technology" (letter), *Science* (February 28, 1986), p. 907.

17. William Hartung and Rosy Nimroody, *Star Wars: Pentagon Invades Academia* (New York: Council on Economic Priorities), table 2.
18. On basic science percentages: Sanger, "Campuses' Role"; U.S. Congress, Office of Technology Assessment, *Ballistic Missile Defense Technologies* (Washington, D.C.: Government Printing Office, 1985), pp. 292–93. On AI programs: Jonathan B. Tucker, "The Strategic Computer Initiative: A Double-Edged Sword," *Science for the People* (March–April 1985), p. 22.
19. Personal interview with Vera Kistiakowsky, March 12, 1986. Additional Kistiakowsky quotations are from this interview.
20. Personal interview with Frank Perkins, March 26, 1986. Additional Perkins quotations are from this interview.
21. SDIO/IST, "Strategic Defense Initiative Organization, Innovative Science and Technology Office" (29-page typed prospectus), March 1985, p. 9.
22. Lester C. Thurow, "The Economic Case against Star Wars," *Technology Review* (February–March 1986), p. 11; "Will Star Wars Reward or Retard Science?" *Economist* (September 7, 1985), p. 95.
23. "No Pigs in Pokes" (editorial), *Nature* (December 12, 1985), p. 496.
24. Thomas Roach quotation, cited in Keith B. Richburg, "U.S. Finds Takers"; Paul E. Gray, "Star Wars and the University," *MIT Report* (December 1985), p. 3.
25. Personal interview with Fran Bagenal, March 20, 1986. Additional Bagenal quotations are from this interview.
26. Lisbeth Gronlund, John Kogut, Michael Weissman, and David Wright, "A Status Report on the Boycott of Star Wars Research by Academic Scientists and Engineers," May 13, 1986.
27. Ruina, "SDI," p. 13; Sidney Hook, "Unacademic Campus Tactics," *New York Times* (October 3, 1985).
28. Colin Norman, "Lab Chief's Memo Stirs Unease at Illinois," *Science* (August 16, 1985), p. 634; R. Jeffrey Smith, "Hicks Attacks SDI Critics," *Science* (April 25, 1986), p. 444.
29. Telephone interview with John Kogut, April 16, 1986. Additional Kogut quotations are from this interview.
30. Jacques Ellul, *The Technological Society*, trans. John Wilkinson (New York: Alfred A. Knopf, 1964), pp. 313, 317, 318.

Chapter 3: Command and Control for SDI

1. Martin Van Creveld, *Command in War* (Cambridge: Harvard University Press, 1985), pp. 268–75.
2. Paul Bracken, *The Command and Control of Nuclear Forces* (New Haven, Conn.: Yale University Press, 1983), p. 55.
3. Iver Peterson, "U.S. Activates Unit for Space Defense," *New York Times* (August 24, 1985), p. A28.
4. John Steinbruner, "Launch under Attack," *Scientific American* (January 1984), p. 43.
5. Michael D. Wallace, Brian L. Crissey, and Linn I. Sennot, "Accidental Nuclear War: A Risk Assessment," draft (February 1985), table 1.
6. For both examples see Bracken, *Command and Control*, pp. 54–55.
7. Desmond Ball, "Can Nuclear War Be Controlled?" *Adelphi Papers* (no. 169), p. 36.
8. Bracken, *Command and Control*, p. 118.
9. Ball, "Can Nuclear War Be Controlled?", p. 36.
10. See for instance John Steinbruner, "Nuclear Decapitation," *Foreign Policy* (Winter 1981–82), pp. 16–28.
11. For both examples see Bracken, *Command and Control*, pp. 54–55.
12. Charles Perrow, "Normal Accident at Three Mile Island," *Transaction: Social Science and Modern Society* (July–August 1981), p. 17.
13. See Bracken, *Command and Control*, pp. 58–59.
14. For a further explanation of this see ibid., p. 68.
15. Federation of American Scientists, "The Emperor's Newest Clothing: Changes to the SDI as a Result of Phase-I Architecture Studies," *News from F.A.S.* (February 16, 1986), p. 10.
16. "Senate Report Draws SDIO Fire," *Military Space* (April 14, 1986), p. 2.
17. B. Waller, J. Bruce, and D. Cook, *SDI: Progress and Challenges*, Report submitted to Senators Proxmire, Johnston, and Lawton (March 17, 1986), p. 2.
18. Eastport Study Group, *Summer Study 1985: A Report to the Director, Strategic Defense Initiative Organization* (December 1985), p. 11.
19. J. C. Fletcher, study chairman; B. McMillan, panel chairman, *Report of the Study on Eliminating the Threat Posed by Nuclear Ballistic Missiles, vol. 5: Battle Management, Communications, and Data Processing*, Department of Defense (Washington, D.C.: Government Printing Office, 1984), p. 7.
20. Waller et al., *SDI*, p. 40.
21. Quoted in John A. Adam and Paul Wallich, "Mind-Boggling Complexity," *IEEE Spectrum* (September 1985), p. 44.

22. Sean K. Collins, "Preferential Boost Phase Defense," *National Defense* (December 1985), p. 36.
23. Adams and Wallich, "Mind-Boggling Complexity," p. 44.
24. Quoted in ibid.
25. See Philip M. Boffey, "Dark Side of 'Star Wars': System Could Also Attack," *New York Times* (March 7, 1985), p. A24.
26. Richard Halloran, "U.S. Studies Plan to Integrate Nuclear Arms With a Missile Shield," *New York Times* (May 29, 1985), p. A8.

Chapter 4: Could We Trust the SDI Software?

1. J.C. Fletcher, study chairman, B. McMillan, panel chairman, *Report of the Study on Eliminating the Threat Posed by Nuclear Ballistic Missiles, vol. 5: Battle Management, Communications, and Data Processing*, Department of Defense (Washington, D.C.: Government Printing Office, 1984), p. 4.
2. Eastport Study Group, "Summer Study 1985: A Report to the Director, Strategic Defense Initiative Organization" (December 1985); D. L. Parnas, "Software Aspects of Strategic Defense Systems," *American Scientist* (September–October 1985), pp. 432–40; W. Myers, "The Star Wars Software Debate," *Bulletin of the Atomic Scientists* (February 1986).

   An interesting indication of the controversy can be found in "Star Wars: Can the Computing Requirements be Met?" Transcript of a debate held on October 21, 1985 at MIT. Available from Computer Professionals for Social Responsibility, P.O. Box 717, Palo Alto, Calif. 94301.
3. L. J. Gawron, "System Error Control," *Bell Labs Technical Journal* (Special Supplement, 1975), pp. S127, S129.
4. "USAF Plans SDI BM/C3 Work" *Military Space* (July 22, 1985), p. 2.
5. On the difficulty of a software project being more than proportional to its size, see B. W. Boehm, *Software Engineering Economics* (Englewood Cliffs, N.J.: Prentice-Hall, 1981); and H. Lin, "The Development of Software for Ballistic Missile Defense," *Scientific American* (December 1985). Regarding the differing complexity for the same size program, see F. P. Brooks, Jr., *The Mythical Man-Month: Essays on Software Engineering* (Reading, Mass.: Addison-Wesley, 1975).
6. C. A. Zraket, "Strategic Defense: A Systems Perspective," *Daedalus* (Spring 1985), pp. 109–26.
7. Quoted in Myers, "Software Debate," p. 35.
8. Eastport Study Group, "Report to the Director," p. 23.
9. J. C. Knight and N. G. Leveson, "An Experimental Evaluation of the Assumption of Independence in Multiversion Programming,"

IEEE Transactions on Software Engineering (January 1986), pp. 96–109.

10. Lin, "Development of Software," p. 49.
11. William J. Broad, *Star Warriors* (New York: Simon and Schuster, 1985), p. 137; J. Fallows, *National Defense* (New York: Vintage Books, 1982), p. 149.
12. C. A. R. Hoare, "Turing Award Lecture," *Communications of the ACM* (February 1981).

Chapter 5: The ASAT-SDI Link

1. Michael Getler, "Science Adviser Sees Lasers and Mirrors As a Missile Defense," *Washington Post* (March 26, 1986), p. 8.
2. Paul B. Stares, *The Militarization of Space: U.S. Policy, 1945–84* (Ithaca, N.Y.: Cornell University Press, 1985), p. 106. Stares's excellent history is used for this section on the early ASAT programs. Also see U.S. Congress, Office of Technology Assessment, *Ballistic Missile Defense Technologies* (Washington, D.C.: Government Printing Office, 1985), pp. 45–66; and its companion volume, *Anti-Satellite Weapons, Countermeasures, and Arms Control.*
3. Ashton Carter, "Satellites and Anti-Satellites: Limits of the Possible," draft, pp. 39–40 (subsequently published in *International Security*, Spring 1986); Colin Gray, *American Military Space Policy: Information Systems, Weapons Systems, and Arms Control* (Cambridge, Mass.: Abt Books, 1982), p. 69.

   This assessment of space mines is almost universally held. For example, the OTA report cited earlier states: "There appears to be no relatively economical means of protecting large satellites against a surprise attack by such mines." *Antisatellite Weapons, Countermeasures, and Arms Control*, p. 65.
4. On the Soviet ASAT, see U.S. Department of Defense, *Soviet Miltiary Power, 1984* (Washington, D.C.: Government Printing Office, 1984), p. 36. Abrahamson's comment: "Statement on the Strategic Defense Initiative," Subcommittee on Research and Development, Committee on Armed Services, House of Representatives, 99th Cong., 2d sess. (March 4, 1986), p. 10.
5. Cited in William Broad, *Star Warriors* (New York: Simon and Schuster, 1985), pp. 162ff.
6. Donald Lambertson, Testimony before the Senate Armed Services Committee, 98th Cong., 1st sess. (March 23, 1983), *Hearings, Fiscal Year 1984*, pt. 2, p. 2647. Robert Cooper, Testimony before the Committee on Appropriations, U.S. Senate, 97th Cong., 2d sess. (April 28, 1982), *Hearings, Fiscal Year 1983*, pt. 2, pp. 347–84.

7. Hans Bethe and Richard Garwin, "Appendix A: New BMD Technologies," *Daedalus* (Summer 1985), pp. 360–61. Useful discussions of ASAT and BMD technologies are also found in both volumes of the OTA report.
8. D. Waller, J. Bruce, and D. Cook, "SDI: Progress and Challenges," Staff Report Submitted to Sens. Proxmire, Johnston, and Chiles (March 17, 1986), pp. 40, 43. See also "SDI Survivability: 'We're Not There Yet,' " *Military Space* (November 11, 1985); and Michael May, "Safeguarding Our Military Space Systems," *Science* (April 18, 1986), pp. 336–40.
9. "In Focus," *Air Force Magazine* (June 1985), p. 32.
10. The paper reportedly was authored by Lowell Wood and Roderick Hyde. See *Military Space* (Dec. 10, 1984), p. 3.
11. Ashton Carter, "The Relationship of ASAT and BMD Systems," *Daedalus* (Spring 1985), p. 188.
12. Richard Garwin, Kurt Gottfried, and Donald Hafner, "Antisatellite Weapons," *Scientific American* (June 1984), pp. 51–52. They cite Adm. Noel Gayler's argument that other means are available to counter satellites, and that it is a poor bargain for the United States to legitimize ASATs on both sides in order for the United States to be able to threaten the Soviet satellites used for hostile non-nuclear conflicts. Also see *The Fallacy of Star Wars*, pt. 3, for a complete discussion of these issues. There is virtually no disagreement with the proposition that the United States is more dependent on satellites than is the USSR.

Chapter 6: The Soviet Response

1. General Abrahamson, in testimony before a House Armed Services Subcommittee on March 4, 1986, acknowledged that the Soviets could launch a "threat cloud . . . of frightening proportions," which would include chaff, decoys, balloons, and other countermeasures. In the same testimony, however, he dismissed fast-burn boosters. See Fred Hiatt, "SDI Chief Says Soviet Decoys Pose Missile Shield Challenge," *Washington Post* (March 5, 1986). Hiatt writes: " 'I have to say, I'm frankly a little bored with some of the superficial criticism that still is going on,' [Abrahamson] said, citing specifically those who say that fast-burning Soviet rockets could escape detection or destruction by leaving the atmosphere quickly. 'We have left all of that so far behind," he said, without explanation."

   The same month, contractors and other scientists actually working on the fast-burn booster (FBB) had a decisively different opinion about it, as reported in the industry newsletter *SDI Monitor* (March 1986), pp. 8–9. The evidence cited by the report includes a classified Defense Intelligence Agency study leaked to the *Boston Globe* stating that the Soviets are capable of building FBBs by 1993. Also, analysts in the Defense Department cite the twenty-year-old Sprint technology that was reconfigured in assessments by a DOD "red team" (and that included confirmation by several aerospace firms) to serve as effective FBBs against space-based lasers. Finally, Rex Finke of the Institute for Defense Analysis stated that FBBs need not suffer significant payload penalties, and may in other respects be more efficient than currently deployed missiles. Said Finke: "We need a closer look at such countermeasures and responses to them. . . . We could find some unexpected cost tradeoffs. SDIO needs a system model for such trades. But that's not been encouraged, since some people feel that an uncontrolled analysis might come out against SDI. Such a model might surface such minimum-cost countermeasures."

2. Martin Marietta, "Laser Shielding of Soviet ICBMs—Performance Implications" (undated); described by R. L. Garwin, *Physics Today* (July, 1986).
3. The study was cited in "Visions of Star Wars," a combined broadcast of *Nova* and *Frontline*, produced by WGBH-TV, Boston, April 22, 1986.
4. Each meter-per-second velocity error would cause the warhead to miss its target by some 6 km; a miss distance larger than 0.2 km would reduce the warhead's effectiveness against a hardened silo. Hence one would need to correct the staging (or "tipoff") error to a tolerable error of 0.02 m/second for the landing accuracy desired against hard targets.
5. Of the entire atmosphere, only 1.6 millionths lies above 90-km altitude. One might imagine that the sleek warhead and decoys need spend only 1.6 millionth as much energy in penetrating this thin layer as in ploughing through the entire atmosphere at constant speed; this would be true, for instance, for the 1% of the atmosphere above 30 km. But at 90 km altitude the sleek shape no longer helps to reduce the drag, as the molecules of air freely collide with and reemerge from the surface. The 4 m/second speed loss and the 35 grams of fuel are about 20 times higher than would be estimated if the sleek cone worked in the rarefied gas as it does in denser gas. In actuality, not all streamlining is lost at 90 km; one can estimate that a drag-makeup engine on each decoy could compensate air drag by burning a total 20g of fuel for each decoy and the RV. A 100g allowance for rocket engine and its fuel is not a great burden on a decoy weighing 1700g. Instead of "drag-makeup engines" on each decoy, the designer may choose to put a larger drag-simulating engine on the single warhead, which will

have to burn as much as 700 grams of fuel in 4 seconds to make the warhead seem as light as a decoy. Naturally, the decoys would have a range of masses so that the precisely slowed warhead (to maintain impact accuracy) need not match exactly the slowing of a decoy.

6. Although it may not please the advocates of infrared homing technology, a better approach to midcourse intercept would be to have the system that actually detects reentry vehicles and discriminates from decoys (if such exist) then uses a low-power laser designator to designate the reentry vehicle assigned to a particular kinetic kill vehicle (KKV). Each KKV would be assigned a particular time and pattern "code" so that it would attack its designated target and none other. This laser target designation, of course, has been practiced since 1967 for laser-guided bombs. The benefit is that the KKV need have no infrared detector, would not be confused by stellar background, and so forth. One difficulty is that the designating system must survive and coordinate with the KKV throughout the flight of the KKV, thus presumably earning the criticism of the SDI computing panel.
7. Although much is made of the technological desirability and benefit of rail guns, that would propel a homing kill vehicle by the magnetic field between the two rails, it is clear that normal multistage rocket propulsion is cheaper and preferable at least up to added speed of 16 km/second. Of fifteen propositions agreed on May 23, 1985, between the author and E. T. Gerry, head of boost-phase systems for the Fletcher panel, the fifth reads, "The energy efficiency considerations favor chemically propelled homing kill vehicles over rail guns up to an added velocity implied by the following equation. . . . under assumptions of an electrical generation efficiency of 30%, rail gun efficiency of 30%, chemical rocket specific impulse of 300 seconds and stage-mass fraction of 90%, this velocity is approximately 16 km/second."
8. See, for example, Z. Brzezinski, R. Jastrow, and M. Kampelman "Defense in Space Is Not 'Star Wars,' " *New York Times Magazine* (January 28, 1985), pp. 28ff. Brzezinski was national security adviser to President Carter, Jastrow is professor of earth sciences at Dartmouth College, and Kampelman is the U.S. negotiator at the strategic arms talks in Geneva. They propose a boost-phase layer consisting of 100 satellites carrying 150 interceptors each, plus 4 geosynchronous satellites and 10 low-orbit satellites for tracking, etc. A second terminal layer, including 5,000 interceptors and 10 aircraft for tracking, would complete the two-tier defense. The price for the boost-phase layer, they estimate, would be $45 billion; for the terminal defense, an additional $15 billion.
9. This point is discussed in R. L. Garwin, "Enforcing Ballistic

Missile Defense against a Determined Adversary," Paper presented at the Stockholm International Peach Research Institute, July 5–7, 1985.

Chapter 7: Limited Defense

1. See, for example, William J. Broad, "Reduced Goal Set on Reagan's Plan for Space Defense," *New York Times* (December 23, 1984), p. 1; David B. Ottaway, " 'Star Wars' Project May be Slowed: Researchers Consider 2-Generation Plan," *Washington Post* (May 12, 1985), p. 1; and Fred Hiatt, "New SDI Scenario: Several 'Generations' of Weapons in Space," *Washington Post* (May 4, 1986), p. 12.
2. Department of Defense, *Report to Congress on the Strategic Defense Initiative* (Washington, D.C.: Government Printing Office, 1985), p. 20.
3. James Fletcher (letter), *Issues in Science and Technology* (Spring 1985), pp. 15–16.
4. See John Pike, "The Emperor's Newest Clothing: Changes to the SDI as a Result of Phase I Architecture Studies," Federation of American Scientists, Feb. 16, 1986. Even this first generation SDI, it should be stressed, is far from being demonstrated as feasible. Major problems remain, especially discrimination of warheads and decoys in midcourse and in the upper atmosphere, and susceptibility to precursor nuclear explosions and other Soviet countermeasures. For a general discussion of overlay defenses, see Ashton Carter, "BMD Applications," in Ashton Carter and David Schwartz, eds., *Ballistic Missile Defense* (Washington, D.C.: Brookings Institution, 1984), pp. 128–37.
5. Fred Hiatt, "SDI Chief Says Soviet Decoys Pose Missile-Shield Challenge," *Washington Post* (March 5, 1986), p. 1. Abrahamson suggested that an initial deployment of one hundred of these interceptors could be installed within the constraints of the ABM treaty. However, full testing and deployment of the range of first-generation SDI technologies now under development would violate numerous treaty restrictions, including those prohibiting territorial defense, mobile and air-based sensors, and multiple warhead interceptors (which is the likely deployment mode for ERIS). An effective terminal defense layer could require deployment of thousands of exoatmospheric, and perhaps tens of thousands of endoatmospheric interceptors.
6. See Sayre Stevens, "The Soviet BMD Program," in Carter and Schwartz, *Ballistic Missile Defense*, pp. 182ff.
7. The following discussion draws from Peter A. Clausen, "SDI in Search of a Mission," *World Policy Journal* (Spring 1985).

8. *Report of the President's Commission on Strategic Forces*, April 1983, pp. 8–9. Moreover, given the many operational uncertainties involved in an actual countersilo attack, the vulnerability of land-based missiles in practice may be considerably less than indicated by abstract calculations. See Matthew Bunn and Kosta Tsipis, "The Uncertainties of a Preemptive Nuclear Attack," *Scientific American* (November 1983).
9. This view is expressed with particular vigor in Z. Brzezinski, R. Jastrow, and M. Kampelman, "Defense in Space Is Not 'Star Wars,' " *New York Times Magazine* (January 27, 1985).
10. See Jack Kalish, "The Technologies of Hard-Site Defense," *Issues in Science and Technology* (Winter 1986), p. 122.
11. See Coit D. Blacker, "Defending Missiles, Not People," *Issues in Science and Technology* (Fall 1985).
12. Fred S. Hoffman, study director, *Ballistic Missile Defense and U.S. National Security: Summary Report*, Future Security Strategy Study (1983), pp. 10–11.

Chapter 9: Arms Control and SDI

1. Paul Nitze, "On the Road to a More Stable Peace," *Current Policy*, U.S. Department of State, Bureau of Public Affairs (February 20, 1985), p. 2.
2. *U.S. News and World Report* (March 18, 1985), p. 26, cited in U.S. Congress, Office of Technology Assessment, *Ballistic Missile Defense Technologies* (Washington, D.C.: Government Printing Office, 1985), p. 133.
3. Paul Nitze, "The Nuclear and Space Arms Talks: Where We Are after the Summit," *Current Policy* (December 1985), p. 3.
4. Nitze, "A More Stable Peace."
5. Cited in Walter Pincus, "Weinberger Urges Buildup Over Soviet 'Violations,' " *Washington Post* (November 11, 1985), p. 1. Also in sharp contrast to official rhetoric about a defensive transition are Pentagon plans for adapting U.S. nuclear war-fighting doctrine to a mixed offense-defense strategic environment. See Richard Halloran, "U.S. Studies Plan to Integrate Nuclear Arms With a Missile Shield," *New York Times* (May 29, 1985), p. A8; and Fred Hiatt, "Air Force Manual Seeks Space Superiority," *Washington Post* (January 15, 1985), p. 13. The assumption of ongoing superpower rivalry, and the probable offensive weapons applications of many SDI technologies, have produced strong skepticism in the defense community toward technology sharing with the Soviets. See David E. Sanger, "Many Hesitant to Share 'Star Wars,' " *New York Times* (November 30, 1985), p. 3.

6. Department of State, Bureau of Public Affairs, "The Strategic Defense Initiative," *Special Report* (June 1985), pp. 1–2. This report is the unclassified version of National Security Decision Document 172, the official statement of administration SDI policy.
7. See Stephen Meyer, "Soviet Views on SDI," *Survival* (November–December 1985), pp. 274–92.
8. Douglas Waller, James Bruce, and Douglas Cook, "SDI: Prospects and Challenges," Staff Report submitted to Sens. Proxmire, Johnston, and Chiles (March 17, 1986), p. 61.
9. Cited in James Fletcher, "The Technologies for Ballistic Missile Defense," *Issues in Science and Technology* (Fall 1984), p. 25. Elaborating on this point, Fletcher states that "if the Soviet Union agreed to reduce its force of intercontinental ballistic missiles, then an effective missile defense would be less expensive and would pose fewer technical challenges." Ibid, pp. 25–26.
10. Fred Hoffman, study director, *Ballistic Missile Defenses and U.S. National Security, Summary Report* (1983), p. 8, emphasis added. On the administration's tendency to invert this point by portraying SDI as a catalyst to arms control, see Donald L. Hafner, "Assessing the President's Vision," in "Weapons in Space," *Daedalus* (Spring 1985), p. 102.
11. See, for example, Walter Pincus, "Panel Told 'Star Wars' May Spark Increase in Soviet Offensive Forces," *Washington Post* (February 22, 1985), p. A24; and Walter Pincus, "Rise in Soviet Missiles Likely," *Washington Post* (April 23, 1985), p. A10.
12. Hoffman, *Ballistic Missile Defenses*, p. 11.
13. Walter Pincus, "SDI Expected to Require Changes in 1972 Treaty," *Washington Post* (November 18, 1985), p. A1. Nitze has said it will take "at least 10 years" to determine SDI feasibility and before U.S. would be prepared to "negotiate ways and means such a system could be introduced." Walter Pincus, "Decade of Study Seen for 'Star Wars,' " *Washington Post* (April 27, 1985), p. A10.
14. Department of Defense, *Report to the Congress on the Strategic Defense Initiative* (Washington, D.C.: Government Printing Office, 1985), Appendix B. For a critique of this report, see Abram Chayes, Antonia Chayes, and Eliot Spitzer, "Space Weapons: The Legal Context," in "Weapons in Space," *Daedalus* (Summer 1985), pp. 201–10. See also Thomas K. Longstreth, John E. Pike, and John B. Rhinelander, *The Impact of U.S. and Soviet Ballistic Missile Defense Programs on the ABM Treaty* (Washington, D.C.: National Campaign to Save the ABM Treaty, 1985).
15. Cited in Jeffrey Smith, " 'Star Wars' Tests and the ABM Treaty," *Science* (July 5, 1985), p. 30.

16. John B. Rhinelander, "Reagan's 'Exotic' Interpretation of the ABM Treaty," *Arms Control Today* (October 1985), p. 3. See also Alan B. Sherr, *A Legal Analysis of the 'New Interpretation' of the Anti-Ballistic Missile Treaty* (Boston: Lawyers Alliance for Nuclear Arms Control, 1986). The reinterpretation was instigated in the Department of Defense under the sponsorship of Under Secretary Fred Ikle and Assistant Secretary Richard Perle—both outspoken critics of the ABM Treaty and of arms control generally. The final position was developed by State Department legal adviser Abraham Sofaer. See Don Oberdorfer, "ABM Reinterpretation: A Quick Study," *Washington Post* (October 22, 1985), p. 1.
17. See Michael Krepon, "Dormant Threat to the ABM Treaty," *Bulletin of the Atomic Scientists* (January 1986), p. 31.
18. Arguing for the new version—and contradicting the official SDI policy line—Richard Perle has said that "an intelligent decision" on whether to proceed with SDI development cannot be made within the restrictive interpretation. Cited in Walter Pincus, "SDI Testing Is Reviewed in Light of Treaty Terms," *Washington Post* (March 26, 1986), p. A6.
19. The administration's December 1985 report on Soviet arms control compliance charges that the Soviets "may be preparing an ABM territorial defense." In support of this charge, the report cites a number of activities said to constitute "potential or probable Soviet violations or other ambiguous activity." These include the testing and development of rapidly deployable ABM components, concurrent testing of air defense and ABM components, endowment of the SA-X-12 air defense system with ABM capabilities, and development of rapid-reload ABM interceptors. See Department of State, Bureau of Public Affairs, "Soviet Noncompliance with Arms Control Agreements," *Special Report* (December 1985), pp. 2–3.
20. One SDI advocate argues that a U.S. offensive advantage would be "a key to maintaining stability during the initial years of the 'defense transition,'" since the Soviets are likely to have the early advantage in ABM deployments. See Keith B. Payne, *Strategic Defense: "Star Wars" in Perspective* (Boston: Hamilton Press, 1986), p. 124.
21. Strategic analyst Glen Kent of the Rand Corporation has drawn attention to this issue. For discussion, see the report of the Office of Technology Assessment, *Ballistic Missile Defense Technologies*, pp. 107–8.
22. George Keyworth, "An Option for a Disarmed World," *Issues in Science and Technology* (Fall 1984), p. 42.

Contributors

JOHN TIRMAN, executive director of the Winston Foundation for World Peace, Boston, is editor of this volume. From 1982 to 1986 he was senior editor at the Union of Concerned Scientists. Dr. Tirman's articles on nuclear policy have appeared in the *Los Angeles Times*, the *Chicago Tribune*, *Esquire*, *The Nation*, the *Bulletin of the Atomic Scientists*, and elsewhere. He edited and contributed to *The Fallacy of Star Wars* and edited and coauthored *The Militarization of High Technology*.

PETER A. CLAUSEN joined the Union of Concerned Scientists as its senior arms analyst in 1983 and is now director of research. Previously, he was an analyst with the Central Intelligence Agency and the Department of Energy. In 1982–83 Dr. Clausen was a fellow of the Wilson International Center for Scholars in Washington, D.C. He coauthored *The Fallacy of Star Wars* and was study director of the 1986 UCS report *In Search of Stability: An Assessment of New U.S. Nuclear Forces*.

JONATHAN DEAN is arms control adviser to the Union of Concerned Scientists. In his distinguished diplomatic career, he served as the U.S. representative to the NATO–Warsaw Pact Force Reduction Negotiations in Vienna in 1978–81, having served as deputy representative from the beginning of those talks in 1973. Ambassador Dean has held diplomatic posts in Bonn, Prague, and Elisabethville, Katanga. He is the author of *Watershed in Europe: Dismantling the East-West Military Confrontation* (1986).

PETER DIDISHEIM was research associate from 1983 to 1986 with the Union of Concerned Scientists in Washington, D.C., where he specialized in space weapons policy, and published articles and one of the UCS Papers on Strategic Defense. He is now legislative assistant to Rep. George E. Brown, Jr., of California.

RICHARD L. GARWIN is a longtime consultant to the Defense Department as well as an IBM fellow at the Thomas J. Watson Research Center. Dr. Garwin, a physicist, was twice a member of the president's Science Advisory Committee, was a member of the Defense Science Board, and has held appointments at Columbia, Cornell, and Harvard universities. He has authored numerous articles on strategic defense and was a major contributor to *The Fallacy of Star Wars*.

GREG NELSON is a computer scientist at the Digital Equipment Corporation's Systems Research Center in Palo Alto, California. After earning his Ph.D. in computer science at Stanford University, he was a lecturer in that field at Princeton University and was also a researcher at Xerox PARC.

DAVID REDELL received his doctorate in computer science from the University of California at Berkeley. He was professor of computer science at MIT and was later software manager in Xerox's Office Systems Division. He is now with the Digital Equipment Corporation's Systems Research Center in Palo Alto, California.

JONATHAN B. TUCKER was a senior editor with *High Technology* magazine and is now in the doctoral program at MIT's Center for International Studies. He has written widely on science policy, including articles for *Foreign Policy*, *The Nation*, and *Technology Review*. During the summer of 1986, Tucker was a research fellow at the Committee on Science, Arms Control and National Security of the American Association for the Advancement of Science in Washington, D.C.

ROBERT ZIRKLE coauthored the UCS study *In Search of Stability: An Assessment of New U.S. Nuclear Forces* (1986). He is now an arms analyst with the Union of Concerned Scientists and a Ph.D. candidate at MIT's Center for International Studies.

• • •

Founded from an informal group of faculty and graduate students at MIT in 1969, the UNION OF CONCERNED SCIENTISTS has grown into one of the largest and most effective public policy organizations in the United States. With headquarters in Cambridge, Massachusetts, and an office in Washington, D.C., UCS's staff of more than thirty work in the areas of nuclear arms control, energy policy, and nuclear reactor safety. UCS sponsorship totals 100,000 nationwide. The organization's activities include research, public education, and lobbying.

Index